Primary Education

Assessing and Planning Learning

Edited by Anna Craft
at The Open University

ROUTLEDGE

London and New York
in association with
The Open University

First published 1996
by Routledge
11 New Fetter Lane, London EC4P 4EE

Simultaneously published in the USA and Canada
by Routledge
29 West 35th Street, New York, NY 10001

Typeset in Garamond by Florencetype Ltd, Stoodleigh, Devon
Printed and bound in Great Britain by
Biddles Ltd, Guildford and King's Lynn

British Library Cataloguing in Publication Data
A catalogue record for this book is available from the British
Library

Library of Congress Cataloguing in Publication Data
A catalogue record for this book has been requested

ISBN 0–415–13527–3

Contents

Notes on contributors

Robin Alexander is Professor of Education at the University of Leeds.

Ian Birnbaum is Assistant Director of Education and Chief Inspector, London Borough of Sutton.

Robert A. Boyle is PhD Candidate, Combined Program in Education and Psychology, The University of Michigan, USA.

Patricia Broadfoot is Professor of Education at the School of Education, Bristol University.

Margaret Brown is Professor of Education at the University of London, King's College.

Arlette Bucher is an Educational Psychologist in Marseilles.

Elizabeth Clayden is Assistant Director at the School of Education, University of Exeter.

Cesar Coll, PhD, is Full Professor of Psychology of Development and Education, University of Barcelona, Spain.

Barry Cooper is Senior Lecturer in Education at University of Sussex, Institute of Education.

Anna Craft is Lecturer in Education at the Open University School of Education. She is Director of the Certificate of Professional Development in Education Programme at the Open University.

Kurt Czerwenka is Professor of Psychology at the University of Lyneburg. He writes in the area of pedagogy in schools, educational psychology and educational theory.

Charles Desforges is Director at the School of Education, University of Exeter.

Alejandro Tiana Ferrer, PhD, Professor of Theory and History of Education, National Distance Teaching University (UNED), Madrid, is currently Director of INCE (National Institute for Quality and Evaluation), Ministry of Education and Science, Madrid, Spain.

Philip Gammage is Professor of Education at the University of Nottingham.

Michel Gilly is at the Centre de Recherche en Psychologie d'Education, Université de Provence.

Caroline Gipps is Professor of Education and Dean of Research at the Institute of Education, University of London.

Jenefer Joseph is an Early Years Consultant in Hertfordshire.

Shelley McAlister is Research Assistant of Evaluation of National Assessment in Primary Schools at the Institute of Education, University of London.

Bet McCallum is Research Officer of Evaluation of National Assessment in Primary Schools at the Institute of Education, University of London.

Barbara MacGilchrist is Dean of Initial Teacher Education at the Institute of Education, University of London

Elena Martín, PhD, is Professor of Psychology of Development and Education, Autonomous University of Madrid, currently Head of the Cabinet of the Secretary of State for Education, Ministry of Education and Science, Spain.

Ronald W. Marx is Professor and Chair, Educational Studies Program, School of Education, The University of Michigan, USA.

Colin Mills is Assistant Warden at the School of Education, University of Exeter.

Keith Morrison is Lecturer in Education at the School of Education, University of Durham.

Peter Mortimore, OBE, is Professor of Education and Director of the Institute of Education, University of London.

Marilyn Osborn is at the School of Education, University of Bristol.

Paul R. Pintrich is Associate Professor, Combined Program in Education and Psychology, The University of Michigan, USA.

Andrew Pollard is Professor of Education at the University of West of England.

Richard Pring is Professor of Education at the University of Oxford's Department of Educational Studies.

William Rawson is Lecturer in Education at the School of Education, University of Exeter.

Acknowledgements

While the publishers have made every effort to contact copyright holders of material used in this volume, they would be grateful to hear from any they were unable to contact.

Chapter 1 Abridged version of Pring, R. (1992) 'Standards in education', *British Journal of Educational Studies*, XXXX, 1, February, Oxford: Blackwell Publishing Ltd. Reprinted with permission.

Chapter 2 Mortimore, P. (1992) 'Quality control in education and schools', *British Journal of Educational Studies*, XXXX, 1, February, Oxford: Blackwell Publishing Ltd. Reprinted with permission.

Chapter 3 Birnbaum, I. (1994) 'The non-league table method', *Education*, 1 July, 1994, London: Pitman. Reprinted with permission.

Chapter 4 Broadfoot, P. (1995) 'Performance assessment in perspective: international trends and current English experience', in Torrance, H. (ed.), *Evaluating Authentic Assessment*, Buckingham: Open University Press. Reprinted with permission.

Chapter 5 Commissioned chapter.

Chapter 6 McCallum, B., Gipps, C. McAlister, S. and Brown, M. (1995) 'National assessment at 7: emerging models of teacher assessment in the classroom', in Torrance, H. (ed.), *Evaluating Authentic Assessment*, Buckingham: Open University Press. Reprinted with permission.

Chapter 7 Clayden, E., Desforges, C., Mills, C. and Rawson, W. (1994) 'Authentic activity and learning', *British Journal of Educational Studies*, XXXXII, 2, June, Oxford: Blackwell Publishing Ltd. Reprinted with permission.

Chapter 8 Edited version of Pintrich, P.R., Marx, R.W. and Boyle, R.A. (1993) 'Beyond cold conceptual change: the role of motivational beliefs and classroom contextual factors in the process of conceptual change', *Review of Educational Research*, 63, 2, 167–99, Washington, USA: American Educational Research Association. Reprinted with permission.

Chapter 9 Abridged from Coll, C. and Martín, E. (1993) 'La evaluación del aprendizaje en el currículum escolar: una perspectiva constructivista', in *El constructivismo en al aula*, pp. 163–83, Barcelona: Editorial Graó. Translated by Susan Mushin. Reprinted with permission.

Chapter 10 Gammage, P. (1993) 'What school is really for: revisiting values' in Day, C., Hall, C., Gammage, P. and Coles, M., *Leadership and Curriculum in the Primary Schools*, London: Paul Chapman Publishing. Reprinted with permission.

Chapter 11 Czerwenka, K. (1994) 'How learning-effective is "free work"? Ways to observe the effects and results of open classroom situations', *European Education: A Journal of Translations*, Summer, Armonk, New York: M. E. Sharpe. German text first published as 'Wie lernweksam ist "freie Arbeit?"', *Pädagogische Welt*, no. 9, 395–9, 1991, Donauwoerth, Germany.

Chapter 12 Broadfoot, P. and Osborn, M., with Gilly, M. and Bucher, A. (1993) 'Teachers' working environment and classroom practice', in *Perceptions of Teaching: Primary School Teachers in England and France*, London: Cassell. Reprinted with permission.

Chapter 13 This chapter is based on the 1994 OFSTED discussion paper *Primary Matters* which has been adapted by kind permission of OFSTED.

Chapter 14 Morrison, K. (1994) 'International developments in assessment'. This chapter originally appeared under the title of 'Uniformity and diversity in assessment: an international perspective and agenda', *Compare*, 24, 1, 1994, Carfax Publishing Company, PO Box 25, Abingdon, Oxfordshire, OX14 3UE. Reprinted with permission.

Chapter 15 Cooper, B. (1994) 'Authentic testing in mathematics? The boundary between everyday and mathematical knowledge in National Curriculum testing in English schools', *Assessment in Education*, 1, 2, Carfax Publishing Company, PO Box 25, Abingdon, Oxfordshire, OX14 3UE. Reprinted with permission. Tables 15.1 and 15.2 and Figures 15.1 and 15.3–15.10, originally published by SEAC, are reproduced by kind permission of the School Curriculum and Assessment Authority.

Chapter 16 Edited version of Pollard, A. (1990) 'The challenge of the 1990s' in *Learning in Primary Schools*, London: Cassell. Reprinted with permission.

Chapter 17 Alexander, R. (1995) 'The third revolution?', in *Versions of Primary Education*, London: Routledge. Reprinted with permission.

Chapter 18   Joseph, J. (1993) 'Four-year-olds in school: cause for concern', in Gammage, P. and Meighan, J., *Early Childhood Education: Taking Stock. An Education Now Special Report*, Derbyshire: Education Now Publishing Cooperative. Reprinted with permission.

Chapter 19   Edited version of MacGilchrist, B. *Managing access and entitlement in primary education*, ASPE Paper No. 3, Stoke-on-Trent: Trentham Books. Reprinted with permission.

Introduction

Anna Craft

The approach of the millennium is providing the teaching profession with the somewhat artificial, but nevertheless powerful stimulus to consider and create agendas for the future within primary education; these include agendas for curriculum and assessment.

Around the world, education systems are placing greater emphasis on the re-definition of the school curriculum for primary-aged children. As the curriculum is redefined to reflect and to foster change in the wider social and economic context in which primary schools exist, teachers are faced with how to plan the total learning environment, and how to assess children's learning within it. Policy-level changes have been introduced in many countries. Some are represented to a degree in this book: mainly Australia, Canada, the UK, France, Germany, Spain, and the United States, with some reference to others.

Many aspects of the policy development in each country have become part of public discourse, although in each country different aspects have been perceived as significant. For example, in England and Wales there has been public debate about appropriate uses of outcomes of summative assessment; and questions raised about the extent to which publication of raw assessment outcomes tell us anything about the quality of a school. The debate includes attempts to define what makes a school 'effective', and has raised questions both within and without the teaching profession, and in education more generally, of how to define quality. Teachers, policy-makers, parents, governors, business people and members of the wider community are all engaged in the continuous debate about how 'standards' of achievement are defined, and how to 'raise' them.

On the other hand, to take another example, in Spain the reforms in curriculum and assessment have led to discussions within the profession only, without wider public debate. The issues which are most pressing are first how to relate teachers' initial teacher training (currently undertaken by universities, and involving a transmission model of teaching, learning and assessment) to the demands of the reformed curriculum and its assessment. Teachers are not well prepared in their initial training for the demands of a new, politically imposed curriculum which has at its core a constructivist model of teaching, learning and assessment. A second major issue for the Spanish teaching profession is the *resourcing* of change. A decentralized model of implementation in Spain was intended to give each of the seventeen Autonomous Regions of Spain, and each of the schools within it, greater local flexibility. It has meant great pressure on schools and teachers to interpret the national and regional frameworks. Although some resourcing is offered to each Autonomous Region, it is a matter of debate as to whether funding is sufficient to carry out the task of re-educating and persuading all teachers to take on a curriculum based on principles opposite to those with which they themselves were educated and which they have used all of their professional lives.

As these two examples demonstrate, differences in what is contentious reflect cultural values about the nature of learning in primary schools, the purposes of assessing learning and the professional standing of the teacher, in relation to policy-makers and in relation to society as a whole.

As the educational community develops its practice in assessing and planning learning, some similarities are also emerging. For example, in assessing learning, there is an increasing emphasis on assessment to inform planning for children's next steps in learning. This is reflected in the title of this text: *Primary Education: Assessing and Planning Learning*. Indeed the Open University Master's course, which this book was designed to support, explores assessment first and planning second for this reason. Another cross-national similarity is the increasing recognition given to social constructivist models of learning built on the work of Piaget and Vygotsky, the implications of which are that teachers need to offer children opportunities to make personal sense and meaning of the school curriculum.

Common to primary schools all over the world is debate about the staffing of primary schools, including the role of the teacher. The rapid growth in information technology, and erosion of the boundaries between in-school and outside-school learning, are two of the forces which are raising questions of how best to 'manage' learning in the primary classroom, and throughout the primary school.

This collection of readings explores some of the issues at the heart of assessing and planning learning in primary schools. Included in the book are readings drawn from a range of different cultural contexts, although the main focus is the United Kingdom. The texts have been selected to enable critical reflection on the central issues. Since assessment of achievement must lie at the heart of planning and supporting children's learning, the book is structured with assessment at the beginning.

The book is divided into four parts. Part I focuses on assessment issues and practice. The first three chapters (Pring, Mortimore and Birnbaum) offer differing perspectives on the nature of standards and quality in education. The next three chapters look at how assessment is made 'authentic' by primary teachers, so that each child's actual understanding and performance is assessed.

Broadfoot's paper (Chapter 4) widens the context by looking at international trends. The picture of policy and practice in Spain (where social constructivist theory has been a driving force in the development of curriculum and assessment, and where education thinkers and academics have been key players in the curricular reforms) is described in Chapter 5 by Ferrer. Evidence of how teachers in England have been developing their own assessment practice is described in Chapter 6 by McCallum, Gipps, McAlister and Brown.

Part II looks at enabling learning. The first chapter (7) looks at children's learning in relation to the nature of knowledge, and thus involves discussion of the relationship between subject content and classroom practice (Clayden, Desforges, Mills and Rawson). This general theme is continued in the next chapter, from the United States, by Pintrich, Marx and Boyle, who explore the interaction between conceptual change and the social context of learning (Chapter 8). The learning theories which are based on social constructivism are explored by Spanish writers Coll and Martin in Chapter 9, where they consider the implications which social constructivism has for assessing and planning learning. Some of the potential tensions between adults' classification frameworks and values, and the creation of meaningful learning experiences for children, are taken up by Gammage in Chapter 10.

The final two chapters in Part II look at aspects of pedagogy, first in Germany (Czerwenka, Chapter 11) and then England and France (Broadfoot, Osborn, Gilly and Bucher, Chapter 12).

Part III looks first at the current development of policy in assessing and planning learning, beginning in England (Craft, Chapter 13). Morrison (Chapter 14) then widens the debate to trace a number of similar international trends in the development of policy, and puts forward an international agenda for debate in the field. The final two chapters offer contrasting documentation of the impact of policy development on practice. In Chapter 15, Cooper looks at what testing in England has thrown up about the boundaries between common-sense, or everyday, knowledge, and mathematical discourse. With a much broader focus, Andrew Pollard, in Chapter 16, attempts to foretell the challenges of the 1990s in England and Wales, in the light of recent policy reforms.

Finally, in Part IV we turn to the future, beginning with Alexander (Chapter 17), a key figure in English and Welsh curriculum rationalization at policy level. He calls for a redefinition of the rationale for primary education, and of the scope of its curriculum, for critical contemplation of the divisions between sectors of education, of funding and of teacher roles, and for primary practice to be underpinned with theoretical integrity. The experiences and learning of the youngest children in school are the focus of Joseph's chapter (Chapter 18), and the equal opportunities issues which her chapter raises are taken further by MacGilchrist in the final chapter (Chapter 19). She addresses some of the issues involved in managing access and entitlement against a backdrop of increasing diversity and change, considering the extent to which policies can be translated into practice.

This book does not attempt to hold up any one particular approach to policy development and implementation in assessing and planning learning in the primary curriculum as more appropriate than any other. It does bring together a disparate collection of current research and reflection on experience in primary education from several different countries. By doing so, I intend to stimulate thinking and practice in how one might most appropriately define, teach and assess the primary curriculum in a variety of local and national contexts, as we move toward and enter the twenty-first century.

Anna Craft
The Open University

Part I

Assessing learning

Chapter 1

Standards and quality in education

Richard Pring

*This is an edited version of a much more substantial article in which Pring examines political arguments made about falling standards in education, and ways of monitoring and measuring this supposed phenomenon.**

POLITICAL CONTEXT

There has in the last fifteen years been a steady flow of warnings from government about 'declining standards'. The 1977 consultative document *Education in Schools* commented on Callaghan's Ruskin speech in the following way:

> [it] was made against a background of strongly critical comment in the press and elsewhere on education and educational standards. Children's standards of performance in their school work was said to have declined. The curriculum, it was argued, paid too little attention to the basic skills of reading, writing and arithmetic, and was overloaded with fringe subjects.
>
> (DES, 1977)

Already we see two kinds of decline in standards – poor performance in the basic skills (children not writing, reading, adding and subtracting as well as a similar cohort of children would have done in a previous age) and the neglect of more traditional subjects as these were usurped by fringe subjects (no doubt peace studies and other forms of integrated studies). But the document goes on to mention poor discipline and behaviour and the neglect of economic relevance.

The consultative document was produced by a Labour government, but one which was reacting, *first*, to well-orchestrated populist appeals from the political right and, *second*, to the concerns of commerce and industry which argued that the output of the educational system – yes, even those who came up to *traditional* standards – were ill-prepared for the economic world they

---

* 'Standards in education', *British Journal of Educational Studies*, vol. XXXX, no. 1 (February 1992), Oxford: Blackwell.

were entering into. Therefore, there were four areas of quality concern – basic skills, traditional learning, discipline, and economic relevance. 'Quality' is reflected in the standards, explicit or implicit, to which reference is made when performance is judged. In that sense quality and standards are logically related concepts, and therefore the four areas of quality concern picked out in Callaghan's speech reflect four different kinds of standard – which kinds may not, as we shall see, always be compatible with each other.

'Standards' and 'quality' have been rallying calls to all political parties and government initiatives ever since. One will recall Sir Keith Joseph's (then Secretary of State) North of England Conference speech in January 1984, when, deeply concerned with the poor standards of many young people, he affirmed the aim of bringing 80–90 per cent of *all* pupils at least to the level which is now expected and achieved in the 16+ examination by pupils of average ability in individual subjects. In thus raising standards, Sir Keith first proposed the need to define the objectives of the 5 to 16 curriculum so that everyone would know the levels that should be achieved. And, following this line of reasoning, the Secretary of State argued for the change in 16+ examinations so that they would measure 'absolute' rather than 'relative' performance. The same message was reiterated by the succeeding Secretary of State, Kenneth Baker, who argued for greater standardization and higher standards in anticipation of the 1987 Consultation Document which thus stated:

> The government has concluded that these advantages and consistent improvements in standards can be guaranteed only within a national framework for the secular curriculum. . . . The imaginative application of professional skills at all levels of the education service, within a statutory framework which sets clear objectives, will raise standards.

Let us pause to see where the argument is developing. There is wide concern about standards. Generally speaking these need to be higher. This concern, however, is about different sorts of standards – those relating to traditional learning, those relating to 'basic skills', those relating to behaviour, and those relating to economic relevance. And presumably standards need to be higher in each of these independent areas. To raise standards requires expressing these standards quite explicitly – they thus become the clearly stated objectives (the absolute benchmarks) against which a pupil's performance might be judged. There might, within any one *area* of standards (let us say, within the area of the basic skill of reading or within the traditional learning area of history), be logically related standards pitched at different levels or in a hierarchy. In that sense one can talk of differentiated and higher standards. Thus, for example, Mr Eggar, in addressing the fifth annual conference of the Joint Council for the GCSE, said that 'many of the challenges which have to be faced have to do with standards. There is the need for adequate differentiation, particularly for more able pupils' (Eggar, 1991). This requires the introduction of level 10 in National Assessment 'which is demonstrably more demanding than the existing Grade A of GCSE'. It is the job of schools, therefore, to make sure that the performance of pupils, in each of these general standards areas, improves in the sense of measuring up to standards further up the hierarchy. Thus presumably the standard expressed in 'can read fluently most words with four syllables' is higher than the standard expressed in 'can read fluently most words with three syllables' because the one would seem to subsume the other (but this is not necessarily true).

Two questions therefore seem to be appropriate: why choose a particular objective of performance as *the* standard of measurement? And why choose one level, in the hierarchy of levels, rather than another as the appropriate standard for a particular age group? The first question would itself seem to raise two subsidiary questions: why are these particular statements of objectives chosen out of an infinite number of possible statements (that is, is there anything in the nature of historical enquiry or economic relevance which makes these rather than those the appropriate standard bearers)? And who has the authority for deciding which, amongst many competitors, are to be the appropriate standards? The National Curriculum, and the subsequent reports on the Foundation Subjects, do not on the whole address these questions. . .

MONITORING OF STANDARDS

. . . In meeting the public concern over standards, the government has pursued several courses of action. It has established 'absolute standards', hierarchically related, in areas of traditional learning. It has re-asserted the 'flagship role' of 'A' levels. It has expressed confidence in the standards set by the degree awards of higher education, despite the decline in the unit of resource.

Nonetheless, it is one thing to assert these things. It is quite another to check that the assertions are correct – to monitor what is in fact the case. Monitoring standards in schools and in higher education has been of several different kinds.

First, this has been a central role of HMI (and of local advisers). It would be argued that the accumulation of experience, the corporate awareness of what is good work, the sense of judgement established through constant critical discussion in the context of widely observed practice – that such professional activity gives insight and judgement that escapes others. Wide experience enables them to have a comparative perspective. They are reluctant to be too specific in what they say about a school or a department, partly because of the political consequences of being so specific, but partly because of the difficulties in capturing the immensely complicated process of children's learning within a few well-chosen words.

Second, there are the results of public examinations. Thus, the examinations at GCSE or at 'A' level are graded; grades are totted up or averaged;

league tables are produced in the Good School Guides. Each year one knows school by school, or nationally, or regionally, whether there are more or fewer students achieving particular grades. These grades, then, become the test of quality. They set the standards, and evidently there are more young people now coming up to these standards. But the standards are set by the examiners: first, in their setting of questions and agreeing of marking schemes, and, second, in the discussion of individual and marginal cases – guided (though not totally determined) by norms of grade distribution. It is a sophisticated system, but it is ultimately based on the judgement of experienced examiners, speaking with the authority of those who have been initiated into a particular tradition within a recognized area of learning. Indeed, becoming an 'A' level examiner requires a kind of apprenticeship, with the forming, through criticism, of a sense of judgement which outstrips explicit criteria and which depends upon comparisons across candidates and over the years. Difficulties arise, of course, in the comparing of grades of different examination systems – in the calibration, for example, of CSE Grade 1 with GCE Grade C, or GCE Grade C with GCSE Grade C, or different modes of the same examination (e.g. Mode 1 with Mode 3 CSE in French), or different Examination Boards. But these difficulties were tackled with technical skills and statistical devices of, first, the Schools Examination Council and, then, of the Schools Examination and Assessment Council.

Third, there have been, in the last fifteen years, the attempts by the Assessment of Performance Unit to provide longitudinal comparisons of performance across the curriculum and, on a very light sampling basis, across the country at different ages. The reports on languages, on science and on mathematics have provided us with the very best evidence available on what pupils can or cannot do. But it is impossible to draw from these simple conclusions of the kind 'standards have done down in mathematics' because, as was pointed out earlier, aims change over time and, thus, so do what are to count as appropriate standards. An attempt to provide a unitary and mathematical yardstick of comparison in the Rasch model was shown to be both conceptually and technically flawed. None the less, the APU evidence on pupil performance in general terms provided valuable information on the basis of which any one school, by drawing upon the item bank, could look comparatively at its own achievement.

Fourth, the educational system has been monitored by the occasional evaluation study – the in-depth probe by researchers. By and large, however, quality has been ascertained through inspection and through examination of individual performance, and by the anecdotal account and the 'general impression' that the public and government receive through the media.

The major weakness in these ways of monitoring standards, pointed to by critics, is the lack of explicit and detailed criteria by which judgements are made. Just as a knife is judged good or bad according to how well it cuts –

and the criteria for cutting well can be established beforehand (does it slice through this tomato without the juice spitting out?) – so too might any performance be judged by its 'fitness for purpose'. That being so, then the purpose of the activity needs to be clearly spelt out, and the criteria for successfully achieving that purpose established. How can you know that a knife is good or bad unless you know whether it cuts and, then, in turn, know what is to count as good cutting? How can you know whether a person is good at maths unless you know what specific mathematical understandings and skills are worth learning, and, then, in turn, know what that person has to do to demonstrate that he or she has those understandings and those skills? What (the critics will say) is lacking from the judgements of HMI and from the gradings of examination boards are the 'performance criteria' or 'performance indicators' according to which judgements are made. GCSE was intended to shift the norm-guided judgements of GCE to the criterion-referred judgements of GCSE, from the intuitive judgements of the one to the performance-related judgements of the other. Thus, whereas under GCE the possession of a GCE History Grade C gave little indication of what the possessor of the certificate could do or understand, under GCSE (so it was argued) one would be able to tell what a person so graded knew or could do.

Therefore, quality is now to be 'assured' through the application of 'performance indicators', and such indicators are to permeate the system of education at every level. Each institution should have such indicators. *One* performance indicator will be examination results, but these examination results in turn will arise from the application of performance indicators to the students. Furthermore, these performance indicators will be explicit and justified against the purposes that the institution or examined subject is trying to serve – and, hence, the importance of 'mission statements', a mixture of ethical judgements (about what is worthwhile) and specific goals, which pin that worthwhileness down to attainable objectives.

This quality assurance requires a system – a mechanism for establishing the purposes, for deciding upon the criteria which demonstrate the achievement of those purposes, and for checking whether those criteria have been applied. Such a mechanism is increasingly modelled on that of industry. Thus, distinctions are made between quality control and quality assurance. 'Quality' is seen in terms of fitness for purpose, that purpose being established partly by the customers of the service but mainly by the government as the custodian of the interests of the customer. 'Quality control' refers to the particular procedures for ensuring that those purposes are established and that the performances conform to specifications (that, for example, x number of students obtain the grades in different subjects which indicate that the learning objectives have been met). 'Quality assurance' refers to the mechanism for ensuring that the 'quality control' techniques are carried out – the 'audit' of this second tier of performance (for example, the monitoring meetings and the external evaluation). Finally, the whole system should be geared to 'quality improvement' – getting institutions to set higher goals in their mission statements, to teach a greater proportion of students to achieve these goals, but above all to increase the 'value addedness' of the teaching – to widen the gap, in other words, between what the learners can do or understand before teaching and what they can do afterwards. Quality control (and thus quality assurance) needs constantly to monitor the 'value addedness' of the institution. There have to be measurements, and measurements of performance both before and afterwards (both at the input and at the output stages) should be provided under the quality control system. Quality requires therefore the adoption of business practice – and business language: fitness for purpose, quality control and assurance, mission statements and performance indicators, value addedness and audits. And there is a competition between major political parties to put forward the most effective and credible scheme for ensuring this happens. . .

In each of the three contexts [of academic, vocational and 'capability'], quality, and thereby the standards implicit within our assessment of quality, presupposes some objective basis for judgement – some base from which might be evaluated the achievement of the learner. Indeed, the very word 'achievement' has built into it the idea of standard, of good or bad performance, of *mastery* of something which is worthwhile, of improvement, and often of struggle as one feels dissatisfied with one's performance (in painting, say, or in playing a game). It is not clear what sense can be given to achievement, to improvement, to dissatisfaction, to struggle, to effort without the implicit recognition of standards against which one judges what one has done or produced. Part of being educated is to come to recognize these standards and to internalize them – to apply them to oneself. In that sense, standards imply an objectivity, a comparative dimension to one's own performance that cannot be simply the product of whim, of one's own wishes, of what lies in one's own self-interest. This may seem a rather exiguous sense of objectivity, but it is important. It indicates that the standards implicit in all judgement cannot simply be created at one's convenience. One's performance has to measure up to standards which are inseparable from the activity as one perceives it and these perceptions have themselves been internalized from participation in a form of life shared with others. The tennis player, dissatisfied with her performance, is dissatisfied because she has internalized the rules and expectations of good tennis playing – not simply the rules of winning but also the rules, if you like, of playing elegantly, stylishly, with economy of effort, with aesthetic pleasure for both player and audience. Even though she wins, she may feel that, set against these expectations, she has not quite come up to scratch.

The academic, vocational and pre-vocational traditions agree on this general point about the objectivity of judgement – and *therefore* on the objectivity (in this sense) of standards.

There is, however, a competing tradition which seeks to place standards in a very different context – a context which embraces relativism as the only rational position to adopt on matters of value. Thus, it would be argued, there is no rational base for saying that one area of learning is more worthwhile than another, or that one activity is superior to another, or that one form of understanding is more valuable than another. In that case, there are no standards, objectively speaking, to be maintained by the masters of those standards, by those who are authorities within the educational world. In a strange and contradictory way, that seems to be partly the position of this government despite its frequent concern for standards. Let me explain.

A government which has claimed that the improvement of standards is a priority is also the government which has proclaimed the superiority of market forces in determining what those standards should be. The general suspicion of the professional (in social work and in law, as well as in teaching and in higher education) is one and the same as a suspicion of 'authority' within areas of professional concern and within the areas of traditional learning. On such a view, the guardians of standards are really the guardians of self-interest; by an interesting twist of irony, the sociological theory associated with the left, which produced critiques of knowledge and its control, have been appropriated by the right. And thus, in the absence of authorities, in the absence of defensible values whereby those already initiated into the academic and vocational traditions can lay down and apply their standards, we are given market forces as both the definers and the maintainers of standards.

Frequent reference is now made to consumer choice as that which will ensure the raising of standards. It is assumed that, as the consumers hunt around for 'the best' service, so the competition for selling what is offered will result in greater efficiency, more effective teaching. But the corollary of market forces operating in a world of moral scepticism is that market forces define as well as promote standards, for the consumer always knows best. Quality is that which pleases the consumer – whether it be the top ten in music or Harold Robbins in literature. There are no authorities of what is good in education; only technicians competent in delivering that which the consumer wants.

There is an ambivalence in political thinking on this issue. The explicit recognition of market forces as the definers of standards does not come easy to Secretaries of State who have a sneaking suspicion that values are not simply what people choose to value – hence, a National Curriculum with well-defined standards built into it. But, in suspecting the authority of those who traditionally have been guardians of those values (those on the inside of the conversation that has taken place between the generations of poets, of philosophers, of historians, of scientists, namely, the academics and the teachers who have been apprenticed to that conversation), there is little alternative to market forces other than the rather arbitrary political definition of standards. And this is apparent to those who have followed the debate concerned with the geography and history National Curriculum working parties' recommendations and over the slimming down of the attainment targets in science and mathematics.

To conclude this section, I have placed the debate on standards, and thus on the quality of education, within the context of different traditions concerning the aims and values of education and training. Each tradition sees quality (and thereby standards) in a very different way, affecting how we conceive of teaching and of the institutional framework within which teaching should take place.

The academic tradition understands standards as the measures, certainly, of correctness, appropriateness, stylishness, validity, within distinctive disciplines of enquiry, but measures which more often than not are implicit only within these enquiries, teased out, not by politicians and civil servants, but by philosophers of science or of history as they reflect on the processes of science and the process of thinking historically. They can be applied without being explicitly acknowledged; they are acquired slowly over a period of time and always are only more or less understood; they are passed on to the next generation of students through example, through the correction of the particular, not through the definition of the universal.

The vocational tradition, which, when properly restricted, can sit happily alongside the academic tradition, is concerned with 'fitness for purpose' where those purposes are clear and specific. They are derived from an analysis of the economic task. Standards concern the competences which demonstrably are the means for achieving those purposes. In theory, there should be nothing controversial about such standards – or in ascertaining whether they have been reached, for they are spelt out in terms of performance indicators, and performances, on standardized tasks, can easily be observed.

However, this task has not proved to be easy, and there is a third and importantly different tradition which trades on the vocational but wants to expand into the academic, thereby transforming it into something different. This tradition speaks of more general competences – not those specific to plumbing or to hairdressing, but those specific to life in general. These are partly captured in the core skills of the Further Education Unit, partly in the General National Vocational Qualifications of the NCVQ, partly in the enterprise and entrepreneurial qualities of the Training Enterprise and Education Department, partly in the life skills of pre-vocational courses. But, trading on the language of vocational competences, they are seeking assessment through performance indicators and these (for life competency, problem-solving and the like) are hard to come by. . .

CONCEPT OF STANDARDS

In this final section, I want briefly to pull together various strands of the argument, for, in pointing to these competing traditions, I have failed to say exactly what standards are or what is meant by standards. That, of course, must be the case because the meaning of any word is related logically to its use within a language or within a field of discourse. Hence the importance of locating 'standards' within different traditions and wide discourses – including the dominant metaphors of each one.

Nonetheless, there are certain logical features of the word and certain philosophical considerations about human action which help us decide between different traditions – or at least the limitation of each.

First, there is something odd about standards going up or down. The *performance* of pupils, as measured by standards, goes up or down, but not the standards themselves. If standards were to rise or fall, that rise or fall could only be judged to be so against a different type of standard – viz. those standards whereby one assesses the standard of standards, and thus one is into an infinite regress.

Second, however, one might see 'standards declining' as meaning that *performance* is not coming up to standard to the extent that it once did or that performance is coming up to a standard which is different from that which once it came up to – and different in the sense that it is less demanding than the other standards. Levels of standard, as in the National Curriculum, must mean something of this kind – that is, the same kind of activity envisaged at various levels of difficulty and thus differentiated in some norm-referenced way. For example, one can see how long division presupposes a range of arithmetical activities, such that there is some logical progression from simple addition and subtraction to the more complex operation. Each level represents a different standard, but the standards are logically related in so far as success in one presupposes success in the others. In this way one has differentiated, hierarchically related standards.

Third, however, standards are benchmarks, they are criteria whereby one assesses or evaluates the quality of a particular activity or process. And that quality must depend upon the identification and the purpose of the activity – upon the values that are embodied within it. Strictly speaking, there are as many standards as there are activities; there are as many activities as there are intentions and purposes that drive people on. There are standards peculiar to house cleaning, painting landscapes, writing Shakespearian sonnets, appreciating the impact of science on the environment. Moreover, as purposes and values change, so too must the standards whereby we assess those activities. As mathematicians reflect on the nature of mathematics, as employers require different sorts of mathematics in order to meet a changing technological world, so does the value that we attach to mathematics change and so does the nature of the activity – and so, too, therefore, do the standards whereby we judge achievement within mathematics. Similarly, just as society comes to value different forms of life, just as we come to embrace different virtues (enterprise rather than modesty, autonomy rather than obedience), so do our moral purposes change, and so too do the standards whereby we assess moral worth. Standards have neither gone up nor come down. They have simply changed. Such considerations make nonsense of the aggregate of marks whereby we talk of the standard in mathematics or *the* standard of morals. And it makes it logically impossible to make sensible comparisons of standards across the generations – or, indeed, across cultures unless those cultures and those generations share a common set of values with regard to that activity.

CONCLUSION

The difficulty in talking about standards is that the concept is, like 'truth', or 'goodness', or 'beauty', both logically indispensable and yet impossible to define without considerable philosophical elaboration. That worries those with a narrow conception of rationalism who believe that all concepts can be operationally defined and their use made clear and unambiguous. Governments whether to the right or left who seek to control outcomes – to bureaucratize education and turn it into something else, to transform teachers into deliverers of a curriculum – will no doubt be seduced by this temptation. They will ignore the complexity of these notions and treat them as though they can be reduced to simple definitions.

But that is to abstract them from the wider social and educational traditions in which they have their meaning. I have simply articulated a little those different traditions. To ignore these differences can so easily distort what teachers have traditionally been about, namely, to introduce the next generation to those ideas and skills and beliefs that have survived critical scrutiny. And to be aware of this is important for, in failing to be aware, there are attempts to change our educational institutions out of all recognition.

Thus, dominated by such narrowly conceived understanding of standards as 'fit for purpose', it is argued that educational achievement after 16 should be reduced to a range of competences pitched at different levels (five levels of NVQ), that attainment targets of the National Curriculum, core skills, BTCs, 'A' levels, degrees, etc. should be defined in terms of these, that clear routes should be charted through these, that units of teaching (like colleges and universities) should become TAPs (or Training Access Points), that through regular assessment of prior learning or APLs individual action plans should be charted and credits granted which make courses of pre-defined content and duration an anomaly. What room then for universities in a world dominated instead by independent assessment centres leading to training points, by performance indicators of competence and credit accumulations, by individualized programmes geared to credits delivered where the performance counts, namely, in the real world of the workplace. Courses like coats will be cut and trimmed accordingly. Indeed, there will be little place for courses as these are traditionally seen.

But all this depends on the failure to understand that there is a broader educational vision, which cannot be analysed out in this way and which incorporates a quite different concept of standards – one which cannot be eliminated from an understanding of human activity.

REFERENCES

DES (Department of Education and Science) (1977) *Education in Schools*, London: HMSO.
Eggar, T. (1991) Address to the Joint Board for GCSE, 27 September.

Chapter 2

Quality control in education and schools

Peter Mortimore

Here, Mortimore extends the discussion by Pring in Chapter 1 on quality and standards. Mortimore calls for the de-politicization of education, and explores quality control in schools. He suggests schools should themselves be able actively to define what they consider to be quality, to pinpoint clear standards of achievement, and to decide exactly how these are measured. He rejects league tables which compare raw achievement scores, because no account is taken in these statistics of how far a child has developed.*

INTRODUCTION

In current debates about education, the terms 'quality control' and 'standards' are frequently heard. They are used interchangeably in relation to claims about whether things are getting better or worse. Given that education is one of the major spending departments of government, it is not surprising that there is so much debate about whether value for money is being achieved. Yet one unfortunate characteristic of much of the debate carried out in recent times is that the message has been premised more on rhetoric than on evidence. Underpinning this rhetoric, however, are some fundamental questions. In his paper, Richard Pring (1991) draws attention to the debate between different views of education, liberal education and vocational education. Whilst using slightly different terms, in a recent article Carolyn Stone and I described the conflict between seeing education as an instrumental activity designed to achieve specifiable and uncontroversial educational goals and the Aristotelian view of education as an ethical activity guided by values which, themselves, are open to continual debate and refinement by those practitioners and other members of society (Mortimore and Stone, 1991). These views represent contrasting positions. For many people, however, education must be about both elements. It must be about the development, to the maximum potential, of all individuals just as it must be about developing

* Originally published in *British Journal of Educational Studies*, vol. XXXX, no. 1 (February 1992), Oxford: Blackwell (edited for this volume).

the maximum potential of our society with its specific needs and requirements. Ideally, there would be little conflict between these two needs and it
would be possible to develop to the maximum individuals within a context
that is good for society as a whole.

In his paper, Pring discusses the concept of standards. In this paper, I shall
be discussing the concept of quality and its control. Is there a difference
between the two? Both terms are difficult. The word 'standard' probably
comes from the French 'estandard' meaning, literally, a rallying point; it is
frequently taken to indicate a specified level as in the use of the term British
Standards (discussed later in this paper). The term 'quality' is usually used,
in everyday language, to indicate a high standard, something that is very
good. But as an international paper prepared by the Organization for
Economic Cooperation and Development (OECD) has stated, at least four
uses of the term can be identified:

- an attribute or defining essence;
- a degree of relative worth;
- a description of something good or excellent;
- a non-quantified trait (in contrast, for instance, with quantity).

Here, I shall be using the term to indicate the worth or excellence of the
education service and I shall be pointing to the means by which it can be
monitored. Even so, its meaning is still relatively unclear, as the contribution
by Sweden to the OECD paper notes:

> The meaning of quality is unclear, and the term is variously used by
> different interests. Statements, some more precise than others, concerning
> the quality of education are made in various contexts, but systematic studies
> on the subject are few and far between. As a result, statements concerning
> quality are not always well-founded, whatever the sense in which the term
> is used.
>
> (OECD, 1989)

A quite different approach to the definition of quality comes from the literature of 'total quality management' (Juran, 1988). This approach has
developed out of the application of behaviourist principles to management.
Used largely in Japanese industry, the idea of total quality management
(TQM) has been incorporated into the British Standards 5750 kite marking
system used in manufacturing.

The ideas of TQM and of the use of British Standard kite marking have
been adopted by some higher education institutions, notably by Huddersfield
Polytechnic. As correspondence to the *Times Higher Education Supplement*
(12 July 1991) illustrates, however, the matter is seen as being highly controversial.

The underlying concept that quality is to do with the whole management
of the institution, fits well with the view of school effectiveness which will

be developed within this paper. The definition used by TQM that quality = fitness for purpose can easily be applied to the school setting, and I differ from Pring's view that such a definition is always inappropriate.

In his paper, Pring also draws attention to the wider educational and political debate in which the question of standards is frequently discussed. I accept that such a debate is inevitable in a democratic society where there is a pluralism of views and opinions are strongly held. What I find increasingly disturbing, however, is the 'party political' nature of such debate.

Whilst I accept that an element of party political campaigning is inevitable in our society, I find it profoundly depressing that as important an area as education is used to secure electoral advantage. This tendency has meant that open and detailed debate on educational grounds has been increasingly discouraged. Dogma has overtaken the use of evidence, and disagreement is itself viewed in party political terms. In my view, this is no way to plan an education service and is quite contrary to the Aristotelian view defined earlier in this paper. Yet such a party political view dominates the education debate and, in my view, has stultified the proper discussion of the 1988 Education Reform Act and its implications for the education service. That is regrettable.

In this [chapter], I will focus on the question of quality control as applied to schools . . . My strategy will be to ask two questions:

- how is quality monitored?
- has the quality of schooling changed over recent years?

MONITORING QUALITY

The quality of schooling is monitored in a number of different ways:

- through Her Majesty's Inspectorate (HMI) and LEA Inspectorates;
- through various forms of educational testing and examination;
- through informal comments by parents; and,
- through research.

Each of these approaches has both strengths and limitations.

HMI and other inspectors

HMI have been in existence for over 150 years. Its major role has always been to report to the Senior Education Minister, that is, currently, the Secretary of State in the education service.

It also has an independent role, managed by itself, as the arbiter of the quality of individual schools and, more recently, local education authorities (LEAs) as well as of the system as a whole. Whilst in the past, school inspection reports by HMI were confidential to the school, since 1983 these reports have been published and the criteria adopted for judgements have been made more apparent. A recent governmental review of the work of the Inspectorate recommended fundamental change in its structure but these recommendations have now been overtaken by the publication by the government of the Parent's Charter (DES, 1991a) in which the role of HMI is seen mainly as acting as a training and accrediting body for other privatized teams of inspectors. It will still, however, retain a duty to report to the Secretary of State although, because of the proposed reduction in its size, its database for doing so will be severely limited.

LEAs have also had a tradition of recruiting and training advisers although, in recent years, there has been a tendency to switch to the term (and the role) of inspectors. Their duty has been to report to the Authority, usually through its Chief Education Officer.

Inspectors are recruited from successful practitioners able to draw on a wealth of national experience as well as a detailed subject knowledge. In its external inspections, HMI has brought to the schools a great deal of understanding and an awareness of comparative levels. However, as anyone who has been inspected knows, HM Inspectors are not just ordinary visitors to schools and their status can inhibit them from seeing schooling as it really is. At one level this does not matter and HM inspections have been able to describe both excellence and very poor quality as they have found them in schools. At another level, it means that fine-grained analysis within the extremes of quality – and lack of it – are less accessible. Furthermore, because of the difficulty of interpreting the quality of examination results without taking account of the nature of pupil intake to schools, HM Inspectors have, on occasion, been accused of unfairness.

As Carolyn Stone and I have argued, however, the greatest value of the HMI is its ability to make holistic judgements. Some aspects of school life cannot be atomized into components – each to be judged separately – without a distortion taking place, as Pring's paper makes clear. In this case, the whole is greater than the sum of the parts and HMI has been in an excellent position to describe that whole (Mortimore and Stone, 1991). This is also true of LEA inspection teams.

Tests and examinations

The use of testing has been common in schools since the advent of the earliest psychological tests. Though common, it is still subject to many problems concerned with the difficulties of ensuring the validity and reliability of tests (Gipps et al., 1983). Similarly, public examinations have been used in schools since 1850 and this method too has been vulnerable to many problems (Mortimore et al., 1986). Since 1988, the assessment of the National Curriculum has been a potential area for similar testing. The last three years have seen a series of developments designed to create assessments for two of the key stages of the National Curriculum. This too has been an area of some controversy (BERA, 1990) and the aims and conditions of such assessment created by the then Secretary of State, Kenneth Baker, have frequently been altered by his two successors John MacGregor and Kenneth Clarke.

Underpinning all attempts to monitor quality through the use of the assessments of individual pupils is a particular problem. It has been found, in many countries and at many different times, that if the method of assessment is competitive, a correlation is found between success and social advantage. Not surprisingly, pupils whose conditions of life enable them to be well-fed and well-housed, and for their parents to be well-informed and confident about dealing with the system, tend to do well. Pupils with the opposite characteristics tend, on the whole, to do much less well; although exceptional, talented and well-motivated pupils will buck this trend. The result of this phenomenon is that assessment frequently tests the background of pupils rather than the quality of their education. That said, there is clear evidence from a variety of studies that individual schools can have a positive impact in promoting the progress of pupils (see Rutter *et al.*, 1979 and Mortimore *et al.*, 1988). Whilst the individual school cannot compensate for the large-scale differences in pupil background, it can, and does, influence the progress made by pupils regardless of their background. Thus, measures of progress are much less susceptible to the influence of family and background than are measures of attainment. Unfortunately, most test and public examination results are tests of attainment rather than of progress.

Current debate about the value of examination league tables in the judgement of schools brings these issues to the surface. In my judgement, league tables of individual pupils' results can say little about the quality of schooling: they provide, instead, a good indication of the background and amount of prior learning of pupils.

In TQM terms, the fitness for purpose of schools taking pupils with very varied backgrounds and levels of prior learning may be quite different. This is not to patronize schools in disadvantaged areas or to pursue the disastrous course followed in the 1970s whereby the lower streams of schools were diverted away from mainstream academic achievement into a form of social education. Rather, it is to recognize that the task facing the schools will be rather different, although the ultimate aim of enabling as many pupils as possible to maximize their potential remains the same. The fitness for purpose definition is helpful in this context. Provided that both 'fitness' and 'purpose' are defined carefully, the definition can be used usefully in the evaluation of the quality of any aspect of the education service.

Whilst it is perfectly right for parents to receive full 'raw' information on the achievement of their children, for those parents to judge the quality of the school they need something else. In my view they need a judgement of how good the school is, taking into account the nature of its pupils. Such an analysis is able to distinguish between the school that has given a net value (over and above its pupil intake) to achievement and those that, although ostensibly successful, are underachieving. The inclusion of the term 'league tables' within the Parent's Charter (DES, 1991a) is, in my view, most unfortunate, particularly at a time when statistical advances have provided suitable methods for dealing with this problem (see, for instance, the work of Goldstein, 1987).

Parents' judgements

The third method of monitoring the quality of schools draws on the common-sense judgement of parents. Parents frequently get to know schools extremely well – especially if they have more than one child attend the same school. They see pupils on the street, they read about them in their local papers, and they hear from their offspring accounts of school life. Inevitably these views will be subjective. Their children will be successful or unsuccessful pupils in the school and their judgement will be coloured by this fact. Other pupils they see and recognize in the streets will be an unrepresentative sample of the main pupil body and the stories they read in local papers will draw attention only to particular aspects of school life. Only if the school has been inspected, will they see the holistic view of the inspectors and have this to set against their own subjective view.

Parents' views of a school are extremely important when taken as a whole and I welcome the systematic attempts that have been made by some schools to collect these data. However, random views by random parents may well be biased as parents, whose offspring have done well, are far more likely to be positive about a school than are those whose children have been less successful.

Research

Research into individual schools is common and there have been many studies, including a series of case studies, published over the years (Hargreaves, 1967; Lacey, 1970; Ball, 1981). Since the early 1970s, however, there has also been a series of studies seeking to compare groups of schools against each other and, as a result, to define effectiveness. These studies have taken place on both sides of the Atlantic. Amongst the UK studies, the work of Reynolds (1982), Rutter *et al.* (1979) and Mortimore *et al.* (1988) stand out. In these cases the researchers looked at schools over a period of years and collected a variety of measures of quality based on pupil outcomes related to intake differences.

In the United States there has also been a series of outstanding studies reported in the comprehensive review by Clark *et al.* (1984) and in the register compiled by the North West Regional Educational Laboratory (NREL, 1990).

Whilst educational research has many advantages over the other methods of judging the quality of schools, clearly it cannot be used in a routine way across the system. It is far too expensive for this. Its value, therefore, lies in its ability to pioneer methods of judgement and to analyse ways of improving effectiveness, rather than in contributing to the picture of overall quality. One of the major spin-offs of such research has been the development of performance indicators. An economic term used in the commercial world, it was adopted by educationalist with the publication in 1984 of a set of performance indicators by the Chartered Institute of Public Finance and Accountancy. The idea has been developed by the DES which published a set of indicators in 1989 and by the OECD which is involved in a project on international indicators involving twenty-three countries.

Whilst indicators have the obvious dangers of focusing only on those aspects of a school's work that are observable, and, like other measures, are subject to the values of those devising them, they offer considerable potential to those in schools wishing to judge themselves systematically. Like so much in education, their value lies as much in the process of defining what is important and attempting to measure it, as in any results which emerge from the exercise.

In my judgement, but clearly not in Pring's, it is a sign of a healthy school if the Head and staff are concerned with creating a set of performance indicators acceptable to them to use over time in order to examine progress.

Having defined the particular purpose of the school (in relation to its pupil body) the school can then set its broad objectives related to this mission. Performance indicators can then be used to monitor the progress towards this. However, as Crawford (1991) has argued, monitoring without feed-back and follow-up action is useless. Performance indicators provide the means to understand many of the processes (though not all) operating in schools. They are thus a powerful tool for the use of those working within the school. They cannot be a panacea, and used casually they can be of little value but, if incorporated into a whole school plan, they can be very valuable. The relationship with school development planning (DES, 1989) is obvious.

School development planning has been espoused by government and adopted by many LEAs as a means of improving quality. What is now needed is an evaluation of how effective the process of planning has been in improving the quality of the classroom, as well as of the management of the school.

These then are the main methods which exist for monitoring the quality of schools. As has been noted, they each have strengths and weaknesses. Some are controlled by government. Others, like performance indicators, rest in the hands of Heads and teachers within schools. As I have argued, these have considerable potential for schools and, in the long term, provided they are used with sensitivity, will improve quality.

CHANGE IN THE QUALITY OF SCHOOLING OVER TIME

The previous section dealt with the available methods of monitoring the quality of schools. This section will focus on the question of whether there have been changes in quality over the last few years.

Phases of schooling – primary schools

In attempting to judge whether the quality of primary schools has changed over recent years one encounters the problem of a lack of comparable data. No standardized measures of curriculum subjects have been used systematically within primary schools. The only exception to this is the work of the DES Assessment and Performance Unit (APU) which in the area of mathematics and language development has sampled the work of primary pupils over time (DES, 1976).

The major source of data, therefore, must be the reports of HMI and the research studies that have addressed the primary phase of schooling. The last major survey of primary education was undertaken by HMI in 1978. Since then various smaller-scale follow-up studies have indicated that standards have been improving. The most recent annual report by the Senior Chief HMI (1991) provides a detailed profile of strengths and weaknesses.

One aspect of development that has featured in public debate is that of reading. The publication by Martin Turner of a report (1990) implying a fall in reading standards led to the commissioning of two reports: one from the NFER designed to review evidence from local education authorities; and the other, from HMI, drawing on their inspections of schools (NFER, 1991 and HMI, 1990). It is not appropriate to review, in detail, the findings of these two reports here, but it is important to state that their overall conclusions are that the case for the fall in standards has not been proven. Because of a lack of national data on reading, it is difficult to give a precise answer to this question. It is also difficult to find a group reading text sufficiently sensitive to serve the purpose of national monitoring. Furthermore, it is unlikely that the reading test being included as part of Key Stage I of the National Curriculum will be useful as a monitoring instrument.

This is not to say that the quality of primary education is satisfactory. Indeed, the latest research (Alexander, 1991) like that of Bennett (1976), Galton and Simon (1980), Mortimore et al. (1988) and papers from the Leverhulme Primary Project at Exeter (Leverhulme, 1990), shows how variable it can be. Planning, despite the growth of school development plans, is still haphazard. The teaching of history, geography and technology is, all too often, weak and disjointed. Collaborative learning is seldom achieved despite the appearance of groups seemingly working well together. Change based on the need for more focused time, greater structure, higher level of challenge and more adequate feedback, appears necessary.

Secondary schools

There have been two overall evaluations of this age phase by HMI. The first, carried out in 1979, drew attention to variations between schools in provision, and to the inappropriateness of the curriculum for a high proportion of secondary pupils (HMI 1979). The second survey, which covered the years

1982–1986, found that almost three-quarters of the schools visited by HMI were performing satisfactorily: 'Gradual but uneven progress by Secondary Schools since the 1970s' (HMI, 1988: 4).

Drawing on the 1991 report by the HMI Chief Inspector, it is clear that almost seventy-five per cent of the work seen in secondary schools is satisfactory or better even though there are still many problem areas: 'much remains to be done, however, before all pupils, in particular lower achieving pupils, can be said to be receiving education of a satisfactory quality' (p. 8).

The unevenness of the effectiveness of schools found by HMI is entirely in line with the major research studies of secondary schools' effectiveness (Rutter *et al.*, 1979 and Smith and Tomlinson, 1988).

Another important source of information about the process of secondary education is the Hargreaves' report, written for the Inner London Education Authority and published in 1984. Apart from providing helpful definitions of achievement (broken down into four distinct components), this report made a number of proposals about the organization of schools and about the curriculum. Drawing on three research studies concerned with the attitudes of fifth-year students; of parents of new secondary pupils; and of secondary school teachers, the report identified a series of major weaknesses in the structure of secondary education.

The implementation of the report, in the form of a phased plan for school improvement, was interrupted by the abolition of the Inner London Education Authority in 1990.

One way round the lack of general school information is to focus on pupil outcomes as recorded in the results of public examinations. From the DES annual report of results (DES, 1991b), it is clear that, overall, across all subjects there was considerable improvement over the preceding ten years. At 16, for instance, there was an increase from 23 to 30 per cent for boys and from 24 to 34 per cent for girls in the proportions of pupils obtaining five or more higher grades in the public examinations. Similarly, the overall percentage with no graded results fell from 13 per cent to 9 per cent. Likewise, over the ten-year period, the proportion of 18-year-olds gaining at least one A level rose from 18 per cent to 21.5 per cent.

Other developments

Attendance rates are often used as indicators of positive attitudes towards schooling and, as such, provide a tool for monitoring. Whilst truancy is frequently a feature of public debate, there is a lack of available data on its frequency. The now abolished ILEA used to carry out an annual survey from which it was possible to infer overall trends. Such trends showed a gradual increase in attendance rates from the dip experienced in the year following the raising of the school leaving age (1974) up to the 1990s. These surveys, however, were not able to distinguish between absence due to illness and absence due to truancy and, therefore, can only provide a general indication of improved 'average' attitudes to schooling. The Parent's Charter will require schools to publish information about truancy rates but, as yet, there are few means – other than the individual judgement of an education social worker – able to discriminate between truancy and other forms of non-attendance.

The behaviour of pupils is also frequently the focus of public debate. Two sources of data exist about the overall level of behaviour: the HMI appraisal of secondary schools, and the work of the Elton Committee (1989). In its report on secondary schools, HMI stated: 'the general picture was of civilised institutions, where most pupils conducted themselves well . . . with only five per cent where there were substantial difficulties' (1988: 72). Similarly, the Elton Report found that – unlike the accounts presented by the media – serious behaviour problems were not common: '. . . teachers in our survey were most concerned about the cumulative effects of disruption to their lessons caused by relatively trivial but persistent behaviour. . .' (1989: 11).

Although it is possible to study the attitudes of school pupils (see for instance, Mortimore, 1988 and ILEA, 1984) there are few national databases available from which inferences of changes over time can be drawn. Indirect measures of attitudes such as the proportion of pupils choosing to remain at school beyond the statutory leaving age or transferring to a Further Education College, however, are available. In the early 1990s, there was a rise in the proportion of young people remaining in education (either school or further education) after the the end of statutory schooling, although the level of 47 per cent rejecting full-time education is still very disturbing. However, the proportion going on to higher education has recently increased.

In summary, then, whilst the available data on secondary schooling are partial and inadequate for the task of national monitoring, there is little evidence and inadequate for the task of national monitoring, there is little evidence of a decline in the quality of any of the measurable outcomes. Rather, there appears to have been a slow but gradual improvement in most of these measures over the last few years. This judgement fits with information provided annually by the Senior Chief Inspector of the HMI on the quality of lessons observed by Inspectors during the year. A summary based on analysis compiled by John Gray (1990) shows that from 1982 to 1990 . . . between 70 per cent and 80 per cent of all the lessons observed by HMI were judged to be satisfactory or better.

There is little room, however, for complacency. Despite the progress that has been made, secondary schools, in my judgement, need to be re-thought to fit the modern world. Research has shown that they can be very effective with pupils who are able and motivated. They are not so good with those who lack these traits, and the system, therefore, inevitably creates unmotivated students who show learning problems. Our concept of ability is still wedded to a notion of the normal distribution curve, and teachers tend to rank-order pupils with the result that some must be at the bottom.

Because of the competitive examination system, the chances of rewards for such pupils are very slight. It is not surprising, therefore, that their own assessment of the situation leads them to seek rewards in areas *other* than school achievement – for which they have little chance of success – and positive behaviour.

Furthermore, the very organization of secondary schools with relatively large numbers of groups of pupils working with a single adult, rather like a Prussian military academy, means that conformity is essential. It also means that conventional learners are well served, and less conventional learners are more likely to experience difficulties and to be seen as poorly motivated and, perhaps, less able.

It is difficult for schools to alter these patterns. Heads and teachers are as trapped by the overall system as are the pupils and, with the best will in the world, their room for manoeuvre is limited. In my view, the time is now right – not for more selection or further categorization of pupils but for a radical change to the organization of learning. Such an approach could learn much from the TVE and various work-based training schemes. It could also learn from the newly established City Technology Colleges and the patterns of organization being adopted in such well-resourced settings.

Special education

Since the publication of the Warnock Report by the Warnock Committee in 1978 and the 1981 Education Act, many Heads and teachers in special schools have been uncertain as to their role in the education service. Whilst the principle of the integration of pupils with special educational needs with their fellows has generally been accepted, local education authorities have varied considerably in the implementation of this idea. Depending on the number of schools and their geographical position, as well as on the traditions of the Authority and the attitude of parents, varying levels of integration have been achieved.

Whilst many pupils with special educational needs have now been integrated into units within mainstream schools, if not always into mainstream classes, special schools frequently have been left with those pupils with multiple needs or with the severest conditions. In monitoring the quality of such schools, the system of statementing introduced by the 1981 Act provides a means of reviewing the success of the school in promoting the progress of individual pupils, though this is seldom done. The John Fish Report, published by the ILEA in 1985, drew upon three research studies carried out by the ILEA in reaching its conclusions that many of the special educational needs of pupils were not being met. The HMI Chief Inspector's latest report, however, whilst recognizing the variability of work in schools, found 'signs of improvement'.

CONCLUSION

. . . Our society needs higher quality schooling. Most teachers, in my experience, are devoted to achieving that higher quality. Whilst they, like others, need to feel appreciated (both in terms of salary reward and perceived status) they accept that a future society will need more young people with higher levels of skill and more positive motivation. Given the right support and encouragement, I am confident that this can be achieved by our schools. Part of the task, however, will be the design of more sensitive mechanisms of quality control. These are not likely to be crude league tables of examination results which take no account of a 'value-added' component, as the recently published Audit Commission Working Paper makes clear (Audit Commission, 1991). They are likely to draw on a series of carefully thought-out performance indicators constructed from across the range of pupil outcomes.

. . . The debate on standards – with respect to schools – has been confused and unhelpful. Heads and teachers, except those of schools with very advantaged intakes of pupils, feel unfairly treated. In the future, parents are likely to be given information, in the form of league tables, which could mask considerable under-achievement or, alternatively, conceal genuine school effectiveness. The majority of pupils, for whom the various educational reforms have been designed and, on whose behalf the public debates have been held, may well come to feel that they have been used as guinea-pigs or as pawns in a series of political games.

REFERENCES

Alexander, R. (1991) *Primary Education in Leeds*, Leeds: University of Leeds.

Audit Commission (1991) *Two Bs or Not . . . ? Schools' and Colleges' A-level Performance, Working Paper*, London: Audit Commission.

Ball, S. (1980) *Beachside Comprehensive*, Cambridge: Cambridge University Press.

Bennett, N. (1976) *Teaching Styles and Pupil Progress*, London: Open Books.

Bennett, N. and Desforges, C. (1985) *Recent Advances in Classroom Research*, Edinburgh: Scottish Authentic Press.

BERA (British Educational Research Association) (1990) Policy Task Group Report on Assessment, *Research Intelligence*, Spring.

Chartered Institute of Public Finance and Accountancy (1984) *Performance Indicators in the Education Service*, London: CIPA.

Clark, D. L., Lotto, L. S. and Astuto, T. A. (1984) 'Effective schools and school improvement: a comparative analysis of two lines of enquiry', *Educational Administration Quarterly*, 20(3): 41–68.

Crawford, F. (1991) *White Paper on Higher Education: Quality Issuing Total Quality Management*, Discussion paper prepared for the Committee of Vice Chancellors and Committee of Principals (CVCP).

DES (Department of Education and Science) (1976) *The APU an Introduction*, London: DES.

—— (1989) *Planning for School Development*, London: Central Office of Information.

—— (1991a) *The Parent's Charter: You and Your Child's Education*, London: DES.

—— (1991b) *School Examinations Survey Statistical Bulletin 1/91*, London: DES.

Elton Report (1989) *Discipline in Schools*, London: HMSO.

Galton, M. and Simon, B. (1980) *Progress and Performance in the Primary Classroom*, London: Routledge & Kegan Paul.

Gipps, C., Steadman, S., Blackstone, T. and Stierer, B. (1983) *Testing Children*, London: Heinemann Educational.

Goldstein, H. (1987) *Multilevel Models and Social Research*, London: Charles Griffin.

Gray, J. (1990) 'The quality of schooling: frameworks for judgement', *British Journal of Educational Studies*, 38(3): 204–23.

Hargreaves, D. (1967) *Social Relations in a Secondary School*, London: Routledge & Kegan Paul.

—— (1984) *Improving Secondary Schools* (London, ILEA).

HMI (Her Majesty's Inspectorate of Schools) (1978) *Primary Education in England*, London: HMSO.

—— (1979) *Aspects of Secondary Education in England*, London: HMSO.

—— (1988) *Secondary Schools: An Appraisal by HMI*, London: HMSO.

—— (1990) *The Teaching and Learning of Reading in Primary Schools*, London: DES.

—— (1991) *Standards in Education*, Annual Report of HM Senior Chief Inspector of Schools, London: DES.

ILEA (Inner London Education Authority) (1985) *Educational Opportunities for All*, John Fish Report, London: ILEA.

Juran, J. (1988) *Quality Control Handbook*, New York: McGraw Hill.

Lacey, C. (1970) *Hightown Grammar: The School as a Social System*, Manchester: Manchester University Press.

Leverhulme Primary Project (1990) *Occasional Paper Autumn 1990*, Exeter, School of Education, University of Exeter.

Mortimore, J., Mortimore, P. and Chitty, C. (1986) *Secondary School Examinations*, Bedford Way Papers 18, London: Institute of Education, University of London.

Mortimore, P., Sammons, P., Stoll, L., Lewis, D. and Ecob, R. (1988) *School Matters*, Wells: Open Books.

Mortimore, P. and Stone, C. (1991) 'Measuring educational quality', *British Journal of Educational Studies*, 39(1): 67–82.

NFER (National Foundation for Educational Research) (1991) *An Enquiry into LEA Evidence on Standards of Reading of Seven Year Old Children*, London: DES.

NREL (Northwest Regional Educational Laboratory) (1990) *Effective Schooling Practices Update*, Portland, Oregon: NREL.

OECD (Organisation for Economic Cooperation and Development) (1989) *Schools and Quality – An International Report*, Paris: OECD.

Pring, R. (1991) 'Standards and quality in education', Paper presented at the Annual Conference of the Standing Conference on Studies in Education, 8 November (Chapter 1 of this volume).

Reynolds, D. (1982) 'The search for effective schools', *Schools Organisation*, 2(3): 215–37.

Rutter, M., Maughan, B., Mortimore, P. and Ouston, J. (1979) *Fifteen Thousand Hours*, London: Open Books.

Smith, D. and Tomlinson, S. (1989) *The School Effect: A Study of Multi-Racial Comprehensives*, London: Policy Studies Institute.

Tizard, B., Blatchford, P., Burke, J., Farquhar, C. and Plewis, I. (1988) *Young Children at School in the Inner City*, Hove: Lawrence Erlbaum Associates.

Turner, Martin (1990) *Sponsored Reading Failure: An Object Lesson*, London: IPSET Education Unit.

Warnock, M. (1978) *Committee of Enquiry into the Education of Handicapped Children and Young People*, London: HMSO.

Chapter 3

The non-league table method

Ian Birnbaum

Written with secondary schools in mind, Birnbaum proposes that the composite pupil assessment outcomes could be used by schools to work out how much value is added by the school in each subject area. In this way, he suggests, teachers would be able to work out a picture of each individual pupil's relative strengths across the curriculum. This kind of quantitative information would, he argues, throw light on potential areas for management development within each school.*

Many schools and LEAs are interested in carrying out a value-added analysis, but lack the basic measurement of attainment and ability of each individual student. This prompted me to describe an easy-to-use technique that deserves to be better known. Its purpose is to estimate the relative value added by subject area, and any school, LEA or national body could use it straight away.

Let us begin with a simple example. Table 3.1 below shows the GCSE results of three students, Ben, Naina and Rosa. In the table, grade A has been scored as 7, grade B as 6, etc. The final column gives the average score for each student (obtained by adding up his/her scores and dividing by the number of GCSEs taken).

Table 3.2 shows the GCSE scores for the same three students with the average score for the student taken off each GCSE score. So for example –0.29 under art is obtained by subtracting 3.29 (Ben's average score) from 3 (Ben's art score). These relative scores basically represent how much better or worse the students did in each of their subjects compared to their average result overall.

The last row of Table 3.2 sets out the average relative scores for each subject across the three students. For example, the art average relative score is obtained by adding Ben's relative score to Rosa's (since Naina did not take art) and dividing by two. The English Language average is obtained by adding all three scores and dividing by three.

* Originally published in *Education* (1 July 1994).

Table 3.1

	Art	Eng Lang	Eng Lit	Fren	Geog	Hist	Maths	Sci	Tech	Ave
Ben	3	4	2	3	–	4	3	4	–	3.29
Naina	–	3	3	5	6	3	4	5	4	4.13
Rosa	2	4	–	5	4	–	3	3	4	3.57

Table 3.2

	Art	Eng Lang	Eng Lit	Fren	Geog	Hist	Maths	Sci	Tech
Ben	−0.29	0.71	−1.29	−0.29	–	0.71	−0.29	0.71	–
Naina	–	−1.13	−1.13	0.87	1.87	−1.13	−0.13	0.87	−0.13
Rosa	−1.57	0.43	–	1.43	0.43	–	−0.57	−0.57	0.43
Total	−0.93	0.00	−1.21	0.67	1.15	−0.22	−0.33	0.37	0.15

One can easily imagine extending the above analysis to all Y11 students in a school, LEA or even the country as a whole. Something similar could also be done for A level or for National Curriculum assessment results. What does the analysis tell us?

Figure 3.1 expresses in chart form the relative scores across a whole school. This shows, for example, that students in this school score on average around 0.4 of a grade more on art than each of them does across all the subjects they take. The chart also shows that girls are doing better at art relative to each of their average subject achievements than boys are relative to each of theirs.

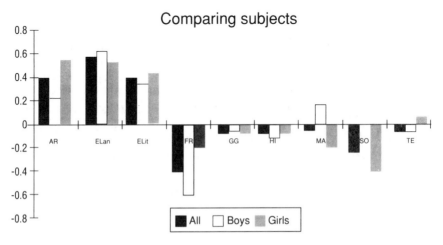

Figure 3.1

One of the great advantages of this approach is that it provides a reasonably pure record of value added for each subject. This is because it is an ipsative analysis, which uses each student's own results as the basis of comparison. It therefore removes the effect of most of the confounding variables, such as overall prior ability/attainment and socio-economic factors, which usually beset value-added comparisons. For example, overall ability or socio-economic factors are unlikely to explain why Ben in Table 3.2 has done relatively worse at art than his overall average. Were this the case, we would expect them to affect his results in all subjects, so the effects will cancel out when the relative score is calculated. Of course Ben's prior ability might partly explain his art result and this should be explored with him as part of the school's formative review of student progress.

However, unless the school specially selects its students in this way, such specific ability is unlikely to show through across the students as a whole in relation to the average overall ability in the school.

Similarly, social factors might explain Rosa's relative underperformance in art (in comparison, remember, to her performance overall), but it is most unlikely that over the student body as a whole such subject-specific social factors will show through in relation to the overall socio-economic effects. In the same way, while myriad 'chance' factors might account for an individual student's relative under- or over-performance in a subject, the effect of these should cancel out over the whole school, although with small numbers of students statistical tests might have to be used.

Is it, therefore, fair to infer from Figure 3.1 that, for example, more value is being added on average in the school to students' development in art than it is in French? The answer is yes, as long as results in art are comparable nationally to those in French. If this is not so, the Head of modern languages at the school might validly say that results are worse in French because French is relatively harder.

The way to resolve this doubt is to do the same analysis nationally and publish the results. Since the data exist for this now, there is much to be said for SCAA or the DFE carrying it out. It would provide revealing information on subject comparability which could greatly contribute to national policy. In the meantime, it is probably down to LEAs to compile and publish such data for all its schools. The overall school figures in an LEA should be a reasonably reliable indicator of relative subject difficulty, particularly in a large LEA.

It is important to underline that this sort of analysis will only allow valid comparisons to be made within one chart, not across charts. So if another school's chart (or, indeed, the national chart) records, say, 0.5 of a grade below average for art, we cannot infer that the first school is adding more value to its students' art development. Assuming the subjects are of comparable difficulty, all we can say is that the first school is adding more value in art than it is in, say, geography.

We cannot get round this by examining the average overall level of achievements in the two schools and making the necessary allowances, because this amounts to reverting to raw art scores. We move the baseline away from each student's average score, and it is only by using this baseline that we can validate the value-added interpretation in the first place. Moving the baseline to overall achievement at school level taints any comparison with the effects of socio-economic and other factors.

This technique therefore only allows comparisons to be made across different subjects for the same group of students. Comparisons cannot be made across different groups of students for the same subject. This means that the method is of limited use for league tables, but offers highly beneficial information for the management of any school. Perhaps this is to its advantage.

Chapter 4

Performance assessment in perspective
International trends and current English experience

Patricia Broadfoot

A comparative piece, Patricia Broadfoot examines international trends in assessment. Drawing on data from Australia, Canada, the USA, the UK and France, she identifies five international trends in the changing 'culture' of assessement.

She then goes on to examine some of the problems in assessing 'authentic' performance with young children, and draws on a research project carried out in England in 1991 and 1992, monitoring the impact of the National Curriculum and its assessment. Here she concentrates on the SATs (Standard Assessment Tasks) for seven-year-olds, to look at some of the tensions which teachers in fact experienced in attempting 'authentic assessment'. *

INTRODUCTION: A CHANGING ASSESSMENT AGENDA

The development of performance assessment techniques is an increasingly characteristic feature of the education systems of the developed world. The urgent need to promote the learning of skills and competences *that cannot be tested by more traditional techniques*, and to report on these, lies behind a range of related developments in international assessment and reporting practice.

Historically, the practice of educational assessment has been largely driven by a perceived need to *measure* individual intellectual capacity. When educational assessment first began to be widely used in the nineteenth century, this was in response to the institution of mass educational provision and the associated need to provide a 'ladder of opportunity' into the expanding industrial economies of that era. The pressing need to find mechanisms of selection that would be both socially acceptable and identify the 'best' candidates, led to a premium being put on assessment techniques that appeared to be fair and objective, that had high levels of reliability.

---

* Originally published in H. Torrance (ed.) (1995) *Evaluating Authentic Assessment*, Buckingham: Open University Press (edited slightly for this volume).

In such a 'high stakes' environment in which, to a very significant extent, test results determined life chances, it was inevitable that there should be an overwhelming emphasis on reliability so that the assessment might be seen to operate fairly and consistently. The question of validity – whether the test does indeed measure what it is intended to measure – has arguably been subordinated to the overwhelming need for comparability of results. The preoccupation with reliability has, in turn, tended to lead to a concentration on that which is more readily measurable – such as knowledge and understanding and a relative, if not absolute, neglect of higher-level intellectual skills, of personal and social competencies and attitudes (Wilson, 1992).

The prevailing assessment culture is still steeped in these preoccupations despite the fact that the social imperatives for assessment today are very different from those of a century ago. Curriculum goals have changed and broadened. There is a higher priority on encouraging people to continue their education rather than on excluding them. Above all, there is an urgent need for education systems to train people who will have the appropriate range of skills and attitudes to be capable of undertaking a variety of work roles in a climate of rapid technological change. Problem-solving ability, personal effectiveness, thinking skills and willingness to accept change are typical of the general competencies straddling cognitive and affective domains that are now being sought in young people. To the extent that the assessment industry falls short of matching these new educational priorities with appropriate new techniques, so it will also inhibit the pursuit of such new educational goals.

As a growing international awareness of the need for change in assessment priorities is leading to a range of significant initiatives, so the problems of bringing about such a major change in the way we think about assessment are becoming increasingly apparent. At the heart of the problems is the *Zeitgeist* of a previous age – a set of unquestioned assumptions concerning assessment priorities which in turn inform judgements concerning the merits of particular techniques. As Nisbet (1992) suggests:

> Public and professional attitudes to assessment in education constitute an 'assessment culture' which, like other cultures, rests on a common set of assumptions and beliefs, and depends on familiarity and long established practices. It is not surprising that the process of change is slow and difficult.

In what follows I explore, first, some of the *policy issues* in performance assessment. The aim will be to examine the rationale for performance assessment as it is embodied in different national initiatives and, in so doing, to classify the nature and scale of the changes currently taking place. The second part of the chapter focuses more directly on some of the technical issues in performance assessment as these have been identified in the particular example of National Curriculum assessment in England and Wales.

POLICY ISSUES IN PERFORMANCE ASSESSMENT

One of the difficulties inherent in any attempt to examine issues concerning performance assessment is the problem of precise definition and boundaries. In particular, I shall argue here that many of the technical problems which we are beginning to identify concerning performance assessment are caused by its inappropriate use, rather than by shortcomings in the approach *per se*. Or, to put it another way, while it may prove possible in the longer term to develop performance assessments which are sufficiently reliable to bear the weight of 'high stakes' selection decisions for individual careers and/or 'high stakes' institutional judgements, it remains doubtful whether it is possible to design performance assessments of this kind which are also useful for diagnostic and formative purposes. It may be, as Stiggins (1992) suggests, that large-scale assessment programmes cannot meet teachers' very different assessment needs.

Evidence that this may be so is increasingly being provided by the attempts of a number of different countries to increase the element of performance assessment within traditional certificate examinations and by the much more novel and radical initiatives aimed at both monitoring and indeed raising national standards of achievement by the assiduous use of assessment. The rationale for both these developments is rooted in the changing assessment culture referred to above which prioritizes the promotion of higher and more appropriate learning outcomes rather than the search for the most accurate ways of measuring these.

International comparisons provide for a more detailed definition of the elements of this new culture as follows:

1   An increasing emphasis on formative, learning-integrated assessment throughout the process of education.
2   A commitment to raising the level of teacher understanding and of expertise in assessment procedures associated with the devolution of responsibility for quality assurance in the certification process.
3   An increasing emphasis on validity in the assessment process which allows the full range of curriculum objectives including cognitive, psychomotor and even affective domains of learning to be addressed by the use of a wider range of more 'authentic' techniques for gathering evidence of learning outcomes.
4   An increasing emphasis on describing learning outcomes in terms of particular standards achieved – often associated with the pre-specification of such outcomes in a way that reflects the integration of curriculum and assessment planning.
5   An increasing emphasis on using the assessment of individual pupils' learning outcomes as an indicator of the quality of educational provision, whether this be at the level of the individual classroom, the institution, the state, the nation or for international comparisons.

Some examples from Australia are cited here since they are indicative of these trends; then some brief comparative comments are offered on some of the initiatives in a number of other countries before I deal with the experience of National Curriculum assessment in England and Wales in detail.

Australia

Concern to monitor standards on a national basis in Australia, as well as in individual states, is reflected in the Australasian Cooperative Assessment Programme which is involved in devising national subject profiles for mathematics and literacy/English. The origins of this initiative are described in the report of the Working Party on Basic Skills and Program Evaluation of the Australian Education Council 1989 as follows:

> The development of national subject profiles must be closely linked with national curriculum development. It would then be possible to develop a framework comprising a sequence of levels through which students progress. . . . Levels could be established for each major component of a subject. For example, literacy could be thought of as a composite of reading, writing, listening and speaking, each with its own sequence of levels. . . . The levels could be defined by a set of *assessment tasks* which could be standardised and widely publicised among schools and the community generally. These tasks could include pencil and paper tests, observation of student performance against set criteria, assignments, etc. Various systems may have a preference for various modes of assessment.

The crucial point to note here is that standardization of the assessments is not to be the product of common tasks but is rather to be achieved by the provision of extensive illustrative material which teachers can use as a basis for judging their own students' performance.

Individual states have also taken their own initiatives in this respect. In Western Australia, for example, a Monitoring Standards in Education Program has produced benchmarks for English and mathematics and has developed assessment tasks to assess the performance of students in Years 3, 7 and 10. These assessments show system-wide performance but *not* individual, school or area-based results. The same materials can also be used by teachers, however, as part of their normal classroom assessment or as part of school development planning. The approach is illustrated in Appendices 4.1 and 4.2 (from *Monitoring Standards in Education*, Ministry of Education, Western Australia, 1990).

> The approach of the Western Australian MSE is different from the approach taken in the Victorian and NSW testing programs [i.e. those of the States of Victoria and New South Wales] in that it begins with the attempt to make explicit the levels of performance expected of students in

Years 3, 7 and 10. In this sense, the 'benchmarks' resemble the 'attainment targets' of the English National Curriculum. In contrast, the Victorian and NSW programs estimate and report levels of student achievement without reference to pre-specified standards. Any judgements about minimum acceptable levels of performance are likely to be made only after test results are available.

A second feature of the MSE project is that it is designed to make standard assessment tasks available to teachers for their own monitoring purposes. Assessment tasks used as part of the 1990 testing will be made available free-of-charge to all government schools in Western Australia [WA] in Term 4, 1990. Because these tasks will have been used with a sample of WA schools, teachers using them will be able to compare the performances of their own students with results for the state.

In common with NSW and Victoria, the WA Monitoring Standards in Education program uses item response theory (IRT) as the basis for defining levels of achievement within each of a number of subject profile components.

(Masters, 1990)

The assumption behind this approach is that performance assessment can best be made by a combination of verbal descriptions of achievement levels with examples of the kinds of task and behaviour that illustrate those levels. Sadler (1987) argues that

> verbal descriptions, on the one hand, have a significant role to play in drawing attention to the particular criteria that are salient at different points on a grading scale. They therefore provide valuable keys into complex evaluative frameworks. But because of the variable interpretation of terms, *verbal statements need concrete referents*. The respective strengths of exemplars on the one hand and verbal descriptions on the other suggest the possibility of specifying standards efficiently by a combination of the two.

A slightly different approach to performance assessment which relies more heavily on observation in a number of routine classroom situations than on specially organized assessment events is illustrated by the Victorian literacy profiles, as Figure 4.1 shows. This is essentially a way of structuring teachers' observations within a hierarchical set of benchmarks to make explicit the professional monitoring of individual children's progress that is an integral part of teaching.

This use of benchmarks and verbal descriptions as the basis for performance assessment is being developed in many other countries as well. A very similar approach is to be found in the Toronto 'benchmark' Standards of Student Achievement in Canada, as Appendix 4.3 illustrates. In this initiative, empirically derived standards are used to provide level descriptors in a number of set tasks in key curriculum areas. Teachers use the task to standardize their reporting of student achievement to gauge how well their students are doing.

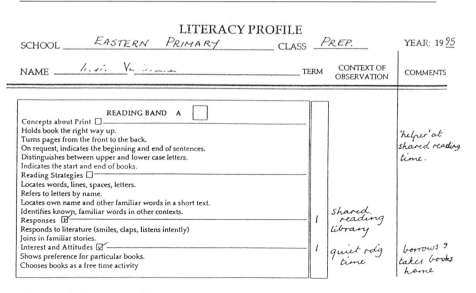

Figure 4.1 Literacy profile

Source: Ministry of Education, Victoria, *Literacy Profiles Handbook,* 1990

In New Zealand, the 1990 Tomorrow's Standards Report recommended the use of 'standard assessment tasks' to sample learning outcomes for students of 8 and 12 years of age on a four-year cycle (Crookes, 1993). The recently launched 'Achievement Initiative' is designed to meet this need by providing teachers with specially developed tasks on which to base their classroom assessment.

United States

The United States provides extensive evidence for the existence of a changing assessment agenda. For example, in California the new state-wide student assessment program takes the ambitious view that performance assessment which includes asking students to speak, research, create and experiment as well as write, can be a basis for state-wide testing. According to Bill Honig, California's former State Superintendent of Public Instruction:

> The assumption was that a subjective grading process was appropriate for classroom assessment, but not for public accountability. But we can and must standardize these more valid assessments – it's either that or live with the results of narrow assessment and poor accountability.

In addition to the use of open-ended problems, enhanced multiple-choice questions and investigations, portfolios are also a significant development. Such a planned selection of students' work collected from work done throughout the school year not only allows teachers, parents and others to see the developing pattern in students' learning and across a wide range of knowledge and skills, it also allows students to be active in the assessment process, which will help to enhance their metacognitive strategies. Similar initiatives are taking place in many other states, including Vermont, Michigan, Connecticut and Maine (Koretz *et al.*, 1992).

United Kingdom

The United Kingdom provides one of the starkest illustrations of the various policy issues surrounding the introduction of performance assessment in the context of the rather different strategies being employed to provide for national assessment in England and Wales, Scotland and Northern Ireland (Broadfoot *et al.*, 1992).

In England and Wales the 1988 Education Reform Act introduced, for the first time, a National Curriculum for Years 1–10 with defined attainment targets and regular assessment of students against these targets by both continuous teacher assessment (TA) and Standard Assessment Tasks (SATs), the latter to be administered at the end of each of four 'Key Stages' and to be expressed in terms of ten hierarchical levels. The rationale for this assessment was provided by the Task Group on Assessment and Testing (TGAT) whose 1988 report identified four purposes for national assessment: diagnostic, formative, summative and evaluative.

In Northern Ireland, by contrast, the aim is to use a combination of Common Assessment Instruments (CAIs), External Assessment Resources (EARs) and continuous teacher assessment. EARs involve the provision of resources for teachers to use as part of the normal teaching–learning situation but which are specifically arranged and targeted at particular levels of achievement to provide assessment information. In a letter to the Chairman of the Northern Ireland School Examinations and Assessment Council (NISEAC) dated 27 February 1991, Lord Belstead wrote that 'the external assessment resources . . . should produce valuable information for teachers which will help them plan their work with each child, and moreover should be of significant assistance in their evaluation of their teaching strategies'. The CAIs are broadly similar to the SATs used in England and Wales which are described in more detail later in this chapter. Like the SATs, they will become progressively more like conventional tests as students increase in age (NISEAC, 1992).

In Scotland, performance assessment has also been introduced in response to government concerns to improve the assessment and reporting of student learning.

The guidelines on assessment (SOED 1991) provide a theoretical framework for practice in schools which is supported by specific arrangements for the testing of children in P4 and P7 across three curricular areas – reading, writing and mathematics. In the pilot round (1991) and first reported period (1992) of National Testing, the intention was that pupils at the above stages would be tested within specified periods of the school session. Test material is from the 'bank' of units built up and held in the Primary Assessment Unit (PAU) of the Scottish Examination Board (SEB). Scrutiny of such units across the five attainment levels (A–E) reveals in the main, an attractive range of assessment materials which are criterion – rather than norm – referenced.

(Thomson and Ward, 1992)

There was a widespread parental boycott of the tests of 7-year-olds in Scotland. Parents feared too much pressure on children with very little benefit to children, teachers or parents. In consequence, these arrangements have now been changed. As from November 1992 teachers will have a catalogue of assessment resources and can administer their chosen tasks whenever they feel an individual pupil is ready. It remains to be seen if this more individualized approach to assessment is manageable in the context of a large class of children, but whatever the outcome, events in Scotland underline the crucial policy point in relation to performance assessment that where external testing for summative or evaluative purposes is unacceptable *in principle*, increasing the validity of the assessment will be unlikely to change this. In this respect it might be said that Scottish parents' expectations of assessment derived from their experience of a previous culture of assessment, and that they were not prepared to give novel instruments the benefit of the doubt.

France

The opposite point is, interestingly enough, made in France, where comprehensive national assessment has been introduced for explicitly formative purposes. Teachers are required to administer centrally devised tests to their students at the *beginning* of certain 'key stages' – and to use the information so generated as the basis for a more individualized pedagogy (Broadfoot, 1992). Unfortunately, however, because the assessments are not 'integral' either to teachers' ideology or to their classroom practice, neither of which is typically informed by a child-centred perspective, it is proving difficult for teachers to make effective use of the information so generated (Pluvinage, 1992).

PROBLEMS IN IMPLEMENTING PERFORMANCE ASSESSMENT WITH YOUNG CHILDREN

Having briefly reviewed some of the ways in which performance assessment has been incorporated into recent assessment policy initiatives in different countries, it is appropriate to explore in more depth some of the technical problems that have characterized these attempts. In what follows, I draw on the results of a project sponsored by the Economic and Social Research Council which is monitoring the impact of the National Curriculum and its assessment procedures on primary schools, teachers and children. The data were gathered during the 1991 and 1992 SAT administration using a combination of classroom observation and interviews with teachers and pupils in nine classrooms from across England. Data were also gathered from interviews and questionnaires with teachers from a larger nationally representative sample of 48 schools.

It is appropriate to use the particular assessment initiative of SATs at Key Stage 1 (7-year-olds) for close analysis because the tasks set have, from the outset, been intended to represent best practice in performance assessment. Children have been asked to undertake tasks which are open-ended, engrossing and stimulating, designed to enable them to demonstrate the whole range of skills embodied in a particular Attainment Target. That this was generally achieved is borne out by observational data which recorded consistently high levels of student interest and enthusiasm and by interview data in which students said how much they had enjoyed the tasks.

The SAT example to be focused on here is a fairly conventional maths exercise which was chosen for study because it was one of the more standardized SATs and therefore should have had fewer problems of reliability (Appendix 4.4). While the task was designed to be used with large groups, typically teachers assessed the children in small groups with the rest of the class being taken by a colleague or teaching aide, although sometimes such support was not available. Regardless of how they were organized, the administration of the SATs evoked a range of concerns among teachers. These included constraints on normal classroom practice; whether a common stimulus to perform was being provided; whether children who were aware of being tested were underperforming because of anxiety; whether children who did *not* know they were being assessed were therefore also underperforming; and whether teachers were being broadly consistent with different groups of children and in relation to each other in the amount of help being given.

The changes in normal classroom style brought about by the requirements of SATs were much in evidence to the research team, especially teachers not being able to intervene in a testing situation in order to promote learning. Teachers felt they could not engage in their normal classroom behaviour of, for example, listening and showing, when a child intervened into a conversation or activity in some way. Though the official position regarding SATs has, from the outset, been that the SAT activities can be woven into a teacher's half-term theme so that they can constitute learning experiences in themselves, this contradicts the requirements of the test process that teachers must avoid giving children direct help and 'asking questions that lead the child to the correct response'. Teachers found this an unnatural way of working and felt the children could not understand the change in their practice, as our fieldnotes indicate:

> A teacher remarked (St Bede's, 1991): I really find it so frustrating being unable to help them when they don't understand.
>
> At another school the teacher had to rebuke 2 children, Adam and Tracy, who have begun to discuss their work:
>
> · 'Adam, Tracy, if I have to tell you not to talk again, I may get angry.' Which produced in the children a puzzled and slightly hurt reaction at this strange departure from normal classroom practice.

Teachers disliked having to reverse the pattern of co-operative, collaborative work in their classrooms:

> Another teacher was heard to say: No, go away Paul. I don't want you to see this.
>
> Later she commented: He looked at me as if I'd gone mad.

Torrance (1991) similarly reports that teachers in consequence often felt deskilled because pre-specified tasks and the observation of pre-specified outcomes is fundamentally against the logic of the infant classroom. Pupils inevitably noticed the change in the teacher's role.

Other unorthodox features of teachers' classroom practice during SATs may be identified as giving covert messages to children that the activity was not routine even if the children did not know, as many children appeared not to know, especially in 1991, that they were being tested. Indeed, depending on the school, many children appeared to lack the conceptual vocabulary to understand what testing is. For example, one teacher working in a busy classroom differentiated her interaction with the SAT children quite clearly by lowering her voice, a cue that this was not 'normal' work. Unusual seating arrangements – three to a table usually occupied by six children, for example, to prevent collaboration – were other features which not only tended to inhibit teachers' attempts to present SATs as just one of a number of ongoing classroom activities, but also appeared to cause stress to both teachers and pupils to the extent that they represented an imposition of different modes of classroom interaction.

HOW STANDARDIZED WERE THE SATS THEMSELVES?

Variability in the organization in which SATs took place meant that children were given different contexts in which to show their level of achievement. In addition to these variations, our data identify a range of sources of variability within the operation of the task itself which are also likely to have affected children's ability to demonstrate their achievement.

Variability in teacher stimulus

Stage in a given SAT

One whole range of variables clusters around the notion of possible reactions to the experience of testing. One obvious source of potential significance concerns who conducts the tests and the stage reached in the SAT process. Our fieldnotes charted a consistent pattern in relation to subsequent groups of pupils undertaking the same SAT. Typically, this starts with a relative lack of confidence on the part of the teacher caused by lack of familiarity, rising to a peak of performance on the second or third application of a given SAT, when the teacher was sufficiently confident and at ease with a particular SAT task to be able to present it in the most positive way for pupils. In contrast, we documented teachers' flagging enthusiasm and boredom as they commenced the same task, in some cases, for the ninth time, and found themselves unable to stimulate the children to perform in the same way as earlier groups because of this.

It is not without significance either that the children were thought likely to respond differently to someone they know conducting the SATs than to a stranger or other teacher. Teachers were so sensitive to this issue that in one case in 1991 a teacher came back, unpaid, from maternity leave to undertake SATs because

(Mrs AR, Kenwood School): I feel the children need to do SATs with someone who knows them really well.

Whether testing is made explicit

Perhaps the most significant issue in this respect, however, is whether or not the teacher made the reality of testing explicit to the children and what consequences this decision may have had. In some cases the SAT was presented as a game, in others as a learning activity, and in a few as a test. In many classrooms, if you did not know what was going on, you would not have realized that some children were involved in an assessment activity.

In one classroom in 1992 the teacher was so concerned about the impact of the Maths 3 SAT in particular, involving the pressure of both timing and clearly right or wrong answers, that she was prepared to undertake testing the children on a one-to-one basis in a class of 30, even though this caused major administrative problems. Indeed, it is an illustration of the strength of the teacher's commitment to protect the children from anxiety and from a feeling of failure that she was prepared to engage in a lengthy period in which there was relatively little teaching for the rest of the class in order to provide this.

It was particularly noticeable in the more explicit testing materials of 1992 that the unambiguous nature of some of the SATs, notably the maths test, produced a greater tension and anxiety in the children and a greater aware-ness of failure which some teachers took great pains to avoid. This was done by a variety of subterfuges – for example, in one school:

> All of the group have finished Level 2. Teacher says: 'Right, books away.'
> To the others: 'Raymond finished this on Friday so we'll let him go back to class now.'
> It was explained later that this was the exit point from the test for Raymond, disguised as the rest move on to attempt Level 3, to avoid hurting his feelings.
> In this same school, the teacher presented another SAT as a game:
> 'Charles got 5, Raymond got 5, and Graham got 6, so Graham is cham-pion.
> 'OK, mighty Graham, go back to class and tell Mrs P that you are the champion at these. Ten housepoints for you.'
>
> (Fieldnotes, St Anne's School)

How the SATs were presented

On almost all occasions when SATs were observed, activities were presented as fun or as part of normal classroom life, which both observation and later interviews with children suggested were accepted as such. In 1991, although 32 per cent of teachers in our sample reported that some children showed signs of stress, most reported no special reaction (59 per cent) and 63 per cent of the teachers who responded suggested that the children experienced, rather, considerable enjoyment in doing the SATs. Occasionally, children demonstrated awareness of some element of assessment in the activities in such responses as:

> Maybe she wanted to test us out in those things.

or

> To see if we're good at it.

More often, children happily admitted that they had no idea why they had been asked to carry out the activities.

> I don't know. She said, 'Four of you will be with me.' I don't know why.

They seemed to accept this, whether they described the tasks with enthus-iasm:

> It was fun. I really liked it.

or indifference:

> A bit boring, but quite nice.

Teachers' strategies for avoiding stress in children included making no overt reference to, or demonstration of, assessment in their presence. Children were not usually dismissed from a group if they were clearly finding the task too difficult but were allowed to continue with teacher assistance which meant that they would not be considered to have reached the level on which they worked.

Sometimes they were told that they had worked extremely well but that they looked tired and 'could leave this work for now'. So much so that one teacher even wondered whether her children's relaxed attitude to the SATs was conducive to their producing the best work of which they were capable or whether some awareness of being tested might have lent an edge to their performance. The rather unorthodox implementation of the Maths 3 SATs in one school in 1992 bears out this argument to some extent:

> The teacher says: 'We're going to start off nice and easy so Steven won't get his worried face, and Rebecca won't get her frown.' (Funny expressions on his face) 'To help you, you'll have these sheets.'
>
> He reads out: '4 + 2 Ugh!' (pulls a face) '2 + 3 Ugh! They're very easy. As soon as you've finished, turn over your paper and take out your puzzle book. You won't need to look at anyone else's because they're *so* easy. Don't worry if you get left behind. It's only a bit of fun and we'll have another competition later. So, remember the rules: no looking at anyone else's, no showing anyone else. When you've finished I'll come round and give team points.
>
> 'We've all got to start together to make it fair, so put your name on it, but don't start yet. To help you, you can use number trail or counters. It's only a bit of fun to make up some points.
>
> 'When I count 3 you can start – no one must see yours. Otherwise it won't be a fair competition. Don't forget the counters if you need them.'
>
> (In the context of a competition or a game, not being allowed to co-operate seems acceptable to the children, even though it's not the way they normally work.)
>
> He goes round the tables: 'I told you they were easy. Don't forget the top are take-aways and the bottom adds.'
>
> (Carla has already finished and taken out her puzzle.)
>
> 'Jason, ssh! Good girl. She's got her paper turned over so I know she's finished. Let's see which table comes first. If it were Rainbow Table it would be good because there's someone from every team on their table.
>
> 'Carla is finished and Heather and Clare and Steven. OK, Yellow Team is finished and that's 20 points to them.'
>
> (Continuing the competition theme.)
>
> 'Which team will be next? Oh, yes, we're only waiting for Michael on that table now.'

Says to Steven: 'Don't forget, the ones on the bottom are take-aways, *not* add-ups.

'How are we doing now? A couple more minutes then, there'll be a chance to win some more points with another game.

'One more to go – will Red Team get third? No, it's Blue Team who are finished. Well done, Blue Team. Ten more points for Blue Team.

'All right, close your puzzle books. Now, the next one you'll have to be really speedy so switch your brains on.

'Now, there are some silly shapes here.' (Holds up fruits and shows whole class – points out and names each fruit.) 'Not to worry about them, they're just a bit of fun to put the answers in. I'm only going to give you 5 seconds for each answer. Don't worry if you miss out, just jump on to the next one. The apples and oranges are just a funny space to put the answer in. Instead of a box, you've got an apple to put the answer in.'

(Gives out sheets)

Gives an example of how to do it: 'Let's think of an easy sum and we'll all write it down. 2 + 1 – can you write number 3 in the apple shape in the black box. Now, when I ask you another sum, you write the answer in the orange shape. That's all you have to do. Go down the black box side. If you like, you can put your finger on the orange so you know what to write next.'

(Shows cards with sums and numbers. Holds card with number 1 on it.) 'Are you ready for the orange sum? Put your hand over it so other people can't see it. Don't worry – it's only a bit of fun.

'Cover it up.'

(Goes through numbers – tells people not to shout out.)

The next one's even easier. 'This is too easy – write in the lemon shape: 5 + 1.' (Children call out: 6) 'No, no, don't shout out.'

(One child has written the answer on the wrong side. Gives another sheet. Continues to hold up cards with sum on, read it out and explain which shape to write in. In between, he tells funny stories about each fruit.)

'Next to the strawberry: answer 4 + 3. Next the pineapple' (talks about where pineapple comes from). 'This is a special sum: 6 + 2.' (All cards with sums on also have dots on.) (Tells stories about plums and elephants in Africa – elephants got drunk on plums.) 'In the plum shape: 5 + 4. You should have one shape left at the bottom, a peach shape. Here comes an easy sum: 1 + 6.'

(Playtime bell has gone)

(Asks one child on each table to collect papers)

'I think I made that too easy. I'm going to have to give out lots of housepoints. If you like that puzzle, shall we try that again on Monday with some harder sums?'

Children: 'Yes, yes.' (All enjoyed it.)

While the teacher has successfully presented MA 3 as a game/competition which the children appear to have enjoyed, the other Year 2 teacher has taken a different approach. She carried out the SAT in a straightforward way, more like a 'mental arithmetic' test. She commented that the children tightened up a lot, sat back in their seats, drawing in their breath, and appeared rather stressed. 'It was so unlike the way we normally work', she commented.

(Fieldnotes, St Anne's School)

This lack of standardization in the presentation of SATs, even within one school is not unusual.

The effect of pupil anxiety

In other cases, however, it was not possible for teachers either to allay children's anxiety or to reduce the awareness of a testing situation. In some cases, this was because the children were already anxious and aware of what was involved before the testing situation.

Gemma finishes and gives her sheet to the teacher. Afterwards the teacher asks Gemma the 3 subtraction sums she had wrong. Gemma instantly answers perfectly. The teacher discusses this: Should she consider that Gemma knows the work or not? She wonders whether the SAT is chiefly designed to test children's ability to do the calculations involved or their ability to apply their knowledge in the context of using money. Sharon is extremely conscientious in scrupulously keeping to time allowances for 'quick recall' activities and in cases like Gemma's, when she tries to examine the aims behind the task: very different from the situation at Meadway, where the teacher was cheerfully open about 'bending the rules'.

(Fieldnotes, Leigh School)

Anxiety was particularly marked in some maths SATs involving mental arithmetic where children were under pressure to get the right answer in a given time.

Differences between teachers in the amount of help given

As well as the lack of standardization caused by variations in the amount of help that a teacher felt required to give to different children in the class, there was also considerable variability *between* teachers themselves in this respect.

An important source of possible variation in SAT outcomes centres on different practices of teachers in interpreting the performance of children. Despite the strict instructions surrounding the Maths 3 1992 test, for example, in which the context for testing and the criteria of performance were unambiguously defined, the research team observed many variations in the way in which teachers actually introduced and judged the SATs. Some were very flexible in the timing allowed for doing the sums; others allowed children more than one attempt at the task; or provided aids in the form of flashcards; or other kinds of help to facilitate children answering.

In some cases, the teacher may have given less help than she was allowed to.

> The teacher and I look through the Maths sheets. The teacher seems quite upset as she looks at each one. She names children who can do it but they've got muddled up or something.
>
> Some have not concentrated: 'Oh dear, I think they can get one wrong but I'll have to check. It means I won't have many Level 2s. They'll all be Level 1s. I think I may have done it wrong.'
>
> The teacher checks the Teacher's Book for procedures and discovers that she should have helped the children to write in the first example on Sheet 3. This is the one where the children have to give change, that has caught out most children.
>
> 'Oh dear, I've made a mistake.'
>
> We go into the staffroom for coffee, the teacher clutching the Teacher's Book to check for further details. She decides that she will ask individual children to think about their answers to Maths 3 in the afternoon 'to see if the penny drops'.
>
> 'Well, they can do it, I know, but they haven't done it and I should have helped them more so we'll see if they can do it.'
>
> There is a lot of sympathy. Teacher: 'What is it all for?'
>
> Other teachers: 'It's for the parents. It doesn't help us at all.'
>
> The teacher is not trying to cheat. She simply wants the test to reflect validly what she feels the children can do; to the extent that it does not, then she is prepared to manipulate it.
>
> *Later.* The teacher has spent the afternoon checking children who 'had not understood what to do in the morning'. She judged that 6 had been able to pass Level 2 'in fact because they had succeeded when the example was explained'.
>
> (Fieldnotes, St Bede's)

Our fieldnotes record many examples of teachers giving differential degrees of help to different children and groups or interpreting performance in ways more or less different from the regulations because they feel that the child in question is truly worthy of a particular level.

Other examples of more overt departure from the SAT instructions include, for example in the 1992 Maths 3, Sheet 1, children looking at each other's answers and copying; in Maths 3, Sheet 2, children shouting out the answers; or in other schools allowing children to count on their fingers even though this is explicitly not allowed.

Chantelle is doing the change exercise for Maths 3.

CHANTELLE: 'What must I do now?'
TEACHER: 'You take 15p to the shop, put out 15p, now take away your 12p.'

Chantelle does so and enters the right answer. She does the next sum correctly with no help. Chantelle reads: '8p + 6p.' She counts 13p, writes this, puts out 20p, enters 7p as change from 20p. She quickly does the last sum correctly. Jason asks the teacher for help with the first sum. The teacher goes through the steps with him. He arrives at the right answer. The next sum, 12p + 7p, he puts out the coins and writes 1p. He looks at the coins, takes the sheet to the teacher: 'Miss, what do I do next?'

TEACHER: 'What do they cost?'
JASON: '19p.'
TEACHER   (pointing to '20p'):   'How much do you take to the shop?'
JASON: '20p.'
TEACHER: 'So, put out the coins and find out how much you have left.'

Jason returns, puts out 20p, takes out 19p, enters '1'. He goes through the addition 8p + 6p of the next sum correctly and enters 14p. He correctly puts out 20p, takes 14p out, stares at the 14p.

JASON: 'Miss, 14p, take away 20p . . .'
TEACHER: 'No, not 14 . . . 20. You need 20p to start with.'
JASON: 'I haven't got enough.' (He has, in fact.)
TEACHER: 'Get some more, then.'

Jason silently moves the coins around, writes '5' in the box (for 20p −14p). For the last sum, he writes '15' (for 6p + 7p).

TEACHER: 'Will you check that, Jason. Put them out again.'
JASON: 'Will you help me?'
TEACHER: 'I am helping you. Put out 6 and 7.'

Jason does so. Jason: 'It's 13p.'

TEACHER: 'Change your answer to 13, then.'
JASON: 'It *is* 13.'
TEACHER: 'No, you've written 15.'

She alters 13 to 15. Jason waits for further help.

TEACHER: 'Now put out 15p and take 13p away.'

   Jason writes 2p in the box. He takes it to the teacher. Four of the 5 sums are marked right.
   (Chantelle finished in 6 minutes, with very little help. Jason needed help at every step, and took 20 minutes.) The teacher has to deal with

Angus. He hits Chantelle with a brush; she pushes him. The teacher and (Mary) have to pull him off and hold him away.

The teacher (entering the results in her assessment book): 'I'm in a muddle here – I'm not sure I should record them as reaching this level when I've had to help them so much, but I'm going to, anyway.' (All have Level 2.) 'I'll try some on Level 3, but I don't think they're going to get it. I didn't think she'd manage that.'

(Fieldnotes, Meadway School)

A very different kind of variation was illustrated in another classroom where the children were having a discussion, as part of a science SAT in 1991, about pollution.

TEACHER:	'Now, have you seen this?' (Shows big plastic pond liner.)
TEACHER:	'Just a minute, boys.' (Teacher draws girls in to speak.)
TEACHER:	'Do you think a cat will get into our conservation area?'
CHILDREN:	'No, as the cats can't get in.'
TEACHER:	'That's right, so it's a safe place for fish and birds. Yes, how do they come in?'
KEVIN:	'They fly.'
TEACHER:	'Yes, so why is it a safe place?'
CHILD:	'Because the cats can't get in.'
TEACHER:	'Yes, so we've got birds coming in and now we're making something more special with our pond. So what do birds like when you have a pond?'
CHILD:	'Slugs.'
TEACHER:	'Well, so what do all animals like? What do we all need?'
CHILD:	'Water.'
TEACHER:	'Good, because we can't manage without water. It will be special for . . .'
CHILD:	'Fish.'
TEACHER:	'And the birds, yes.'
TEACHER:	'And then we've got to be very careful, haven't we? Any ideas, Maria?'
MARIA:	– (Silence)
TEACHER:	'Well, OK. Laura?'
LAURA:	'Perhaps the fox might come, and dogs could.'
TEACHER:	'Well, it wasn't what I was thinking – once our pond is finished, what do we have to do and be careful of?'

Kevin suggests netting to keep the dogs off.

TEACHER:	'OK, do you think we need a net for our pond?'
EMMA:	'My uncle makes (?) (?) paths.'
TEACHER:	'We are going to make an area that's nice. And what would we have to do if we saw an infant dropping a crisp packet?'

KEVIN: 'Say tidy up.'
TEACHER: 'Yes.'

(Fieldnotes, Meadway School)

These fieldnotes illustrate the situation in which the teacher is seeking the right answer from the children as defined by her in relation to a constantly shifting agenda. The teacher is careful to draw the girls into the discussion and to control the dominance of Kevin but she dominates the discussion herself and the children have to guess her mind. This kind of interpersonal domination by the teacher which may facilitate or discourage the oral performance of children is explored in more detail in Filer (1993) but clearly will have an effect on how capable, orally, the teacher defines the children to be. In relation to the above excerpt the teacher herself said later:

'I found I was chasing them round the houses today to get them to say things.'

Overview

In sum then, we can say that in both years studied there were enormous variations in the manageability, conduct and interpretation of SATs. Variation was caused both by differences in the opportunities provided for children to perform at their best and by the interpretation of that performance by the teachers. The data suggest that SATs conducted with a keen, able group of children, enjoying the teacher's undivided attention, where the teacher herself is confident and still interested in the task, will elicit the children's best performance, avoid most of the anxiety, and provide for reasonable standardization. At the other extreme, where the task itself may involve considerable creativity and thus interpretation in the marking, or collaboration between children, or where it is too difficult for some children or where the teacher has little or no help in the classroom so that she can work with the SAT group, the children are likely to perform well below their optimum level, their performance variously affected by anxiety, distractions, interference from other children, and copying from each other.

The data suggest that teachers who are already working in the more difficult circumstances of larger numbers of more disruptive children, where there are less resources for additional support, are the very teachers who need to guide and intervene more to elicit children's optimum performance. Such teachers are likely to be those who have to intervene more to help children through the task and are likely to be more troubled about the position of levels. The fact that even the highly standardized SATs were subject to very considerable variation, both in the management of the task and in the circumstances in which the children were able to work, suggests that what many would see as the obvious answer of providing more short, sharp tests, may not in fact be the solution to providing greater standardization.

While such tests may superficially appear to meet the perceived need for objective information about children's levels of achievement, they will in practice still embody an enormous amount of variation in the *context* for performance and will in addition have very limited utility. Indeed, they are likely to be quite counterproductive in terms of at least two of the four purposes of national assessment, the diagnostic and the formative. While written tests would appear to offer relative ease of administration and greater comparability between schools, they are also likely to produce extremely limited information. They may also result in teaching to the test and constrain the National Curriculum in ways which would be unacceptable.

In this respect it is interesting to contrast teachers' views of the teacher assessment (TA) component of SATs which was felt to have caused little or no disruption to normal classroom routine, and was felt to be both reasonably accurate and manageable in terms of time. At the same time, these assessments have led to some new insights concerning children's learning for many teachers. Given that all the teachers felt there was a very fair match between the SAT results and TA results, the question must arise of the value of an additional layer of testing which in practice is so unreliable.

The original blueprint for national assessment, which was set out in the TGAT (1988) Report, identified four different purposes for national assessment: diagnostic assessment to identify individual pupils' strengths and weaknesses; formative assessment to give feedback and encouragement; summative assessment to report on a given pupil's attainment at a given stage of schooling; and evaluative assessment to provide aggregated information about the overall level of pupil achievement in any particular school, as a basis for comparing one school with another. It is immediately clear that SATs do not provide very well for any of these purposes. They are not frequent enough, nor sufficiently integrated into the normal routines and curricular emphases of a given classroom to provide guidance for pupils and teachers about appropriate individual learning targets. Nor are they reliable or detailed enough to provide summative and evaluative information that can be confidently trusted by teachers, parents and the public. Since the SATs come only at the end of a Key Stage and since they identify only very broad levels of attainment, this suggests that the latter is their real purpose. Our data suggest that in the context of primary education in England and Wales in which the ideology of child-centred education is still central, it is not possible to devise any assessment task or test to be implemented by teachers which will not be subject to very considerable contextual effects. One might wish to go further and argue that any attempt to test 7-year-olds on a systematic basis is bound to be heavily overlaid in its results by contextual effects, including who does the teaching, in what circumstances, and what is the personal affective state of the child concerned. Even if such tests were superficially reliable – for example, if they were multiple-choice, like those which are used widely in Japan and the USA – their validity would be very questionable.

Yet the many strongly worded criticisms of SATs, which were voiced by teachers, have been almost exclusively concerned with their mode of implementation and use and not with the tasks themselves. Rather, these have been generally appreciated. So has the increased liaison between colleagues, the increased contact with parents and the provision of moderation arrangements which teachers see as the result of a more formal obligation to engage in teacher assessment.

THE WAY FORWARD

It is apparent that there is now an international trend towards more broadly based performance assessment which is conducted by teachers. It would appear that much educational benefit can be derived where teachers are challenged to be more professional in their assessment practice and are provided with materials to support them in their task of identifying the complex web of strengths and needs that characterize the individual learner. But while the policy priorities behind the development of performance assessment initiatives typically include this agenda, they equally tend also to embrace the very different agenda of institutional and system accountability. In this kind of 'high stakes' context, evidence such as that included in this chapter, which suggests that performance assessment cannot be detached in practice from the mediatory effects of teachers' professional strategies and judgement, must give rise for concern. Given the choice between narrow, but relatively reliable, 'high stakes' assessment and valid, but relatively unreliable, 'high stakes' assessment, the only tenable strategy would appear to be to abandon attempts to make aggregated judgements of institutional or system-wide standards on the basis of 'high stakes' assessments. Rather what is needed is a different combination of approaches. For standards monitoring this should involve a light-sample-based and hence 'low stakes' performance assessment approach like that pioneered in England by the APU. Such an approach could be combined with the use of carefully structured, and externally supported, performance assessments backed up by a portfolio of evidence both to facilitate the process of teaching and learning and to improve communication with parents and other users. By contrast, as long as assessment data are used as the basis for league tables and the like, the potential of performance assessment to enhance learning is unlikely to be realized and grave injustices may be done to many schools and children.

ACKNOWLEDGEMENT

This chapter is based on the work of an ESRC research project (grant reference number R000234673) involving Dorothy Abbott, Andrew Pollard, Marilyn Osborn and Paul Croll. More details of the research project reported here are included in Pollard et al. (1994): see references.

APPENDIX 4.1 DEFINING 'BENCHMARKS' (WESTERN AUSTRALIA)

MATERIALS DEVELOPED FOR THE PROGRAM

The benchmarks. What to look for statements and assessment tasks were developed from selected phases/stages of the English and mathematics syllabuses. Because they are linked directly to the respective syllabus documents, the benchmarks reflect the content and methodologies of each subject. They were developed in collaboration with practising teachers and were subject to scrutiny by other educatiors and community representatives..

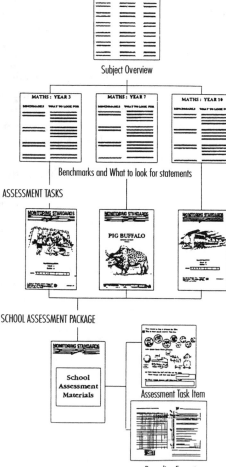

BENCHMARKS

Subject Overview

Benchmarks and What to look for statements

ASSESSMENT TASKS

SCHOOL ASSESSMENT PACKAGE

Assessment Task Item

Recording Format

BENCHMARKS

The benchmarks have been written in behavioural terms to enable observations and judgements to be made about student performance.

WHAT TO LOOK FOR STATEMENTS

What to look for statements provide examples of what to look for when making judgements as to whether or not a student is working at the benchmark.

ASSESSMENT TASKS

Assessment tasks were developed to monitor performance in relation to the benchmarks. They are not intended as 'minimum competency' tests but focus on the range of skills evident within each year level. The tasks have been developed around a theme or within a context which is consistent with the syllabus. This allows the students to write about and solve problems within situations that are meaningful to them. The assessment tasks were administered to a sample of students in Years 3, 7 and 10.

ASSESSMENT MATERIALS

Assessment materials for English and mathematics will be made available to schools during Term 2, 1991. The package will include assessment tasks, marking guides, record sheets and reporting guides, record sheets and reporting guidelines. These will allow teachers and schools to monitor the performance of their students and to compare this performance to system-wide results.

APPENDIX 4.2 DEFINING 'BENCHMARKS' (WESTERN AUSTRALIA)

BENCHMARK	WHAT TO LOOK FOR
7 LEVEL OF UNDERSTANDING Using appropriate texts, the student is able to locate significant information (both implicit and explicit), recall details in a sequential order, summarise the relevant information, recognise relationships between ideas and substantiate personal evaluations.	There is evidence that the student can: • identify the form, e.g., *report, description, graph, myth, interview*; • accurately locate and recall relevant information from print and non-print forms – in a sequential order when appropriate; • infer information from print and non-print forms, i.e., cause/effect and problem/solution relationships; emotion from clues located throughout the text; • infer the meaning of figurative language, e.g., *as light as a feather*; • categorise and classify information; • recognise the underlying concepts of words, e.g., *'magpie' as distinct from the less precise 'bird' may imply a large black and white bird that swoops people*; • identify ambiguous and inconsistent messages in print and non-print forms; • connect and synthesise two ideas separated within a text or between texts; • make simple evaluations and judgements about the text; • substantiate answers to questions using text information and background knowledge where appropriate.
3 LEVEL OF UNDERSTANDING Using appropriate written and graphic texts the student recalls explicit information and infers implicit information. Unsubstantiated judgements may be made.	There is evidence that the student can: • obtain meaning from simple tables and diagrams; • demonstrate understanding by drawing to complement the text; • recognise cause and effect relationships, e.g., *'We can't go to the zoo today because it is raining'*; • retell a few significant events in sequential order; • identify explicit information, e.g., *characters, time and place*; • identify the emotions of characters, e.g., *the man was sad*; • construct meaning from simple figurative language, e.g., *he was as white as a sheet means that he looked pale and unwell or scared*; • elaborate answers to questions, e.g., *it is a scary story because it's about a mean old witch who eats children*; • follow simple written directions.

APPENDIX 4.3 DEFINING 'BENCHMARKS' (ONTARIO, CANADA)

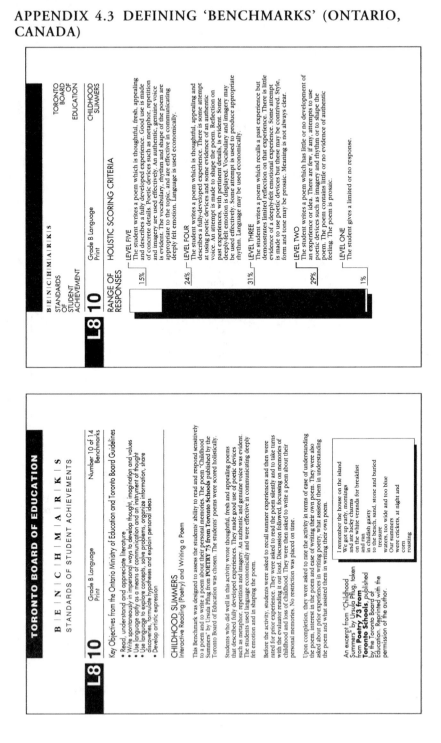

B|E|N|C|H|M|A|R|K|S

STANDARDS OF STUDENT ACHIEVEMENT

TORONTO BOARD OF EDUCATION

L8 10

Grade B Language
Print

CHILDHOOD SUMMERS

RANGE OF RESPONSES

HOLISTIC SCORING CRITERIA

LEVEL FIVE
15% The student writes a poem which is thoughtful, fresh, appealing and describes a fully developed experience. Good use is made of concrete details. Poetic devices such as metaphor, repetition and imagery are used effectively. An authentic, genuine voice is evident. The vocabulary, rhythm and shape of the poem are appropriate to the topic, and are effective in communicating deeply-felt emotion. Language is used economically.

LEVEL FOUR
24% The student writes a poem which is thoughtful, appealing and describes a fully-developed experience. There is some attempt at using poetic devices and some evidence of an authentic voice. An attempt is made to shape the poem. Reflection on past experiences, with pertinent details, is evident. Some deeply-felt emotion is displayed. Vocabulary and imagery may be used effectively. Some attempt is used to produce appropriate rhythm. Language may be used economically.

LEVEL THREE
31% The student writes a poem which recalls a past experience but demonstrates limited reflection on that experience. There is little evidence of a deeply-felt emotional experience. Some attempt is made to use poetic devices but these may be contrived. Style, form and tone may be prosaic. Meaning is not always clear.

LEVEL TWO
29% The student writes a poem which has little or no development of an experience or idea. There are few, if any, attempts to use poetic devices such as imagery and rhythm or to shape the poem. The poem contains little or no evidence of authentic feeling. The poem is prosaic.

LEVEL ONE
1% The student gives a limited or no response.

TORONTO BOARD OF EDUCATION

B|E|N|C|H|M|A|R|K|S

STANDARDS OF STUDENT ACHIEVEMENTS

L8 10

Grade B Language
Print

Number 10 of 14
Benchmarks

Key Objectives from the Ontario Ministry of Education and Toronto Board Guidelines

• Read, understand and appreciate literature
• Write spontaneously in impersonal ways to develop thought, imagination and values
• Use language apply as a means of communication and an instrument of thought
• Use language to explore concepts, solve problems, organize information, share discoveries, formulate hypotheses and explain personal ideas
• Develop artistic expression

CHILDHOOD SUMMERS
Interactive Reading (Poetry) and Writing a Poem

This Benchmark was designed to assess the students' ability to read and respond sensitively to a poem and to write a poem about their personal memories. The poem "Childhood Summers" by Ursula Pflug from **POETRY 73 from Toronto Schools** published by the Toronto Board of Education was chosen. The students' poems were scored holistically.

Students who did well in this activity wrote thoughtful, fresh and appealing poems that described fully developed experiences. They made good use of poetic devices such as metaphor, repetition and imagery. An authentic and genuine voice was evident. The students used language economically and were effective in communicating deeply felt emotion and in shaping the poem.

Before the activity, students were asked to recall summer experiences and then were rated for prior experience. They were asked to read the poem silently and to take turns with the evaluator reading it out loud. Discussion followed, focussing on memories of childhood and loss of childhood. They were then asked to write a poem about their personal memories. No restriction was placed on time.

Upon completion, they were asked to rate the activity in terms of ease of understanding the poem, interest in the poem and ease of writing their own poem. They were also asked about prior experiences in writing poetry, what assisted them in understanding the poem and what assisted them in writing their own poem.

An excerpt from "Childhood Summers" by Ursula Pflug, taken from **Poetry 73 from Toronto Schools**, published by the Toronto Board of Education. Reprinted with the permission of the author.

I remember the house on the island
We got up early, mornings
and ate lucky charms
on the white veranda for breakfast
and ran
in childish gaiety
to the beach, sand, stone and buried
treasure
waters, too wide and too blue
Our summers
were crickets, at night and
corn
roasting

APPENDIX 4.4 STANDARD ASSESSMENT TASKS FOR 7-YEAR-OLDS (ENGLAND AND WALES)

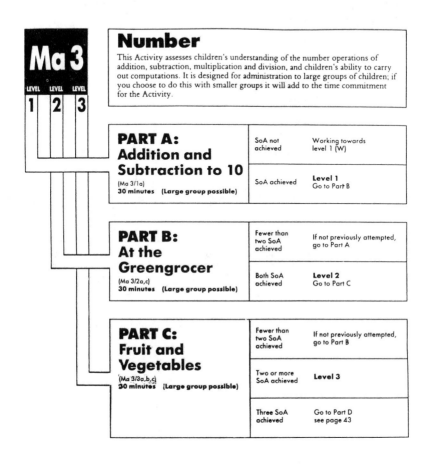

Ma 3

LEVEL 1   LEVEL 2   LEVEL 3

Number

This Activity assesses children's understanding of the number operations of addition, subtraction, multiplication and division, and children's ability to carry out computations. It is designed for administration to large groups of children; if you choose to do this with smaller groups it will add to the time commitment for the Activity.

PART A:
Addition and Subtraction to 10
(Ma 3/1a)
30 minutes (Large group possible)

SoA not achieved	Working towards level 1 (W)
SoA achieved	**Level 1** Go to Part B

PART B:
At the Greengrocer
(Ma 3/2a,c)
30 minutes (Large group possible)

Fewer than two SoA achieved	If not previously attempted, go to Part A
Both SoA achieved	**Level 2** Go to Part C

PART C:
Fruit and Vegetables
(Ma 3/3a,b,c)
30 minutes (Large group possible)

Fewer than two SoA achieved	If not previously attempted, go to Part B
Two or more SoA achieved	**Level 3**
Three SoA achieved	Go to Part D see page 43

PART A:
Addition and Subtraction to 10

Resources

Each child will need a copy of Ma 3 *Pupil Sheet 1*, a pen or pencil, and ten counters, of the kind you normally use.

What to do
Large-group procedure

◆ Help the children to work out the first addition and the first subtraction on Ma 3 *Pupil Sheet 1*, as an introduction.

This is not assessed. Although the additions and subtractions are listed on the same sheet, there is no need for the children to do them all at the same time, or in the order listed.

◆ Ask each child to complete Ma 3 *Pupil Sheet 1*, using counters to work out the answers.

You may give the children any help they need in reading the *Pupil Sheet*, but they must work out the computations without help in order to demonstrate evidence of attainment.

◆ If you are working with a small group, ask each child to perform the computations on Ma 3 *Pupil Sheet 1*.

You may do this orally, or using the *Pupil Sheet*, or rewriting the *Pupil Sheet* in a form with which the children are familiar (for example, 2 and 3 instead of 2 + 3). However you decide to approach it, each child should carry out the same 10 computations without help (after the initial examples) in order to demonstrate evidence of attainment.

Ma 3

LEVEL **2**   LEVEL **3**

PART B:
At the Greengrocer

Resources

Each child will need a copy of Ma 3 *Pupil Sheets 2* and *3* and a pen or pencil. For *Pupil Sheet 3* children may use money or play money or counters if this is your normal practice.

If you decide to work with a small group, you may wish to use real or play fruits marked with the prices.

What to do
Large-group procedure

◆ Give each of the children a copy of Ma 3 *Pupil Sheet 2*.

◆ Explain that you are going to read out some additions and subtractions very quickly, and that they should write each answer in the fruit you name.

In explaining the work, use whatever words you and the children are used to. The fruits are a way of showing children where to write their answers without the possible confusion that might be caused by numbering.

◆ Ask the children to look at the blue column of fruits. Read out '2 + 1'; explain that they should write the answer '3' in the apple. Tell them that the following ones will need to be done very quickly. Explain that they should work down the page filling in the answers in the fruits.

◆ Then read out the following additions, allowing children *no more than 5 seconds to answer each one*:

    4 + 4   (orange)
    1 + 5   (lemon)
    3 + 7   (pear)
    4 + 3   (strawberry)
    6 + 2   (pineapple)
    5 + 4   (plum)
    1 + 6   (peach)

For example, say 'Four plus four; write the answer in the orange', and so on.

This assessment is aimed at children's ability to recall number facts without calculating, so it is important to allow them no more than 5 seconds to answer. Reassure children by telling them that they can leave a blank and move on to the next one if unable to answer quickly. Some children respond well if this is presented as a game or race; in any case, present it in a relaxed way so that children do not become worried if unable to keep up.

Part B continues

Ma 3

LEVEL **2**   LEVEL **3**

Large-group procedure (continued)

You may write the additions and subtractions on flash cards or a chalk board if you wish, but children must not be able to see any one for more than 5 seconds.

◆ Then tell the children to look at the red column of fruits.

◆ Read out '3 – 1'; explain that they should write the answer '2' in the apple. Tell them that the following ones will need to be done very quickly. Explain that they should work down the page, filling in the answers in the fruits.

◆ Then read out the following subtractions, allowing children *no more than 5 seconds to answer each one*:

     9 – 4 (orange)
     7 – 5 (lemon)
     4 – 3 (pear)
     10 – 7 (strawberry)
     9 – 6 (pineapple)
     8 – 2 (plum)
     5 – 3 (peach)

For example, say 'Nine minus four; write the answer in the orange', and so on.

◆ Give each of the children a copy of Ma 3 *Pupil Sheet 3*. Help them to work out the first addition and subtraction and to write the answers in the boxes.

◆ There is not a time limit for this *Pupil Sheet*.

◆ Ask them to complete the rest of the sheet by themselves. They may use counters or money if this is your normal practice.

You may give any help necessary in reading the words on the sheet, but children must perform the calculations without help to demonstrate evidence of attainment.

◆ If you are working with a small group, ask each child all of the eight additions and eight subtractions given above. The first addition and the first subtraction should be discussed as an example and not assessed.

You may do this in oral or written form, and vary the order of the questions, but each of the children should do the same 16 questions that appear above.

Part B continues

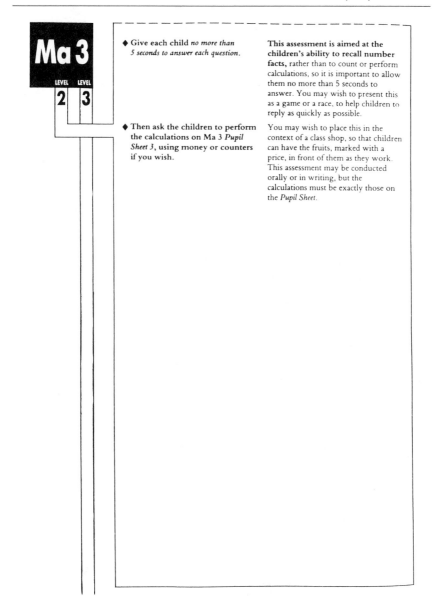

Ma 3

LEVEL **2**   LEVEL **3**

◆ Give each child *no more than 5 seconds to answer each question*.

◆ Then ask the children to perform the calculations on Ma 3 *Pupil Sheet 3*, using money or counters if you wish.

This assessment is aimed at the children's ability to recall number facts, rather than to count or perform calculations, so it is important to allow them no more than 5 seconds to answer. You may wish to present this as a game or a race, to help children to reply as quickly as possible.

You may wish to place this in the context of a class shop, so that children can have the fruits, marked with a price, in front of them as they work. This assessment may be conducted orally or in writing, but the calculations must be exactly those on the *Pupil Sheet*.

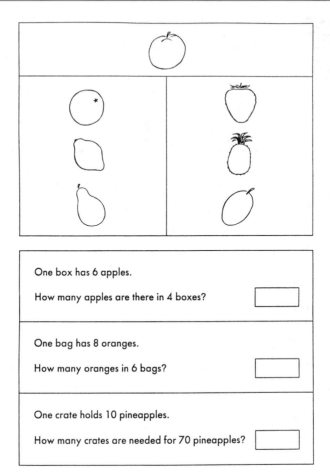

One box has 6 apples.

How many apples are there in 4 boxes?

One bag has 8 oranges.

How many oranges in 6 bags?

One crate holds 10 pineapples.

How many crates are needed for 70 pineapples?

REFERENCES

Australian Educational Council (1989) Report of the Working Party on Basic Skills and Program Evaluation (including student portfolios) cited in G. Masters (1990) 'Subject Profiles as Frameworks for Assessing and Reporting Student Achievement', Discussion Paper for Management Committee of Australian Co-operative Assessment Project, Perth.

Broadfoot, P. (1992) 'Assessment procedures in French education', *Education Review* 44(3): 309–26.

——, Harlen, W., Gipps, C. and Nuttall, D. (1992) 'Assessment and the improvement of education', *The Curriculum Journal* 13(3): 215–30.

Crookes, T. (1993) *New Zealand National Education Monitoring Project*. University of Otago.

Filer, A. (1993) 'Contexts of assessment in a primary classroom,' *British Educational Research Journal* 19(1): 95–107.

Koretz, D., Stecher, B. and Deibert, E. (1992) *The Vermont Portfolio Assessment Program: Interim Report on Implementation and Impact 1991–2 School Year*, CSE Technical Report 350, Los Angeles: University of California.

Masters, G. (1990) 'Subject profiles as frameworks for assessing and reporting student achievement', mimeo, Australian Council for Educational Research.

Ministry of Education, Victoria (1991) (Schools Programs Division) *Literacy Profiles Handbook, Curriculum Frameworks Support Materials*. Victoria: Ministry of Education.

Ministry of Education, Western Australia (1990) *Monitoring Standards in Education Information Bulletins*, Perth: Ministry of Education.

Nisbet, J. (ed.) (1992) *Assessment and Curriculum Reform*, University of Aberdeen.

NISEAC (Northern Ireland Schools Examinations and Assessment Council) (1992) Assessment Arrangements for 1992/3 Pilot Year, Belfast: NISEAC.

Pluvinage, F. (1992) 'L'évaluation dans la gestion des enseignements: commentaires sur l'évaluation 1991 en sixième', Paper given to 15th CESE Congress, Dijon.

Pollard, A., Broadfoot, P., Croll, P., Osborn, M. and Abbott, D. (1994) *Changing English Primary Schools*, London: Cassell.

Sadler, R. (1987) 'Specifying and promulgating achievement standards', *Oxford Review of Education* 13: 191–209.

Stiggins, R. J. (1992) 'Two disciplines of educational assessment,' *Counselling and Development*.

TGAT (Task Group on Assessment and Testing) (1988) *Task Group on Assessment and Testing: A Report*, London: DES.

Thomson, G. and Ward, K. (1992) *Test Material and its Use in the Primary School*, University of Edinburgh.

Torrance, H. (1991) 'Evaluating SATs: the 1990 pilot', *Cambridge Journal of Education* 21(2): 129–40.

Wilson, M. (1992) 'Educational leverage from a political necessity. Implications of new perspectives on student assessment for chapter 1 evaluation', *Educational Evaluation and Policy Analysis* 14(2): 123–45.

Chapter 5

Spanish policy and practice – assessing learning the constructivist way

Alejandro Tiana Ferrer

Reporting on and analysing curriculum reform in Spain, Alejandro Tiana Ferrer explores some of the social constructivist underpinnings of the curriculum and its assessment (or evaluation, as it is known in Spain). He does this by looking at the structures which have been introduced for curriculum planning and assessing learning. *

AN EDUCATION SYSTEM IN A PROCESS OF REFORM

The Spanish education system has been undergoing a process of reform for several years now. The so-called *White Paper for the Reform of the Education System* served as the basis for the drafting of the Law on the General Ruling of the Education System (LOGSE), passed in 1990. This was the start of a far-reaching reform of the education system and curricula.

The process of educational reform is moving in three complementary directions. In the first place, the Law transforms the *structure* of the education system, establishing Primary Education (6–12), followed by the comprehensive Compulsory Secondary Education (12–16), Vocational Training and a two-year Baccalaureate. Both Primary and Secondary levels are divided into two-year cycles. Each one of these is conceived to be a single unit, with the final decision as to whether the pupils move on to the next cycle being taken at the end of each.

The second direction of the reform process refers to the introduction of a new model of *curriculum development*, which will be dealt with in greater detail later on. The third direction is aimed to improve the quality of education, which is considered to be one of the central purposes of the reform carried out.

In fact, the LOGSE devotes a full chapter to the educational factors which contribute to improving the *quality of education*. Specific attention is paid,

---

* This chapter was commissioned specially for this volume. It is based on a paper prepared by the author as a contribution to the CERI-OECD project on Quality, Standards, Curriculum, Assessment (1994).

among others, to in-service teacher training, autonomy of schools, the promotion of research and innovation, provision of academic, psycho-pedagogical and vocational guidance, the redefinition of the role of the inspectorate and the evaluation of the educational system by means of creating the National Institute for Quality and Evaluation (INCE).

THE PROCESS OF CURRICULUM DEVELOPMENT

As well as restructuring the education system and adopting a series of measures aimed at improving quality, the LOGSE has introduced a new model of curriculum development, with the following basic features:

1 It is an open and flexible model, in the development of which Autonomous Regions, schools and teachers had to take an active part.
2 It aims to respond to four fundamental questions which allow the planning and development of educational practice: what to teach, when to teach, how and what to teach, how and when to assess.
3 It is a broad model and is not simply limited to the acquisition of concepts and knowledge, but also includes practical skills, attitudes and values.
4 It has two different functions: that of making the intentions of the educational system explicit and that of serving as a guide to teaching.

First step: setting the Basic Curricular Design or official curriculum

The curriculum is developed through three different levels. The first one is the so-called Basic Curricular Design or official curriculum. This is defined by each Autonomous Region and must incorporate the core curriculum established across the state (which occupies from 55 per cent to 65 per cent of the school timetable).

The core curriculum includes various components. First, it states the *general goals of the level*. They are defined as a series of different abilities (locomotive, cognitive, affective or emotional balance, interpersonal relationships, and social action and integration) which pupils have to develop and/or learn in the course of their schooling as a consequence of their education.

Second, the core curriculum includes broad *curricular areas*. The areas defined for Primary and Compulsory Secondary Education are those set out in Table 5.1.

In each of these areas, the curriculum includes various components:

1 An *overarching statement* or explanation of the sense, approach and the general principles of the area, accompanied by guidelines for its teaching.
2 *General objectives, expressed in terms of abilities*, which the pupil is to have attained by the end of the level. Unlike the level goals, these add an explicit reference to contents.

Table 5.1 Curricular areas in the official curriculum

Primary education	Compulsory secondary education
Knowledge of the natural, social and cultural environment	Natural sciences
	Social sciences, geography and history
Artistic education	
Physical education	Physical education
	Visual and plastic education
Language, official regional language and literature	Language, official regional language and literature
Foreign languages	Foreign languages
Mathematics	Mathematics
	Music
	Technology

Cross-curricular subjects:
- civic and moral education
- education for peace
- education for health
- education for gender equality
- environmental education
- sexual education
- education of the consumer
- road safety

3   The most suitable *contents* to develop the abilities included in the level goals and area objectives. This is not a list of subjects to be dealt with, but is rather a catalogue of blocks to be worked on at different cycles in the level. The area contents do not refer solely to conceptually based contents, but also incorporate contents relating to procedures, values and attitudes.

4   *Attainment targets* or criteria to design activities to enable assessment which are coherent with the general goals of the level and the area objectives.

Second step: drawing up the school Curricular Project

Once the official curriculum has been established by each Autonomous Region, schools have to adapt it to their particular situation. This adaptation takes the form of a document called the Curricular Project, a central feature of the Spanish model of curriculum development. It constitutes an intermediate link between the official curriculum and the teaching activities which take place in classrooms and should reflect the relevant decisions adopted on the following elements of the curriculum:

1   *General goals of the level*: The school must adapt the goals set in the core curriculum to its specific characteristics. Furthermore, the cross-curricular subjects must be incorporated into the curriculum.

2 *Sequence of objectives and contents of each cycle*: The official curriculum does not distribute the general objectives for each area, their contents and attainment targets in cycles. This represents one of the key decisions which teachers have to make when drawing up the Curricular Project. It should set out the abilities and contents which have to be worked on in each cycle.

3 *Methodological strategies*: The Curricular Project must also include references to elements such as methodological principles and options for each curricular area, the criteria adopted to put pupils into groups, organization of space and time at school or selection and criteria for the use of the materials and teaching resources.

4 *Assessment strategies and procedures*: As regards decisions on assessment, the Curricular Project must first tackle the question of what to assess. On the basis of the attainment targets included in the official curriculum, the school should: a) review them according to their own characteristics, adapting these where necessary; b) draw up attainment targets for each cycle, according to the sequence of objectives and contents carried out in the Project itself. Second, the question of how to assess should be tackled, with reference to situations, strategies and procedures. Third, the Curricular Project must decide when to assess, considering at least three basic times: initial, formative, summative. Fourth, the document must decide on the type of report which is to be used at the school and to whom the information regarding the results of the assessment is to be given. Fifth, it must establish criteria for: a) deciding whether or not to move the pupil up to the next cycle or grade; b) supporting the pupils who receive negative assessment; c) deciding if a pupil will or will not attain the final qualification.

5 *Measures to ensure diversity*: The Curricular Project must, finally, establish the contents and structure of the guidance programmes which are to be developed in the school, the optional subjects to be offered (in the case of secondary schools), the way in which curricular diversification will be organized, as well as the organization of resources for pupils with special educational needs.

Third step: drawing up the Classroom Programme

The third level of specification of the curriculum is composed of what are known as Classroom Programmes. These consist of specifying the decisions taken in the level or school Curricular Project for each specific group of pupils. The Programmes are drawn up by each teacher for his/her particular set of pupils and for each year, including the sequence of contents, the teaching units to be developed and the assessment procedures to be applied.

A FLEXIBLE, SCHOOL-BASED SYSTEM OF ASSESSMENT

It can be inferred from this presentation that the Spanish education system does not set universal standards for areas and levels as a whole, but rather sets certain minimum attainment targets which have to be completed, specified and adapted by each school for its own particular pupils. At national level, the State and the Autonomous Regions set the general attainment targets for area and level in the official curriculum. At school level, the Curricular Project presents the attainment targets for level, area and cycle. At classroom level, the teacher sets the specific targets for his/her subject and group of pupils, on the basis of which the assessment procedures and instruments to be applied throughout the year will be decided.

In line with this model for designing and developing the curriculum, the mechanism established for the assessment of students has three basic characteristics:

1 It is a flexible system, since the specific attainment targets and criteria of assessment, accreditation and promotion to the next level are established by each school, through its Curricular Project. This means that the school can adapt the general criteria to its particular circumstances, depending on the particular features of its milieu and its pupils.
2 It is a school-based system, since the assessment takes place entirely within the school itself. In contrast to other countries, Spain has no national or external examinations, either at the end of the Primary or Secondary Education. Pupils are assessed by their own teachers throughout their period of compulsory schooling. The only external examination takes place after the Baccalaureate for those pupils who wish to enter university. Whilst this is a prerequisite of studying at university, it is not necessary when it comes to obtaining the diploma of Secondary Education Graduate or the Baccalaureate.
3 It is a system which emphasizes the need to assess not only the students' outcomes, but also the process of education in the school, the classroom and the teaching carried out by teachers.

From the need for coherence between the curriculum and the assessment of pupils are derived requirements such as the continuous, global and integrated nature of the latter and insistence on the formative, regulatory, guiding and self-correcting nature of the assessment which must be geared to improving processes and results. In daily classroom activities, teaching, learning and assessment are very closely linked, forming part of a teaching and learning continuum.

A MODEL IN A PROCESS OF IMPLEMENTATION

The model presented is a recent innovation in the Spanish education system and one of the central pillars of the current education reform process. However, its introduction will logically be a gradual one, and it is hoped that it will be completed within a few years.

In the last two years, the Ministry of Education and Science has developed an ambitious Monitoring Plan for the process of LOGSE implementation, collecting information from teachers, families, head teachers, inspectors and school support services. The study, based on using opinion questionnaires, accompanied by case studies and a detailed examination of a sample of Curricular Projects, has furnished interesting and useful information. An initial set of conclusions is drawn from these studies:

1 Teachers are experiencing difficulties in drawing up Curricular Projects for their respective schools. In spite of the responsibility and leadership taken on by head teams, the process is not always an easy one, especially for secondary schools.

2 The process is receiving positive evaluation in spite of its difficulty. Curricular Projects are seen as useful, as they encourage team work, adapt teaching to suit pupils and schools' characteristics, and improve teaching. This overall positive assessment is greater among primary school teachers.

3 Deadlines set for preparing the Projects have been considered too tight, which has caused more emphasis to be placed on the product itself than on the process, contrary to the intentions of the education authorities.

4 Quite a few schools consider they have received less than the necessary amount of help in preparing the Project. Irrespective of the efforts made by education authorities, there can be no doubt that, in teachers' views, a limited amount of support has been forthcoming. This has led the authorities to offer additional activities in this respect.

When specifically analysing those aspects related to setting standards and establishing assessment mechanisms, a number of other conclusions should be mentioned:

1 In general, the most innovative aspects of the Curricular Project have presented most difficulties. Decisions and procedures for assessment, accreditation and moving pupils up to higher grades have proved complex, especially in the eyes of secondary school teachers.

2 The adaptation of the area objectives and level goals to the characteristics of the school and their distribution in cycles have not been especially difficult.

3 The sequence of contents according to cycles is the aspect which has caused fewest difficulties, perhaps as a result of its greater similarity to

traditional teaching practice. Nonetheless, this similarity has meant that certain schools have based their activities on the distribution of contents, without carrying out a detailed analysis of the more complex mechanisms for developing abilities. Although there are many schools which recognize that the new curricular approach has its value, they have little confidence when it comes to implementing it and prefer to adopt more conservative stances, even when they believe it to be necessary to review these at a later stage. Implicitly, they are adopting a gradual approach, which is fairly realistic.

4　In contrast to the preceding case, the decisions pertaining to assessment and moving pupils up and dealing with diversity have been a much more difficult matter for schools. Usually, decisions on assessment tend to be limited to very general references on continuous and integrative assessment, without specifying the exact measures (procedures, instruments, times) when these will be used in the classroom. Teachers feel an integrative assessment as set down in the LOGSE to be complicated to achieve.

5　Determining targets according to area and cycle is revealed to be one of the aspects with which teachers have most difficulties. Nor do the Area and Classroom Programmes always contain the necessary degree of specification, often being little more than declarations of a far more general nature than is really required. On occasions, attainment targets have been understood as end goals for each subject and level, as in the old-style curriculum.

6　Schools have generally dealt with decisions on moving pupils up in certain detail. Given the scrutiny to which they are subjected by families and students, it is hardly surprising that schools should have been prudent in this respect. It is perhaps this prudence which has led to a more copious and detailed result than might have been expected. All of this goes to show the difficulties which exist when a really integrative assessment has to be undertaken, although prospects for progress in this respect are positive.

SOME FINAL REMARKS

The model for pupil assessment which is currently being implemented in Spain is, as has been stated, flexible and school-based. As assessment is understood to be a constituent part of teaching and learning processes, this flexibility is very advantageous, since it enables an adequate response to the needs of the different schools, teachers and pupils. A second advantage this model offers is that of involving teachers in decision-making processes. The requirement that specific decisions be made to assess what pupils are learning, automatically entails teachers taking an active part, considering the teaching to be given and the criteria on which the results are to be assessed.

This implies a stimulus for teachers as professionals, although it can present problems in practice.

Together with these advantages, the model presupposes certain risks. The first of these is the possibility of the system splintering and of allowing a loss of control in results. Since schools themselves make the decisions on assessment, promotion and accreditation of students, criteria applied could be too heterogeneous. In an education system like the Spanish one, in which respect for the right to education on conditions of fairness is a fundamental principle, the aggravation of this situation could mean it did not fulfil one of its main aims.

With the intention of taking the utmost advantage of the benefits of this model and circumventing its difficulties, avoiding the risks and disadvantages set out, education administrative bodies have set a number of different mechanisms in motion. Some of these are geared to controlling the system and providing with information, whilst others are targeted at supporting school development.

Overall, it can be said that the coherence between the new model of curriculum design and development introduced in Spain has still not been taken up in an unequivocal way in the classroom. Given the newness of the situation, this should not seem surprising nor give cause for concern. There is, however, no doubt that it will demand constant effort on the part of the national and regional authorities to ensure that the general principles of the new model are put into practice. It is true that, until now, educational practice has not covered the innovations introduced in the reform and that still only limited change is visible, but it can be expected that in the next few years the effects of the implementation and dissemination of the new model, will begin to be noticeable. As has been emphasized on various occasions, this requires continued insistence by authorities and the profession itself on teacher training strategies and support for schools.

Chapter 6

Teachers' own assessments

Bet McCallum, Caroline Gipps, Shelley McAlister and Margaret Brown

This chapter draws on the authors' ESRC-funded project (no. 000 23 2192) in four English Local Education Authorities, which monitored teachers of seven-year-olds in 1991 and 1992 and the development of their assessment practice. The authors describe three models of teacher assessors: 'intuitives', 'evidence gatherers', and 'systematic planners'; models which were endorsed by a group of LEA advisers not involved in the project. *

INTRODUCTION

The Education Reform Act (ERA) of 1988 brought about wide-ranging changes in education in England and Wales. Comparable changes were intro-duced in Scotland and Northern Ireland, which have separate educational systems. A major strand of this reform was the implementation of a national curriculum and national assessment programme.

For each subject, the curriculum is enshrined in law: statutory orders describe the matters, skills and processes to be taught as 'programmes of study' and the knowledge, skills and understanding as 'attainment targets' (ATs) which pupils are expected to have reached at certain stages of schooling. The stages are defined as Key Stage 1 (ages 5–7), 2 (7–11), 3 (11–14) and 4 (14–16).

The ATs are articulated at a series of ten levels. The series of levels is designed to enable progression: most pupils of 7+ are expected to be at level 2 in the system, while most pupils of 11+ are predicted to be at level 4, and so on. The ATs are articulated at each of the ten levels by a series of criteria or statements of attainment which form the basic structure of a criterion-referenced assessment system.

The national assessment programme as outlined in the report of the Task Group on Assessment and Testing (TGAT, 1988) and the statutory orders, requires that pupils be assessed against all the ATs by their teachers and on

* A version of this chapter first appeared in Research Papers in Education (1993) 8 (3): 305–27. H. Torrance (ed.) (1995) *Evaluating Authentic Assessment*, Buckingham: Open University Press.

some ATs by external tests called Standard Assessment Tasks (SATs) at the ages of 7, 11 and 14. At these ages the results are combined and must be reported towards the end of that school year. (At 16 the external test is to be the General Certificate of Secondary Education (GCSE) which is currently taken by approximately 85 per cent of the age group, and the grading system of the GCSE is to be merged with the ten-level National Curriculum scale.) Teachers may make their own assessments in any way they wish, but observation, regular informal assessment and keeping examples of work are all encouraged. The results of individual pupils are confidential to themselves, their parents and teachers; results for a class as a whole and a school as a whole are to be available to the parents; results at school level are to be publicly reported.

National Assessment in Primary Schools (NAPS) is an ESRC-funded research project based jointly at the University of London Institute of Education and at King's College, London. The aim of the project is to monitor the implementation of the new national assessment system, together with the interpretation and use of results. Our focus is on teachers' developing assessment practice and therefore we were particularly interested in how the teacher assessment (TA) element of the national assessment programme was carried out. This chapter focuses on TA at Key Stage 1, in the second year of the statutory implementation of national assessment.

Given the emphasis on TA in the TGAT model, one might have expected the Department for Education to initiate a major programme of in-service training and resource materials to support TA. However, it became clear that the policy of government and the School Examinations and Assessment Council (SEAC) was to give increased weight to the results of the external SATs, leaving teachers with little support in arriving at their own assessments. While SEAC devoted considerable resources to SAT development, the only publications (SEAC, 1990) devoted to teacher assessment (packs A, B and C) were produced rapidly and with insufficient trialling. Both our study and other evaluators (see, for example, Whetton et al., 1991) have demonstrated that they proved of little value to class teachers.

Since teachers were largely left alone to implement TA, with in general only a minimal input from their local education authority advisers (Bennett et al., 1992), it was clearly an interesting question as to what methods would be selected, and on what implicit or explicit beliefs these would be based.

As the following section will make clear, our attempts in 1991 to elicit detailed, explicit accounts of how teachers made their assessments failed. We realized that much of the teachers' practice was implicit and that the standard research techniques of interview and observation were not adequate to render these activities explicit. We therefore developed a different technique which, together with an interview, and supported by observations of case-study teachers and their earlier interviews, allowed us to develop and describe models of assessment practice used by Year 2 (age 7) teachers. These models appear to reflect beliefs about the nature of teaching and learning in young children.

GATHERING DATA ON TEACHER ASSESSMENT

Our fieldwork is based on detailed work with Year 2 teachers in each of 32 schools. These are drawn from four local education authorities which were chosen to represent a range of different settings, both socio-economic and geographic: a northeastern county, a southeastern shire, a London borough and a Midlands metropolitan borough. Both of the last two have substantial numbers of pupils whose first language is not English. Within each school district we have chosen a stratified random sample of eight schools, to include infant, junior, primary, Church of England, Roman Catholic and non-church, and a range of sizes and locations.

Six of the 32 schools, including at least one from each of the four LEAs, were selected for more detailed case study on the basis of illustrating practices which appeared to differ in significant ways.

The data-gathering concerned explicitly with TA has involved: visits to all 32 schools to interview heads and Year 2 teachers about TA (spring 1991); four consecutive days in each of the six case-study schools, focusing on TA methods (autumn 1991); visits to the 25 case-study and non-case-study schools, where the Year 2 teacher had not changed from last year using the 'quote sort' activity to focus on TA (spring 1992); and a postal questionnaire sent to all Year 2 teachers about their 1992 experiences of TA (and SATs) – vignettes of our TA models were sent to all Year 2 teachers as a validation of our observations. (Additional visits were made to schools in both years to gather data about the use of SATs.)

In the 1991 interviews we found teachers unable to describe their TA practices in any detail. Many of the interviews yielded vague descriptions of collecting evidence and details of record-keeping and planning:

> I keep a folder for each child with pieces of work, a bit of this, a bit of that, as you go along.

> I looked at my notebook, my lists, the children's books and exercise books. From that I could work out their level.

In order to obtain more specific information we included in the following year's fieldwork four days of observation in each of the six case-study schools, focusing on TA. These visits still yielded little observable evidence of TA. Teachers found it difficult to describe precisely what they used to determine the level of attainment and how they reached this decision. Even where teachers claimed that they used ATs, it was not clear how they had done so.

One teacher's method of assessing English, for example, was to look at two or three exercise books from one child, 'refer to the Attainment Target' and assign a level.

A way of eliciting more explicit information about their views and practices was therefore needed. For 1992 we developed a sorting activity based on the extraction of quotations about TA which were selected from those made by teachers in our 1991 interviews. Rather than conducting the 'quote sort' as a questionnaire using a Likert scale, we used the activity as a basis for interview, allowing us to combine both qualitative and quantitative methods. This method involved sorting 16 quotes (see Appendix 6.1 for details) into 'like me' or 'not like me' categories. After the teachers had sorted the quotes we had a detailed interview, asking each of them to explain the reasons for the categorization. Altogether, 25 Year 2 teachers were involved: seven from the six case-study schools (one school had a pair of teachers working as a team) and 18 from the non-case-study schools where the Year 2 teacher had not changed between 1991 and 1992.

As a result of this, we have identified three models, or 'ideal types', which vary along the dimensions of *systematicness, integration with teaching* and *ideological underpinning*. We emphasize that the models are not hierarchical in value and that no particular set of views or practices is intended to represent a desired model of TA. Indeed, our informal judgement suggests that there are teachers within each of the groups whose pupils have both relatively high and relatively low standards of attainment.

Although there were some minor difficulties in using authentic quotes (such as confusion resulting from negatives in the wording and the inclusion of more than one idea within the same quote), the teachers engaged with the activity and we were able to analyse their responses. The data from the quote-sort activity and the detailed diagnostic interviews were analysed at several levels. First, a simple count was made of the number of teachers agreeing with each statement (see Appendix 6.2). Then a matrix was drawn up of teachers who agreed with each other in particular quotes. The final quantitative approach was to produce clusters of teachers using the cluster analysis utility on the Datadesk statistical package for the Apple Macintosh. The detailed interview material was analysed using the constant comparative method (Glaser and Strauss, 1967) to produce groups of teachers with similar approaches/profiles. These groupings were matched against both the clusters and our classroom observations of these teachers. The first tentative models were refined several times by the project team.

Three models emerged: 'intuitives', 'evidence gatherers' and 'systematic planners'. These models emerged from the analysis of all the data gathered from Year 2 teachers during the first two phases of the project (interviews, classroom observation, quote-sort activity and related interview, review of records and record-keeping practices, accounts of curriculum planning and detailed descriptions of how levels were arrived at for one child).

Preliminary validation of the models was carried out by presentation to a group of LEA advisers, who were not in the NAPS sample; the models were recognized and endorsed. Further validation was obtained from presenting the models in the form of vignettes (see Appendix 6.3) to our sample of Year 2 teachers. Teachers were asked to choose the vignette which most closely resembled their own practice in order to establish to what extent the descriptions matched their own perceptions. Vignettes seemed an appropriate format to feed back to teachers, as they enabled us to present the essentials of each model, including both behaviour and philosophy, in everyday language with which teachers could identify. They also had the advantage of being brief, which would contribute to the likelihood of response. The wording of each model was considered carefully and we also took care to present the models in an order which was not clearly hierarchical.

Response to the vignettes was requested from all Year 2 teachers we had been dealing with in our 31 sample schools. (One school had withdrawn from the study following the appointment of a new head.) Altogether 31 Year 2 teachers from 24 schools responded to the vignettes, of which 18 were the original Year 2 teachers from the previous year, who had done the quote sort and with whom we were familiar. The remaining 13 teachers were mostly unknown to us, although some had been interviewed or observed for reasons other than the quote sort. Teachers gave us no feedback that the models were unrealistic or that it was difficult to choose one to identify with. Seven teachers did not return a vignette for reasons apparently unconnected with the task, such as resignation, retirement or school closure.

These responses to the vignettes also provided a partial validation of the TA models in the sense that 31 teachers were prepared to commit themselves to a model, thereby recognizing and being able to identify with the models in practice. Furthermore, of the 18 teachers who both did the quote-sort activity and responded to the vignettes, 11 chose the model which we had felt best matched their practice from the data we had available. The extent of the overlap is further validation of the models; we had not expected a complete match since we were aware that the teachers' perceptions of their assessment practice sometimes differed from our descriptions of their practice, based in turn on our own perceptions. In any case, when real teachers are compared with 'ideals', there is rarely a perfect fit (see, for example, MacDonald, 1974). Since the models represent 'ideal types', it will not always be possible to place a particular individual squarely within one of them, nor are the types themselves completely distinct.

THE MODELS OF TEACHER ASSESSMENT

The three models of teacher assessment are described below. For two of the models – intuitives and systematic planners – we feel we have identified two fairly distinct sub-groups: the former can be divided into *children's needs ideologists* and *tried and tested methodologists*; the latter into *systematic assessors* and *systematic integrators*. The names were chosen by the team to represent what we felt to be the best summary of the characteristics of each group.

Model I: intuitives

We have termed the teachers in this group 'intuitives' because they object to the imposed system of national assessment as a disruption to intuitive ways of working. Intuitives fall into two sub-groups: the first, 'children's needs ideologists', show a great deal of confidence and can articulate arguments about assessment which defend a child-centred view of curriculum, teaching and learning; the second, 'tried and tested methodologists', feel secure in modes of teaching and assessing practised before the ERA but are less confident in articulating what these are or their actual basis or uses for teaching or assessment purposes. All of the intuitive group of teachers are minimal adopters of national assessment procedures. The children's needs ideologists resist criterion referencing as being in tension with 'whole-child' philosophy and are often confidently critical of the SAT tasks as being inappropriate and ill-matched to their own ideas of 'levelness'. The tried and tested methodologists resist the whole notion of ongoing recorded TA because it means a radical change in behaviour for them:

> You are either teaching or assessing, you can't be doing both.

However, they are prepared to carry out SATs following the letter of the law because the materials and instructions are provided and this is a type of assessment familiar to them, being test-like and summative. Thus their resistance to change can be seen to derive partly from their view of teaching, but also partly from the still prevailing traditional 'culture' of assessment. . .

For all intuitives, there was a reliance on memory and a lack of observable ongoing TA, and thus we were unable to describe in detail the processes that this group were using to make assessments. Teachers themselves spoke about TA in general terms, without reference to statements of attainment:

> Sitting on my own at night when it's nice and quiet and the children have gone home, I looked through what I had for the child, I called on my memory, plans I'd made for what we'd covered, and looked in their folders at the relevant documentation.

One of the main characteristics of this whole group is their rejection of systematic recorded TA, which is seen as interference with real teaching.

> I just can't bear the thought of breaking off to give them a tick. To be honest, in my classroom, I can't keep breaking off and writing things down.

A systematic approach to assessment is criticized as being 'too formal', 'clinical', 'too structured – down such tramlines', and there seems to be a particular dislike of 'the clipboard syndrome' or going around recording all the time.

The children's needs ideologists find it 'too hard to sit back and let a child struggle' without offering some input 'because it's second nature'. They prefer a holistic approach, seeing teaching and assessment taking place simultaneously and 'recording mentally all the time while watching the processes a child is going through'. These teachers subscribe to an 'exploratory' view of learning (Rowland, 1987) since they initially guide the task to a point where children can be left to arrive at their own solutions to the problem as jointly defined. They prefer the role of 'provider of a stimulating environment' to that of 'instructor'.

Not surprisingly, devising a list of teacher's questions as an assessment technique 'ignores what the child is saying back to you' and focused observation-based note-taking may even be seen as 'damaging' because 'children are left alone and their concentration breaks down'. Curriculum planning is based on what teachers feel are the needs of children and this means there is no need to have internalized either ATs or statements of attainment because 'you can't always follow what you, the teacher, intend to do'. They would stress the importance of combining an individual conference with each child together with their own reflections on the 'whole' child, before making any final recorded assessment.

The tried and tested methodologists believe you cannot be teaching and assessing simultaneously and seem to base their practice on a sequential understanding that they assess what they have taught. This practice is underpinned by a didactic model of learning (Rowland, 1987) in which the teacher defines the child's needs and provides the appropriate instruction. The child responds and the teacher marks and provides feedback. Because the focus is on teaching, they feel that 'you can't record on *ad hoc* assessments you make' so assessment for this group of teachers tends to be summative, taking the form of giving worksheets, scrutinizing tangible evidence like pages of maths from exercise books and doing verbal checks of a child's knowledge by 'getting them on their own and having a little chat about it'. At the end of half terms or terms, they call up their memory and feel that 'if you're worth the name of teacher, you should know your children inside out and be able to recall what children can do'.

In carrying out these summative assessments, intuitives retain and report the value of assessment procedures with which they are familiar such as 'ILEA Checkpoints', teacher-made worksheets and tests, maths worksheets related to published schemes. This is in spite of the fact that the results do not relate to the statements of attainment which form the basis for TA under the National Curriculum.

Teachers' close knowledge (often rooted in long careers in teaching) is the main basis on which tried and tested methodologists in particular make their assessments. There is a strong belief that 'the assessing needs to be done by the actual class teacher' and not someone else; teachers have got to *know* a child to know whether 'what they have done on paper' is good or not, or in order 'to know if the result is really amazing for that child'. Consequently, previous records are not observed to be readily available or consulted and teachers rely mainly on their own personal judgements. Planning based on diagnostic assessment was not observed in their classrooms; rather there was a tendency to 'all start at the same beginning point and then spread out'.

These teachers often have their own implicit standards; for example, in relation to the SAT tasks:

> That was no way a level 3 task. You have to do more to get a level 3. We know what quality work is.

Because of these implicitly held notions of levels of difficulty and ability, intuitives resist criterion referencing, relying rather on 'gut reaction', and an all-round close knowledge of children built up after spending so much time with them. Close knowledge involves children's 'everyday performance, personality, the way they present themselves, their acquisition of knowledge outside of school' and their interactions within groups. This is used as a basis for recording assessment:

> I don't think I can discount what I know about a child from its attainment.

> You have to take account of contextual issues because that's what being a professional is.

Some found it hard to ignore children's attitudes and behaviour when recording attainment, particularly on SATs:

> If a child had really tried hard and put a lot of effort in it, it's very hard not to give it [the NC level] to them.

And allowances were made for age:

> It's so unfair: one of the August birthdays is quite a bright little boy. He just hasn't got there yet. So I feel like giving him a little more leeway.

Because teachers continue to include all these biographical and contextual details and do not 'distil' out attainment when assessing children, one can say that they are passive resisters of the criterion-referenced system characteristic of the national assessment model.

Of all the teachers in the sample, this group has made least adaptation to their preferred ways of working. The ideologists bitterly resent change imposed from outside (Cooper, 1988), wanting to protect 'the human face of teaching' and their personal investment in it (Nias, 1989), and worry that shifting to a focus on assessment could cause damage to children. This 'moral accountability' felt by primary teachers was noted in a comparative study by Broadfoot and Osborn (1986). Collegiality in the schools from which they come has provided them with considerable confidence in their practices and beliefs, which enables them to resist the pressures to change.

Change can threaten to invalidate long years of experience (Marris, 1975), and some long-serving tried and tested methodologists express a strong reluctance to accept the national assessment model:

> I haven't memorized the ATs – they're going to change anyway. I find the jargon difficult.

There is among some of this group a sense of insecurity, often related to lack of personal support within their schools. They report a fear of 'sinking under paper' and an uneasiness with constant educational change, the last few years seeming like

> the Aldershot Assault Course. No sooner do you get over one wall when another looms up.

As one in a long line of recent changes, National Curriculum assessment requires teachers to engage in more detailed work plans and give more attention to techniques which will support criterion referencing for individual pupils. The perceived amount of energy and time required to learn the new skills and roles associated with the innovation has provided a rationale for resistance within this group (House, 1974).

Model EG: evidence gatherers

These teachers have a basic belief in the primacy of teaching, rather than assessing. Their main method of assessment relies on collecting evidence which they only later evaluate. They have gone some way towards adapting the requirements of national assessment and they could be considered rational adapters, in the sense that they have adapted in such a way as to not change their teaching: collecting evidence does not interfere with teaching practice. Evidence gathering is associated with a belief that pupils generally learn what is taught and only what is taught; thus assessment follows teaching in order to check that the process is going according to plan.

One of the main characteristics of evidence gatherers, therefore, is that assessment is accommodated within existing systems and it is not always planned in:

> I don't really plan a task to cover assessment. I plan first what I want to do and then see how it can be fitted into assessment.

The teachers in this group do not often plan assessment activities, but rely on assessment 'opportunities' to arise within their normal classroom teaching:

> You think, 'Oh, that's another Attainment Target'.

This system is dependent on the teacher's ability to recognize tasks which can be 'matched' to the national assessment ATs and to 'vaguely have assessment in mind all the time'. Having recognized an activity as usable for assessment, the teacher then devises a means of gathering evidence:

> A piece of work we did on autumn days, we got to talking about that and a lot of science points came out of it . . . so, quickly we do a weather chart! They covered all the other things really well and it was obvious from the discussion, but we just had to have the weather chart for evidence.

Teachers tend to think in terms of ATs, rather than statements of attainment, and the 'matching' of tasks to ATs usually takes place after the activity itself, either at the end of the day or at the end of term when recording is done:

> I hadn't really planned how this exercise would fit into assessment, but I see now that it does. I will have to look up exactly where and how it fits in. . . . I'll look it up in the book when I get home.

Where teachers do plan assessment activities, such assessment is primarily for the purpose of collecting written evidence, rather than for diagnostic assessment:

> I sometimes set up an activity. Quite often the worksheet is part of that, to prove they can do it.

Evidence is gathered in relation to the ATs and the purpose of assessment is largely seen to be proving National Curriculum coverage:

> I know that if we cover these topics we'll have done all the ATs. I like things done as part of topic work.

Such planning for assessment typically goes on at the same time as planning topic work, usually before each term. Once topics are chosen, ATs are matched against them, although statements of attainment may also be looked at during this planning level. There is a general confidence that national assessment is being 'covered' within the topic work. This may be either an individual teacher's termly plan, or whole-school topic work as part of a 'rolling programme'. The link between assessment and topic work enables teachers to incorporate assessment into their usual way of doing things, and makes assessment more user-friendly:

> It means a lot more to me if it's part of an activity that I'm going to do or part of my topic for the term – to make sure that I'm covering the attainment targets with my topics.

The teacher can identify 'gaps' in the curriculum at the time she records on her assessment record sheets, which is usually done termly in the school holidays.

When you go through and fill in the record sheets you can look at them and just find a little point that you haven't covered, so you make a little note that you have to do this.

Overall, a programme of planned topic work is seen to ensure that both national assessment and National Curriculum have been done.

Not surprisingly, given the title of this model, there is an emphasis on gathering evidence of all kinds:

I keep everything. I'm known as a hoarder.

The main characteristic of this group is the need to gather evidence in abundance, with an emphasis on written work, which enables the teacher to have 'proof' of what has been done. 'Trying to get as much evidence as I can' is the aim of many of these teachers (and may preclude the value of the assessment itself). 'Getting the result down on paper' is seen to be essential, because teachers feel accountable and, under national assessment, are concerned that they may be asked to produce evidence of their assessment of children:

I keep a camera in the cupboard for technology. It is the only record you've got if somebody asked you for evidence.

Evidence may be collected from a variety of sources, including pages from workbooks, worksheets from published schemes, teacher-devised worksheets, children's written work, spelling tests, observation and questioning children on work they have done. There is a heavy reliance on worksheets and maths schemes as written evidence, though teachers tend not to trust such schemes to cover the ATs adequately:

I've yet to see a scheme which has gone into National Curriculum adequately or entirely. Worksheets can support, yes, but that shouldn't be the system by itself. Schemes miss things out, so assessment based on this will miss things out.

Our Nuffield maths scheme, I have put the attainment targets alongside. Nuffield did produce a sheet that did that but I produced a sheet that verified it.

Teachers therefore devise their own worksheets to complement the published schemes:

I still give my own maths tests to cover Scottish Primary Maths. I would never go by just what they have done on the worksheets or in the book. I would want to be sure.

Most of the teachers in this group acknowledge that 'you don't always have a piece of recorded work every time' and that other kinds of evidence, including teachers' notes on observations, may be valid:

I set activities and watch them and then we work on worksheets as well as see what they've done. But the outcome is not just the worksheet, I have assessed the whole process.

I would never rely all on my memory. You must have it backed up with evidence. You've got to have your notes as evidence.

Another key feature of evidence gathering is that assessments are summative, rather than formative in nature:

I would just write it down but I wouldn't go into records until I am ready to record. I leave assessing to the end of term.

Recording assessment is usually done termly, when evidence is gathered in one place and the teacher reflects on the work the child has done over the term:

If I have their pieces of work there I can just sit there and think 'this particular child has achieved that'.

Most, though not all, of the teachers in this group prefer not to rely on memory because

you couldn't possibly call up your memory on each child's performance on every AT – it's just too difficult.

The 'bits and bobs of evidence' which are 'pulled together for the end of term' enable the teacher to sit and reflect on the child's achievements over the term and 'weigh up' performance overall. Despite the emphasis on collecting evidence, though, not all the evidence that has been collected will be used in the awarding of levels and it is possible that in some cases evidence is used selectively to support the teacher's intuition.

Another characteristic of evidence gatherers is that there is an increased awareness of national assessment procedures and, in some cases, a degree of excitement brought on by new developments:

We do observations all the time in the class, we're getting quite familiar with this sort of assessment. Initially you're dying to offer them a bit of help or advice but not now: now I can quite happily sit down and just write down what I see.

The teachers themselves are conscious of their increased awareness of assessment procedures since the implementation of national assessment. Overall, assessment for these teachers is a new and higher priority, although they are not prepared to let it become 'the be-all and end-all', as they are anxious to keep as many of their former ways of working as can be retained within new assessment and curriculum procedures.

The teachers tend not to have internalized the statements of attainment and they do not interrogate the evidence in a systematic way, although they have familiarity with the ATs and are able to recognize how activities fit into them:

> This activity is AT4 or 5. So I've already got that in mind, but I wouldn't have done this time last year.

They are also much more aware of levels:

> You're aware of the level already, even when you first look at what they have made.

> I have a particular awareness of Year 3 children this year as level 3 last year.

Their awareness extends to assessment techniques, where observation and children's talk are recognized as increasingly important for assessment:

> You constantly talk to children and now you're more aware of what they say in response because you've got this in your mind all the time: do they understand what they are talking about? There is a new awareness about the responses.

The teachers have also developed an understanding of the distinction of attainment from other contextual factors such as effort and behaviour, although some admit that this is sometimes hard to accept:

> It is very difficult sometimes to stay unbiased, but one has to. We mustn't let the child's behaviour cloud our thinking.

> Obviously you know the children and what they have put into it, but you still have to keep separate what they can actually *do*. It's not always easy but you have to do it.

Some teachers in this group feel that although attainment is clearly separate from other factors ('effort does not equal attainment'), new assessment procedures require the teacher to suppress what she knows about the 'whole child':

> Before SATs it was the whole child that you were really looking at. Now you still know the whole child but on paper you can only put what they actually do.

It appears that while the teachers are newly aware of the notion of criterion referencing, there are times when contextual factors must be taken into account:

> If you know a child is in some sort of bother, you've got to look at assessment against this context. So if a child has underachieved because of certain circumstances, you wouldn't accept the assessment without considering this.

> If I have given a child a high level all the times before, I will leave that level. I won't change it, because I know what the child is capable of.

A final feature of the evidence-gathering model is that systematic assessment is seen as a threat to relationships with children. The teachers in this group had a fear of national assessment interfering with their relationships with children if they were to 'go over the top' by adopting more systematic assessment practices. Assessing against a can-do list was seen as 'tabulated' and 'judgemental', as well as unnecessarily systematic:

> We haven't broken it down into a can-do list but I think in our minds we know what the children can do because we're observing all the time.

There was also concern that the can-do list might put some children at a disadvantage because either the teacher might be 'missing something' or

> some children might never get on to it because they can't do the things on the can-do list.

Although one teacher kept a list of the ATs and statements of attainment in her handbag and referred to them every week when doing her lesson plans, carrying such a list was seen as interfering with the 'real job' of teaching:

> You'd never get on with your work if you were doing that.

> I feel this is more or less teaching through ATs or statements of attainment.

Similarly, recording or note-taking on the spot was seen sceptically and acceptable only 'providing you just jot it down and don't make a thing of it'. While some teachers acknowledged that recording on the spot was more accurate than reflecting back, they did not see it as a priority and had not incorporated it into their own assessment practice:

> I'm sure it is much more accurate but I just can't find the time to do it.

Finally, some evidence gatherers clearly rejected such practices as note-taking on the spot:

> I think if you are taking notes while you are making candles, you're in for trouble.

Overall, evidence gatherers shared concerns with their critical intuitive colleagues in rejecting the methods of systematic assessors. Rather than rely on memory and intuition for assessment, however, they favoured gathering evidence and then reflecting back over the child's performance during the term in a summative manner.

Their new awareness of national assessment procedures and their willingness to adapt were perceived as accounting for National Curriculum coverage and therefore assessment was accommodated within existing systems, rather than making major changes to their habitual teaching roles.

Model SP: systematic planners

We have called the third group of teachers 'systematic planners'. Planning time specifically for assessment has become part of their practice (although this varies in the degree to which it is integrated with everyday teaching) and the planned assessment of groups and individuals informs future task design and classwork. A constructivist approach to learning underpins this model, with teachers expecting children to learn in idiosyncratic ways; they are willing to try children on higher levels not yet taught, using such opportunities diagnostically. Such teachers also demonstrate social constructivist beliefs (Pollard, 1987) in that they attach importance to interacting and arriving at shared meanings, both with pupils and with their fellow professionals in the context of TA. These teachers have embraced the national assessment requirements and understand the principles of criterion referencing, often breaking down statements of attainment into smaller steps. While upholding the importance of teaching, they report real value in continuous diagnostic assessment as an enhancement to their effectiveness:

> I need to know that at a particular time of day, I am actually going to be assessing one thing. You've got to be structured, you've got to know what you are looking for.

The most significant characteristic of this group of teachers is that they plan for assessment on a systematic basis. This means that the teacher consciously devotes some part of the school week to assessing, and explicitly links the results of assessment and curriculum planning.

There are two identifiable sub-groups in this category. Some teachers, whom we have called 'systematic assessors', give *daily* concentrated time to one group of children at a time and have devised systems to lessen demands made upon them by the rest of the class. Some teachers wear badges or put up a 'busy flag' as a sign they are not to be interrupted. These teachers often make it clear that it is quite permissible to ask peers, not the teacher, for help or they devise an agenda of tasks for the children to work through.

Other teachers, whom we have called 'systematic integrators', do not separate themselves off from the rest of the class but circulate, gathering evidence in different ways which feeds into *weekly* recorded assessment and informs planning. The clearest example of this occurs in the case of two teachers working as a pair and sharing 60 children. They collect assessment data on children throughout the week and have devised a 'Friday sheet' on which is recorded (after consideration and interpretation of each other's comments) their jointly agreed assessments of children. Also on this sheet there will be an agreed plan for children's subsequent work. Thus a cyclical programme develops.

However, in spite of these differences, the two groups of systematic planners have much in common and the remaining descriptions apply to both groups. For all systematic planners assessment is diagnostic:

> You're making some assessment of previous work because you have to assess in order to teach . . . whether they are ready to go on to the next stage.

Children are selected on the basis of previously recorded assessment. The process becomes cyclical. Diagnostic assessment feeds into planning for individual, group and class activities which, in turn, offer opportunities for more diagnostic assessment. Records are generally accessible and used. However, these teachers are often willing to try children 'on the next level' without necessarily teaching first. For example, following on from what two children had attained previously, they were asked to order numbers to 1,000. The teacher left them alone to do this. The task was not presented as a maths 'exercise' but rather as a problem-solving task to be recorded informally. The teacher spent some time in discussion with the children: 'I just want to see how you experiment with this.' She could see the kind of errors one child was making and gave some help. She also took their papers home that evening. Her plan was:

> I'll look through the sheets. I'm going to get Pam to do some more work. I might make her a worksheet. I'll think it out when I go home.

Pam was not given a worksheet next day but the teacher devoted a planned amount of time to working with her.

By giving children work at the next level without specifically teaching first, assessment seems less 'bolted on' to teaching and becomes a learning process for teachers.

> The interesting thing about teacher assessments are that they surprise you.

For this group of teachers assessment techniques are multiple and children are assessed both formatively and summatively through a combination of: observation; open-ended questioning (the questions varying from child to child); teacher–pupil discussion; running records; and scrutiny of classwork. Attention is paid to fitting the assessment technique to the activity being assessed. One of the significant differences between this model and the other two is the sharp focus on statements of attainment. Teachers' self-devised checklists are used, often comprising lists of 'can-do' indicators which represent the teacher's analysis and interpretation of each of the statements of attainment, broken down further into descriptions of what a child might say or do to demonstrate attainment:

> Even with the statements of attainment, there are still smaller steps. Like, the statement of attainment says 'know number facts to 10'. But the steps before that in basic addition – there are all sorts of ways of going about that.

Teachers may assess more than one statement of attainment at a time, perhaps a 'process one and a content one', but these will be planned and not simply noticed in passing (although serendipitous observations of a child's knowledge or understanding are not ignored). Because of the multiple methods in use, evidence of attainment for the final record takes many forms:

> The record would be a drawing together of everything. It would be based on 'can-dos', children's own records, their spontaneous comments and observations.

In addition to the above reported list, critical incidents both noted and memorized, annotated pieces of work, annotated photographs and worksheets 'used for consolidation' may be used.

Unlike the intuitives, relying solely on memory is thought to be untrustworthy:

> I don't think memory is accurate enough. I think that's when you assume things about children.

and note-taking and recording at the time on self-designed formats are favoured:

> We keep boxes of sticky labels at our sides during most activities and we record as we go along or at the end of a session but not at the end of a day, because it's difficult to remember.

One piece of tangible evidence (particularly one published workcard) or one session of observation is thought to be insufficient evidence of attainment because

> you're teaching to the worksheet, you could be missing out chunks. That's not developing children.

In addition, teachers like to have some ownership of the assessment process:

> I suppose assessment to me is something special. . . . I tend to put a little more effort into it myself. I don't use the published workcards.

Teachers may 'revisit' the statements of attainment several times 'to really say if they have attained it', so as 'not [to] push and give a false picture' and may repeat assessments over time often using different techniques 'to double-check, be fair' or 'do a quick stock-take'.

These teachers have now become very familiar with national assessment procedures, have internalized the ATs and statements of attainment or have them permanently displayed for easy reference, either on planning sheets or on assessment proformas they have made. They can often quote them when assessing by observation or recognize national assessment levels when looking at a piece of work:

I think when I'm marking say English 3, it leaps up from the page . . . 'Ah, this is a level 2'.

Systematic planners separate attainment from other factors and are able to 'distil' attainment in the National Curriculum from other aspects of a child's achievement; they prefer to record attainment separately from attitudinal, contextual and biographical details, although these also may be recorded, sometimes within a school policy of records of achievement (ROA). The effort a child makes is not what counts. It is the result that is important:

> You must be quite specific about what a child has attained. The effort goes into ROA. You make notes of it in other places but not in teacher assessment.

> When a particularly difficult child was being teacher-assessed, the teacher might be thinking about his general problems in the classroom. We've found that using the criteria, this child, being assessed on exactly the same thing as everyone else, has actually shown he's doing quite well.

Such teachers have therefore internalized and are using a criterion-referenced model of assessment.

Systematic planners are not resistant to the new methods of assessment imposed by central government. They see systematic diagnostic assessment as adding to their professionalism:

> I think some teachers get hung up on the word 'assessment' and get frightened by it and they undervalue what they are really doing.

They reject the trial-and-error methods and intuitive guessing of the other two groups, stressing that they have teaching in mind but:

> teaching based on assessment done sometime earlier. The greatest thing is to make notes so it informs your teaching.

They do not reject the notion that the child is at the heart of the learning process, nor that the 'whole child' is important:

> I use my knowledge of the child in my *approach* to teaching and assessing but not in my actual assessment.

Of all teachers in the sample, these teachers have made the most progress towards a hypothetical integrated model of teacher assessment. It could be that their own practice before the ERA was bound by particular systems of organization and classroom management (for example, the methods favoured by 'group instructors' and 'rotating changers' described by Galton *et al.*, 1980) and hence was more amenable to the adoption of systematic assessment.

However, the balance of incentives seems, for this group, to outweigh the disincentives and national assessment has offered them a sense of mastery, excitement and accomplishment (Huberman and Miles, 1984). The systems they have devised can be seen as a stage in taking ownership of the innovation, enabling the teachers to retain a feeling of control.

DISCUSSION

Criterion referencing

National assessment is a broadly criterion-referenced model of assessment and is intended to reflect whether or not a child possesses the knowledge, skills and understandings defined by more or less specific criteria (statements of attainment). Criterion referencing represents a new departure for infant teachers, who have previously assessed children in a more normative way, also taking account of contextual factors (such as effort or social background) which may affect a child's performance. We therefore need to consider how the TA models that we have identified address the issue of criterion referencing and to what extent teachers have been prepared to change their former practices in order to embrace this new method of assessment.

A questionnaire sent to Year 2 and Year 3 teachers in autumn 1991 showed that many schools have adopted whole-school record-keeping policies, using records that pass up the school with each child. While the majority of this recording is done at statement of attainment level, our observations revealed that only one group of teachers were using criterion referencing on statements of attainment as part of their classroom practice. This is supported by Her Majesty's Inspectorate (1992), observing that 'few teachers used specific criteria matched to attainment against National Curriculum levels in their day to day marking'.

Across two of the models (evidence gatherers and intuitives), teachers made infrequent or no reference to statements of attainment; this was possibly because of the summative ways of recording at the end of terms. Intuitives, particularly, rejected notions of criterion-referenced assessment by continuing to incorporate effort or background factors when making an assessment, and by their refusal to internalize or make readily available the statements of attainment.

These groups, rather than using statements of attainment, tended to have an overall notion of 'levelness' and therefore relied on implicit norms in relation to ranking children:

From what I know of Debbie, she just isn't a Level 3 child.

The quasi-norm-referenced use of level 3 to indicate children of well above average attainment caused some teachers to ignore or ridicule the possibility of children reaching level 4, although our observations in a few schools, not always in affluent areas, demonstrated that pupils were able to achieve level 4 in some aspects of the SATs.

The more systematic of the systematic planners carried out criterion referencing by use of a 'can-do' list against which children are assessed. This list
originated from the statements of attainment themselves, which had been
interpreted and broken down into simpler and more specific can-do statements so that criterion referencing could be more easily integrated into
classroom practice. (The ongoing use of criterion-referenced assessment
starting from rather broadly defined criteria raises problems of reliability
because of possibly differing interpretations by teachers.) Some systematic
planners, in order to carry out frequent or spontaneous assessment had memorized statements of attainment, or carried a list of the statements with them,
showing that criterion referencing was both clearly understood and being
used in practice.

Overall, though, there is little evidence so far that teachers have widely
accepted criterion referencing, or that they are about to do so. Ideological or
logistic objections, as described in the intuitive and to a lesser extent, in the
evidence-gathering models, are preventing them from moving away from
normative ways of assessing into the criterion-referenced model prescribed by
national assessment.

Use of results for formative purposes

Results passed up to intuitives and evidence gatherers were used as general
guidelines only and not used as a basis for planning classwork or forming
groups. More systematic teachers used 'inherited' results to inform them of
children's attainment on the National Curriculum and thus to place them in
attainment groups.

The degree to which the groups of teachers used assessment results for
formative purposes varied, with intuitives and evidence gatherers retaining
their previous patterns of teaching and preferring a more summative role for
teacher assessment. Systematic integrators, however, incorporated formative
assessment into their weekly forecasts of work, while systematic planners used
assessment to feed into individual and class planning on a daily basis.

Models of teaching and learning

From our interviews and observations of the teachers, we are able to get some
indication of their views of how children learn, which links, of course, with
their preferred style of teaching.

Although intuitives as a group had a child-centred view of curriculum,
teaching and learning, the children's needs ideologists subscribe to an
exploratory or scaffolded view of learning, where they provide a stimulating
environment and guide the child to the point at which they feel that the
child can carry out the task on his or her own; while the tried and tested
methodologists have a more didactic model of learning, where the teacher

herself decides on the child's needs and provides the appropriate instruction. Evidence gatherers similarly tend to believe that pupils learn what is taught and only what is taught. The systematic planners, on the other hand, have a constructivist approach to learning: they expect children to learn in idiosyncratic ways, and not necessarily what is taught; they also believe in arriving at shared meanings with pupils.

This information on learning was collected, not specifically, but as a by-product of the work on TA; it is therefore rather skeletal and we aim to develop this aspect of our research in the future.

CONCLUSIONS

Teacher assessment of the National Curriculum has been particularly difficult for infant teachers because of the lack of training and support materials.

In Northern Ireland teachers have a range of materials called External Assessment Resources which they can use when they wish to support their assessments. The resources are listed in a catalogue and schools may select three per subject. Provision of material such as this would have helped teachers in England in getting to grips with TA (see also Torrance, 1991, for a discussion of this possibility). Of course, the provision of assessment resources to support TA might serve to encourage a style of TA as mini-SAT, always external to the teaching process, a practice which Harlen and Qualter (1991) warn against. Our view, however, is that for many teachers a stage of doing mini-external assessments is just that – a stage – and that as their confidence and experience develop they move on to more informal, integrated, truly formative assessment.

With no offered model of TA it is perhaps not surprising that our teachers came up with a range of approaches. These approaches were related to their espoused views of teaching and learning, their general style of organization and their reaction to the imposition of the National Curriculum and its assessment. They were thus developing assessment practice in line with their general practice and philosophy of primary education. That it should have happened in this way is not surprising. What is particularly interesting to us as researchers is the relationship between teaching, learning and assessment in the teachers' practice; the link between assessment and learning is a crucial one but is not generally widely addressed.

Important, too, is what these teachers are telling us about criterion-referenced assessment. Evidence supporting this reluctance to assess on an overly analytical basis comes also from Year 3 teachers who received the national assessment information along with the Year 2 children who came up to them in September 1991 and 1992. Some of these teachers wanted *more than objective* test results, they wanted subjective information about children which was, they feared, being downgraded in the national assessment programme. Consulting with the previous teacher and looking together at children's work offered an opportunity to look at the whole child; no amount of hard data on a form could replace this activity. Despite its place as a major theme in the development of educational assessment, attempts to develop criterion-referenced assessment from the top have not been particularly successful in the past (Black and Dockrell, 1984; Pennycuick and Murphy, 1988; Brown, 1989). If the philosophy of criterion-referenced assessment does not fit with strongly held philosophies of infant education, then we may expect to find resistance to it which will serve to weaken its principles (for example, by arriving at levels through norming and ranking processes).

National and international debate of issues such as these is critical to the continued development of sound assessment practice in schools. We are fortunate to be able to continue our work over the next 3 years and will use some of these same techniques with Key Stage 2 teachers. We hope thus to validate and extend our understanding of TA at Key Stage 1 to teachers of older children and to explore more fully links between assessment practice and assumptions about learning.

APPENDIX 6.1 HOW WE USED RESPONDENTS' QUOTATIONS TO FOCUS ON TEACHER ASSESSMENT

1 Gather all quotes about TA from our phase 1 and phase 2 visits.
2 Select 16 quotes from data on different aspects of TA.
3 Put the quotes on to cards suitable for sorting.
4 Present cards to Year 2 teacher in pilot school for sorting: tape their comments while sorting and record their responses into 'like me', 'not like me' and 'middle' categories.
5 Present cards for sorting to 25 Year 2 teachers.
6 Transcribe tapes in full and organize responses on a sheet for easy reference, i.e. columns of responses under categories.
7 Make tables of 'like me' and 'not like me' from responses.
8 Match teachers who are most and least like each other.
9 Account for differences in responses and assess methodology.
10 Make a cluster analysis.
11 Match quote choices and cluster groups to our models of TA.

APPENDIX 6.2 QUOTES USED

Quote   *Number of teachers*
                                                agreeing out of 25

A I try to remain unbiased in my assessments, but I find children's
   behavioural problems difficult to ignore.   14
B We have broken down ATs into a can-do list and we observe
   children against this list.   5

C There is a lot of oral work in science and I find you can assess English skills through science activities even though the emphasis is on science.   24

D I don't think I will be able to discount what I know about the child from its attainment. No one can tell the effort behind the result as well as the teacher.   11

E I look at how it all went, how children approached the task, their attitude, whether they were copying or following the leader, whether they attained or covered.   24

F For a lot of ATs you can use written work. For some it's a lot of observation and you have to ask them what they've done because it's processes.   25

G From our maths scheme you can hang quite a lot on the ATs, so I would use those worksheets and I can tell quite a lot through the worksheets.   12

H I set up activities and watch them and once I feel they've understood thoroughly, then I give them a worksheet. After the worksheet, I assess the outcome and award a level.   13

I You observe things and make a note of things that just happen. You think, 'Oh, that's another AT'. You make a note of these things and at the end of the day you put them into your records where relevant.   10

J At the end of each term or half term, I call up my memory of a child's performance on the AT.   8

K I do a lot of talking to the children to see if they exhibit the sort of knowledge that you think fits the AT.   24

L I feel that recording at the time is more accurate than reflecting back.   15

M I look at a statement of attainment (SOA) and devise a small list of questions which will test a child's knowledge of that SOA. I put the list into my diary and, during the activity, ask all the children in the group the same set of questions.   10

N I take a photograph either as a record of work done, like when a child has made a model, or as a trigger to my own memory. The snap triggers my memory back to the questions children were asking or the knowledge they were displaying or the way they were going about something, like on a field trip when the children are involved and enjoying something.   11

O I keep a piece of paper with me with the ATs and SOAs clearly written out.   5

P You are either teaching or assessing, you can't be doing both.   4

APPENDIX 6.3 VIGNETTES

Please tick the model that is MOST like you:

Model A

I prefer to plan the ATs into my topic work and I know that if we cover these topics we'll have done all the ATs. I tend not to plan too many assessment activities because I think one can become too systematic about assessment. I'm quite familiar with the ATs now, which helps me recognize opportunities for assessment.

I think it's very important to gather as much evidence as I can, things like pieces of children's work, worksheets they've done, little notes I have made, anything I have noticed while they are working.

I do my recording at the half term or the end of term when I sit down with all the evidence I have gathered and think about the child's performance. I wouldn't just rely on my memory for that, you have to have it backed up by evidence. I can give them a level using the evidence plus what I remember.

Overall, I prefer to go about my usual teaching and use assessment opportunities as they occur.

Model B

I tend to see assessment as a whole process; it's a part of what teachers do all the time and there is no need to plan it in. I have a general picture of the whole child and what a child can do; this is where the teacher's skills and experience are important.

I prefer assessment to be informal so that spontaneity is not lost. I plan what the children need. I don't have particular ATs or statements of attainment (SOAs) in mind. I'm recording mentally all the time when watching the processes a child is going through. I don't take notes because I think that can interfere with your relationships with children. I might give a worksheet or a little test to check understanding or something I have taught.

As a professional, I think you have to take account of the contextual issues such as attitudes and social background.

When it comes to recording for national assessment, I can reflect on what I know about the child.

Model C

I need to know that at a particular time of day I am actually going to be assessing. I like to be structured and know which SOAs I want to assess. Beforehand, I try to interpret the SOAs and break them down into a kind of can-do list: descriptions of what children might do or say to show they are meeting the National Curriculum criteria. I may assess the same SOA more than once, to double-check and be fair.

I'll observe and question the children while they are working and record at the time or soon afterwards on my own checklists. These notes will inform my future planning because you have to assess in order to teach.

I think you need to be quite specific about what a child has attained on the National Curriculum and record this separately from other things like effort, context and background details; they can be recorded elsewhere, say in a child's record of achievement.

While observing, I am often surprised by what children can do (especially in areas I haven't yet taught) and overall I feel that doing ongoing TA has improved my skills as a teacher.

REFERENCES

Bennett, S. N., Wragg, E. C., Carre, C. G. and Carter, D. S. G. (1992) 'A longitudinal study of primary teachers' perceived competence in, and concerns about, National Curriculum implementation', *Research Papers in Education* 7(1).

Black, H. and Dockrell, W. B. (1984) *Criterion-Referenced Assessment in the Classroom*, Edinburgh: Scottish Council for Research in Education.

Broadfoot, P. and Osborn, M. (1986) 'Teachers' conceptions of their professional responsibility: some international comparisons', Paper presented at BERA conference, Bristol.

Brown, M. (1989) 'The Graded Assessment in Mathematics Project', in D. F. Robitaille (ed.), *Evaluation and Assessment in Mathematics*, Science and Technology Education Series no. 32, Paris: Unesco.

Cooper, M. (1988) 'Whose culture is it anyway?' in A. Lieberman (ed.), *Building a Professional Culture in Schools*, New York: Teachers College Press.

Galton, M., Simon, B. and Croll, P. (1980) *Inside the Primary Classroom*, London: Routledge & Kegan Paul.

Glaser, B. G. and Strass, A. L. (1967) *The Discovery of Grounded Theory*, Chicago: Aldine.

Harlen, W. and Qualter, A. (1991) 'Issues in SAT development and the practice of teacher development assessment', *Cambridge Journal of Education* 21 (2).

Her Majesty's Inspectorate (1992) *The Implementation of the Curricular Requirements of the Education Reform Act. Assessment, Recording and Reporting*, London: HMSO.

House, E. (1974) *The Politics of Educational Innovation*, Berkeley, CA: McCutchan.

MacDonald, B. (1974) 'Evaluation and the control of education', in R. Murphy and H. Torrance (eds) (1987) *Evaluating Education: Issues and Methods*, London: Harper & Row.

Marris, P. (1975) *Loss and Change*, New York: Anchor Press/Doubleday.

Nias, J. (1989) *Primary Teachers Talking*, London: Routledge.

Pennycuick, D. and Murphy, R. (1988) *The Impact of Graded Tests*, London: Falmer Press.

Rowland, S. (1987) 'An interpretative model of teaching and learning,' in A. Pollard (ed.) *Children and their Primary Schools*, London: Falmer Press.

SEAC (Schools Examination and Assessment Council) (1990) *A Guide to Teacher Assessment, Packs A, B & C*, London: Heinemann Educational.

TGAT (Task Group on Assessment and Testing) (1988) *Task Group on Assessment and Testing: A Report*, London: DES.

Torrance, H. (1991) 'Evaluating SATs: the 1990 pilot', *Cambridge Journal of Education* 21(2): 129–40.

Whetton, C., Sainsbury, M., Hopkins, S., Ashby, J., Christopher, U., Clarke, J., Heath, M., Jones, G., Pulcher, J., Shagen, I. and Wilson, J. (1991) *An Evaluation of the 1991 National Curriculum Assessment, Report 1*, NFER/BGC Consortium, London: School Examinations and Assessment Council.

Part II

Enabling learning

Chapter 7

Authentic activity and learning

Elizabeth Clayden, Charles Desforges, Colin Mills and William Rawson

In this article, the authors focus on the relationship between subject content and classroom practice. They put forward an argument for 'situated learning', which involves a re-conceptualization of knowledge itself, and understanding learning as being 'enculturation' into a particular domain of learning.*

LEARNING AND THE STRUCTURE OF CLASSROOM EXPERIENCE

Sam is five years old. He enjoys school and he particularly enjoys maths. Observed during a series of maths activities, he was seen to work extremely hard at the tasks in the commercial scheme used in his classroom. This work predominantly involved drawing objects to make up sets and then colouring the objects in the set. When asked what the work was all about, he said 'colouring'. He called his maths workbook his 'colouring book' (Desforges and Cockburn, 1987). Sam's view is quite common amongst 5- and 6-year-old pupils.

A teacher set out to get her class of 8-year-olds to understand the socially negotiated origins of laws. She asked them to pretend they had been shipwrecked on a desert island and to sort out a set of rules and sanctions to determine people's behaviour. The class worked attentively on this project. They animatedly discussed the rules they would need. They reported clearly to their teacher. Later, when they were asked what they thought they had learned, one said she felt she had learned what to do if she were shipwrecked. Another thought she would never take another boat trip (Edwards and Mercer, 1987). They had missed the abstract content of the teacher's lesson.

Scenes like these are common in classrooms. They raise some extremely important questions about the relationship between experience and learning. They call into question the validity of the old slogan, 'I do and I under-

* Originally published in *British Journal of Educational Studies*, vol. XXXXII, no. 2 (June 1994), Oxford/Cambridge, Mass.: Blackwell.

stand', and they challenge us to think again about the assumed link between hard work and learning.

Of course, in the scenes described, the children were learning something. But they were not learning what their teacher intended. Rather, the children appear to have a much more immediate view of their activities. The interpretations – and what they carry away as learning – are related directly to the activities in which they have engaged.

Edwards and Mercer (1987) reported several detailed case studies which expose the gap between classroom experience and learning. In one class, some 10-year-olds had been set up to explore the periodicity of the pendulum. In the teacher's mind was the aim that the class would discover, or re-invent, the scientific principle of the control of variables. The teacher had given the pupils a range of pendulums made of different lengths of various materials. They also had a range of bobs. The children worked intensively on the problem, but it was clear that they were altering several variables at once, thus precluding their understanding of the factors affecting the rate of swing of the pendulum and manifesting their lack of progress towards understanding the principle of control.

The teacher, feeling he was running out of time, asked each group to alter only one variable so that each would have something to report to the class at the end of the lesson. This they did. They discovered that the length of the pendulum was the factor which determined the rate of swing. However, when asked why they only altered one variable at a time, they each said, in different ways, 'There were four groups and four things so we did one each.' Clearly, they had not learned the notion of control. They had learned how to manage classroom work.

While it is important not to make too much of these accounts, it does seem consistently to be the case that young children focus on the working practices of their activities in making direct interpretations of them. In their efforts to make sense of their classroom experience, the working practices are much more salient than abstract ideas. Colouring, discussion, managing reporting back are important things to sort out in the eyes of these children. What they learn from classroom experience is how to do work, how to be neat, how to finish on time (or sometimes how to spin work out) and how to tidy away.

It is not surprising to observe that children find it very difficult to use their experience in classrooms on problems which require the generalization of knowledge and skills met there. For example, Assessment of Performance Unit (APU) surveys have shown that most 12-year-olds can solve '225 ÷ 15'. What they find difficult is to answer word problems such as, 'If a gardener has 225 bulbs to set equally in 15 beds how many bulbs will there be in each bed?' Many do not realise that this is a division sum. Learning in classrooms is often constrained to the particular formats in which work is set. Generalization or knowledge transfer is frequently extremely limited.

The problems of the relationship between experience, learning and knowledge use or transfer are serious challenges to schooling. Schooling is premised on the concept of transfer. In school, children are supposed to learn bodies of knowledge and skill which they can then use elsewhere. The fact that large numbers of pupils find this extremely difficult is a serious challenge to teachers.

The challenge often comes in the form of accusing teachers of letting standards fall or failing to meet standards set. Teachers are charged with not working hard enough or, perhaps, not working their pupils hard enough. In this view, more work should lead to more learning which would lead to more transfer.

Plausible though this perspective is, it is clear from the case studies reported above that, rather than leading to more learning, it could lead to less. Putting more pressure on classroom workers is likely to urge them to focus even more on working practices rather than conceptual content. It is an understanding of working practices that gets tasks finished. A solution to the challenge of classroom learning and transfer of knowledge might have to involve 'doing different' rather than 'doing more'.

This chapter examines these ideas and presents an argument in favour of 'doing different'. It continues in the following section by focusing on views recently put forward by Brown *et al.* (1989). They describe the tension that exists between the view of learning as a means of knowledge transfer and the alternative idea that it is socially situated and not separable from the activities in which it is developed. They argue that, if knowledge is in part a product of the culture in which it is developed and used, then it is the authentic practices of individual cultures that should be employed in schools to encourage learning, rather than the culture of schooling itself.

Recognizing the relevance of these ideas to the teaching and learning of young children, we continue by exploring ways of identifying and developing authentic activities in the classroom. We suggest that teachers may have difficulty in planning work for children that is authentic to cultures of which they are not a part. Consequently, it is proposed that there should be opportunities for both students and practising teachers to examine, evaluate and develop their own understanding of appropriate cultures.

A SOCIALLY SITUATED VIEW OF LEARNING

In the face of the challenge of transfer, some writers (e.g. Brown *et al.*, 1989) have suggested a fundamental re-think of the problem, starting with a re-conception of the nature of knowledge. Traditional schooling, they argue, is based on a view of knowledge as a 'self-sufficient substance . . . independent of the situations in which it is learned and used'. The aim of schooling is to transfer this 'substance' into the minds of children. 'The activity and context in which learning takes place are thus . . . merely ancillary to learning – useful but fundamentally distinct and even neutral to what is learned' (p. 32).

Brown *et al.* argue that this view of knowledge and its acquisition is no longer tenable. They suggest that recent research in developmental and social psychology and in anthropology indicates that knowledge is not separable from the activities and situations in which it is produced. 'Situations might be said to co-produce knowledge through activity. Learning and cognition . . . are fundamentally situated' (ibid.). By 'situated' they mean that knowledge is an inseparable part of the activity, context and culture in which it is used and generated.

This view of knowledge as socially situated has important implications for our understanding of subject matter knowledge and for how classroom experience might be managed to help children acquire such knowledge. From this perspective, bodies of knowledge (e.g. physics, history) are generated by communities of scholars. Their concepts are not fixed quantities. Rather, they are a 'product of negotiation within the community' (ibid.: 33). Communities of scholars are intimately connected through the work they do. But they are also bound by 'intricate, socially constructed webs of beliefs, which are essential to understanding what they do' (ibid.). To understand an academic subject is to appreciate how the community of scholars in the subject uses the tools (i.e. concepts and procedures) of the domain. Understanding involves entering the community, adopting its perspectives, appreciating how the world looks from within the culture of scholars in the domain.

In the terms of Brown *et al.*, learning is a process of enculturation. 'Unfortunately students are too often asked to use the tools (i.e. the concepts and procedures) of a discipline without being able to adopt its culture. To learn to use tools as practitioners use them, a student, like an apprentice, must enter the community and its culture' (ibid.).

In the main, schools deny pupils the opportunity to engage with the cultures of academic domains. Whilst pupils meet and use some of the tools of academic disciplines, the pervasive culture in which they use them is school life itself. 'The ways schools use maths formulae or dictionaries are very different from the ways in which practitioners use them . . . students may pass exams (a distinctive part of school cultures) but still not be able to use a domain's conceptual tools in authentic practice' (ibid.: 34). This is a way of explaining the lack of transfer of knowledge and procedures learned in school. In order to achieve authentic practice, learners must be engaged in authentic activity. 'Authentic activities [then], are most simply defined as the ordinary practices of the culture' (ibid.).

RECOGNIZING AND SUPPORTING AUTHENTIC ACTIVITY

The claim that pupils in the main are frequently denied the opportunity to engage with the cultures of academic domains requires closer inspection. Such a claim has serious implications for classroom practice. Take, for example, the teaching and learning of mathematics.

Lakatos' view of the ordinary practices of the mathematical culture is described by Lampert (1990: 30):

> mathematics develops as a process of 'conscious guessing' about relationships among quantities and shapes, with proof following a 'zig-zag path starting from conjectures and moving to the examination of premises through the use of counter examples or 'refutations'.

This is in sharp contrast to the following portrayal by Lampert of experiences with mathematics in schools:

> doing mathematics means following the rules laid down by the teacher; knowing mathematics means remembering and applying the correct rule when the teacher asks a question; and mathematical truth is determined when the answer is ratified by the teacher.

(ibid.: 32)

If Lampert's view is accepted, then it seems clear that a serious attempt is necessary to modify instructional practices in the classroom in order to provide for authentic activity in mathematics. Before this can happen, it would be reasonable to expect a teacher to know what the ordinary practices of this particular culture are; to be able to identify and untangle these from all that goes on in the classroom; and to be well equipped to sustain and extend mathematical practice when spotted.

The following snapshot of a classroom event provides a resource on which these issues relating to classroom practice and authentic activity can be examined. It took place in a Year 1 classroom in a city school. As part of the class teacher's repertoire of classroom practice, a short period of time had been set aside for groups of children to share their books. During this time they reported on their current reading and also encouraged others to read too. This was a popular activity among the children and it was viewed by the teacher as an opportunity for them to engage in an activity which would enhance their learning, not only to describe and listen, but also to explain and answer.

The talk amongst members of one group was particularly animated. However, they were not involved with the type of book the class teacher had in mind. These children were busily matching picture cards depicting the antics of popular television characters with spaces in a commercially produced scrap book. By standing back from the group, the class teacher noted that they were handling numbers and shape in ways beyond her expectation. Questions like: 'Do you have a 1, 7, 3?', she felt, were particularly significant.

What does this incident have to do with the culture of a skilled practitioner in mathematics? In the hands of a 6-year-old, one feature – that of struggle – is focused on the way the formal language of place value was replaced by a shared meaning among this group. It was brought about by breaking up a string of digits into individual and identifiable parts. The picture card, therefore, was called 'one seven three'. It served as a description of that particular card separating it from the rest of the collection. (The class teacher suspected that identifying these cards numerically this way did not signify an understanding of a relationship between number and actual quantity.) By accepting the conventional arithmetic symbols as a means of communicating, the children were articulating a situation in such a way as to enable others to participate. Similarly, within the culture of the expert mathematician, the physical construction of symbols assists mental experimentation in learning to construe situations and elaborate relationships.

To support this comparison, further clues to mathematical activity in this classroom episode are seen in the distinctions these children made to identify the various sets to which the family of cards belonged. Studying patterns in numbers reveals characteristics about relationships between quantities. This is precisely what happened with these children. Discarding the '1' and the '7' of the number, they concentrated on the order of the units and organized cards according to this unit digit. Hence, a set of 173, 174, 175 . . . cards became 3, 4 and 5 . . . because according to the children's evaluation of the situation, '1 and 7 are always the same'. From the picture cards being the focus of attention, these were replaced by the numbers associated with them. The numbers eventually became the 'object' of attention and a general relationship between the whole number and its various parts was depicted. Isolating unit digits from the hundreds and tens helped make the generalization that picture cards were ordered in a sequence of 3, 4 and 5. . . .

Other clues to mathematical activity in this incident are seen in matching a picture card to a vacant space upon each page of the scrap book. The manner in which a child tried various positions, either obliquely or laterally, before actually fixing the card to the page seems to indicate a search for congruence. What in the first instance does not appear to be mathematical may indeed be something that is.

This classroom snapshot shows mathematics as an event. It is a collaborative venture embedded in the problems these children encountered as they formulated and executed their decisions. But it arose spontaneously. The class teacher's judicious use of this event provided her with sufficient evidence around which she could prepare further activities to challenge their understanding of the number system far beyond counting up to 10. An awareness of engagement in authentic mathematical activity opened up, for her, a new kind of practice in teaching and learning.

UNDERSTANDING AUTHENTIC ACTIVITIES

The activity above is different from those described previously in this paper which were planned as science or maths, but missed the mark and instead were teaching children how to manage classroom work. The children matching picture cards were immersed within their own culture as children. The teacher recognized that what they were engaged in were authentic maths activities that she could take further, but she had not anticipated that this would happen.

Teachers know well the culture of school and schooling, both from their experiences as students within it and as teachers. They have no difficulty in planning activities for children that are authentic to that culture. The difficulty appears to be when they try to plan an activity for the classroom that is authentic to a culture of which they are not a part or have only a slight understanding – when they need to defy the limitations set by the culture of schooling.

For example, to enable teachers to plan science activities for the classroom which are authentic to the culture of science and scientists, they need to know more about the nature of science, the tools that scientists use in their work and the ways in which they use them. As Claxton (1991: 83) has pointed out, 'the metaphor of learner-as-scientist only works to help form a picture of the learner if we already have a picture of the scientist'. If this picture is a misrepresentation, then planning an activity for the classroom that is authentic to the culture of science will be impossible.

The description of the process of science defined in recent years and set down in National Curriculum documents has somehow missed the point. Science is an essentially human activity but, as Zuckerman has observed: 'the incorrect idea still prevails that the scientific process is always an orderly one, ... that scientists, as it were, constitute a dispassionate body of men and women who, through training and experience, are all but interchangeable' (1970: 13).

LEARNING ABOUT THE CULTURE OF SCIENCE AND SCIENTISTS

For many, the ideas they have about the nature of science were formed by the experience of learning in the laboratory of a secondary school and will remain unchallenged during their adult life, including the time spent training to be a teacher. Many of the experiments observed during these lessons would have been carried out in a sequence based upon the way in which they were to be written up, using the headings, aim, method, result and conclusion. This format has evolved from the layout of the formal communication of their work and findings submitted by scientists to the appropriate journal for publication. But does it bear any relationship to the way in which scientists actually work?

In the first paragraph of his article, 'Is the scientific paper a fraud?', Medawar (1963) states, 'I mean the scientific paper may be a fraud because it misrepresents the processes of thought that accompanied or gave rise to the work that is described in the paper.' The underlying concept of this style of writing, he says, is that scientific discovery is an inductive process where generalizations take shape from simple, unprejudiced observations, not allowing for any hypotheses or expectations of outcome as starting points for enquiry.

An alternative view put forward by Popper (1959) is that scientific work starts with a hypothesis which is formulated in the light of previous experience and knowledge. It may be in the form of a prediction, but certainly further understanding is gained, or deduced, when this hypothesis is put to the test. This hypothetico-deductive process, should, according to Medawar, replace the inductive method as a basis for the scientific paper:

> 'The discussion which in the traditional scientific paper comes last should surely come at the beginning. The scientific facts and scientific acts should follow the discussion, and scientists should not be ashamed to admit . . . that hypotheses appear in their minds along uncharted byways of thought; that they are imaginative and inspirational in character; that they are indeed adventures of the mind.
>
> (Medawar, 1963)

If their image of science and scientists is based on false assumptions, can teachers design activities for young children that are sufficiently intellectually challenging so as to provoke adventures of the mind?

An attempt to analyse and describe the culture of science has been made by Claxton (1991). His description of the scientific method has several different layers (p. 69). The *core processes* are observation, generating ideas and testing ideas. These interact to make up a particular type of thinking which takes place within surrounding 'rings of influence'. These are:

- the *personal context*, involving the personality and temperament of the individual;
- the *scientific context*, provided by other scientists working in the same field; and finally
- the *social context* produced by social pressures and political and economic decisions.

This model includes some ideas rarely used as descriptors of the culture of science and scientists. Words like 'ambition', 'honesty', 'status' and 'public opinion' occur within the 'rings of influence'. It may be one of the most accurate descriptions of the ordinary practices of this culture. It may provide a few clues for teachers bent on knowing more about the culture of science and thus being more able to design authentic activities for the classroom.

The nature of science – or maths or any other curriculum area – should not be seen as something that is only to be read about in books and journals. There are other, more practical, ways of helping teachers to study science so that they begin to understand how to plan classroom activities that are authentic to the culture of this discipline. In-service courses that address their subject knowledge of science are popular with primary teachers. This is understandable, given their task of teaching science as part of the core curriculum and, in most cases, without a background in science.

These courses can provide an opportunity for teachers to learn about the ways in which scientists actually work. Course members can engage in investigations at their own level of understanding and analyse not only their findings but also their procedures. Practising scientists can be invited to talk to the teachers about their work; and can be encouraged to visit schools and classrooms. Similar strategies are appropriate at undergraduate level, where they may be easier to manage and where there may be a greater availability of 'real scientists'.

If learning is a process of enculturation, as Brown *et al.* suggest (1989), then it may not be possible in the context of the classroom for an activity to be totally authentic to an academic culture. A spectrum of authenticity may exist. Sometimes children's work will fall within a band that lies close to the culture of school and schooling. On other occasions, it will be nearer the opposite end of the spectrum, that which represents the academic culture. This means that the classroom work described at the beginning of this chapter would belong in the first group and lie on bands close to the school and schooling end. Some aspects of the activity where the children matched picture cards were very authentic to maths, so at least those parts would lie nearer the end of the spectrum representing the academic culture of maths.

The discussion about teachers' understanding and misunderstanding of the nature of science and the work of scientists indicates that they require a deeper and more accurate appreciation of the culture of the appropriate academic disciplines. Only then will they be able to plan activities for children's learning that are authentic to these cultures.

CONCLUSION

In this article we have suggested that the challenge of transfer – the capacity to use knowledge to learn – lies at the heart of schooling. Traditional approaches to this problem have assumed knowledge to be 'stuff' to be 'possessed' by teachers and 'transmitted' to learners. This has led, we have suggested, to pupils' acquiring bodies of inert knowledge.

We have indicated an alternative view of learning which casts knowledge as the working practices of a domain or discipline and learning as enculturation into these practices. We have recognized that such a view poses problems for teachers and for their professional development. On the other hand, it offers a promising approach to the problem of transfer by putting the pupil into the engine room, as it were, of knowledge creation.

REFERENCES

Brown, J. S., Collins, A. and Duguid, P. (1989) 'Situated cognition and the culture of learning', *Educational Researcher*, Jan./Feb. 32–42.

Claxton, G. (1991) *Educating the Enquiring Mind*, London: Harvester Wheatsheaf.

Desforges, C. and Cockburn, A. (1987) *Understanding the Mathematics Teacher*, London: Falmer Press.

Edwards, D. and Mercer, N. (1987) *Common Knowledge*, London: Methuen.

Lampert, M. (1990) 'When the problem is not the question and the solution is not the answer: mathematical knowing and teaching', *American Educational Research Journal*, 27 (1), 29–63.

Medawar, P. (1963) 'Is the scientific paper a fraud?' In D. Pyke (ed.) (1991) *The Threat and the Glory*, Oxford: Oxford University Press.

Popper, K. (1959) *The Logic of Scientific Discovery*, London: Unwin Hyman.

Zuckerman, S. (1970) *Beyond the Ivory Tower*, London: Weidenfeld & Nicolson.

Chapter 8

Learning as a 'hot' process

Paul R. Pintrich, Ronald W. Marx and Robert A. Boyle

This is a much shortened version of a more substantial article in which the three authors draw on a wide literature of educational research (not exclusively from primary education), mainly from the States, to support their argument that learners draw both on social relationships surrounding learning experiences, and on their own beliefs about the area of learning, in making conceptual change. They describe a model of dynamic and interactive factors in learning, which is summarized in Table 8.1 and then explained in the rest of the chapter. In this model, learning is characterized as a real, 'live' or 'hot' process, enabling learners to feel purposeful and motivated. *

INTRODUCTION

... Research on student cognition has demonstrated that students' prior conceptual knowledge influences all aspects of students' processing of information from their perception of the cues in the environment, to their selective attention to these cues, to their encoding and levels of processing of the information, to their search for retrieval of information and comprehension, to their thinking and problem-solving (Alexander and Judy, 1988; Alexander, Schallert and Hare, 1991; Pintrich, Cross, Kozma and McKeachie, 1986; Winne and Marx, 1989). These cognitive models are relevant and useful for conceptualizing student learning, but their reliance on a model of academic learning as cold and isolated cognition (Brown, Bransford, Ferrara and Campione, 1983) may not adequately describe learning in the classroom context. In particular, cognition-only models of student learning do not adequately explain why students who seem to have the requisite prior conceptual knowledge do not activate this knowledge for many school tasks, let alone out-of-school tasks. In this article, we will discuss both individual

* Originally published as 'Beyond cold conceptual change: the role of motivational beliefs and classroom contextual factors in the process of conceptual change', in *Review of Educational Research* (Summer 1993), 63 (2): 167–99 (edited for this volume).

differences in motivational beliefs as well as classroom contextual factors that may contribute to this problem.

The failure to activate or transfer appropriate knowledge can be attributed to purely cognitive factors, but it is likely that motivational and contextual factors also play a role (Garner, 1990). Models that focus only on cognition tend to avoid including constructs such as an individual's goals, intentions, purposes, expectations or needs (Pintrich, 1990; Searle, 1992). . . . Students can and do adopt different goals and purposes for their school work, and becoming cognitively engaged in the myriad of classroom academic tasks is really a choice they can make for themselves. In addition, their level of engagement and willingness to persist at the task may be a function of motivational beliefs (Pintrich and De Groot, 1990a, 1990b; Pintrich and Schrauben, 1992).

These three aspects of an individual's behaviour – choice of a task, level of engagement or activity in the task, and willingness to persist at the task – are the three traditional behavioural indicators of motivation. Almost all motivational research has been directed at explaining these three aspects of behaviour and has invoked a number of motivational constructs as precursors of motivated behaviour . . . There has been little research or theory development that attempts to link motivation and cognition (Winne and Marx, 1989). Accordingly, it seems important to begin to build the connections between the motivational and cognitive components of student learning.

Besides the intra-individual links between motivational and cognitive components of learning, the actual classroom context may influence students' motivation and cognition and, most importantly, interaction between these two constructs. For example, the tasks that students confront in a classroom are often not as structured conceptually or procedurally as they might be in the experimental setting of a psychology laboratory (Blumenfeld, Mergendoller and Swarthout, 1987; Blumenfeld, Pintrich, Meece and Wessels, 1982; Doyle, 1983). Given that these classroom tasks are often not clearly defined, students must often define the tasks for themselves, providing their own goals and structure. Students may not perceive the tasks in the same way that teachers do and may not understand what cognitive resources are appropriate for different tasks (Marx and Walsh, 1988; Newman, Griffin and Cole, 1989; Winne and Marx, 1982). At the same time other classroom tasks (e.g., drill and practice worksheets) may be so overstructured and repetitive that very little cognitive engagement is required for satisfactory performance (Doyle, 1983). In addition, the overall classroom structure and organization can influence students' perceptions of what is considered learning as well as their actual cognitive engagement (Stodolsky, 1988). However, this contextual analysis still leaves a role for the active individual. As Lave (1989) points out, in many contexts – not just schools and classrooms – individuals often have to make choices about whether they have a problem or not, then make choices about the specification of what constitutes the problem, and finally decide how they will go about solving it in that context. Again, given that this is a choice that individuals make, motivational constructs such as goals and agency beliefs can play a role in helping describe the factors that influence individuals' ability to recognize a problem, define it and attempt to solve it.

The purpose of this article is to present a *conceptual analysis* of the relations between motivational factors and student cognition as well as an analysis of classroom contextual factors that may condition the relations between student motivation and cognition. There are many models of student cognition derived from a variety of theoretical perspectives, but we focus on a model of conceptual change that is important for describing how students' prior knowledge may facilitate or impede actual learning. Of course, there are other perspectives on knowledge change and development, such as nativist views on the origins of knowledge (e.g., Spelke, Breinlinger, Macomber and Jacobson, 1992) and network models based on associationism and connectionism (e.g., Singley and Anderson, 1989), but we focus on conceptual change because of its relevance to conceptual understanding in schools (Gardner, 1991). In addition, conceptual change models have become very popular and useful in research on learning in the subject areas (science, mathematics, social studies; e.g., West and Pines, 1985). At the same time, in contrast to work on students' cognitive learning strategies which has examined the role of motivational beliefs (see Pintrich and De Groot, 1990a, 1990b; Pintrich and Schrauben, 1992), research on students' conceptual change has never explicitly examined the role of an individual's motivational beliefs. Accordingly, the purpose of this article is not to present a comprehensive review of the reseach, given that there is virtually none on motivation and conceptual change, but rather to develop an argument for the importance of examining motivational beliefs as mediators and classroom context as moderators of conceptual change. As part of this argument, we suggest a conceptual framework for future research in this area that includes the interactions between cognitive and motivational constructs as well as classroom factors. We begin with a brief examination of the general conceptual change model as it might be amenable to a motivational analysis, then discuss how different motivational beliefs and classroom contexts may facilitate or impede conceptual change, and suggest directions for future research.

DEFINITION AND DESCRIPTION OF CONCEPTUAL CHANGE

. . . We take the constructivist position that the process of conceptual change is influenced by personal, motivational, social and historical processes, thereby advocating a hot model of individual conceptual change. . . We believe that the actual content of students' theories and models is influenced by personal, motivational, social, and historical factors, as shown by the existence and persistence of students' misconceptions in science. These assumptions underlie our analysis of how students' motivational beliefs and the classroom context influence the process of individual conceptual change. We begin our analysis with a brief description of the traditional model of individual conceptual change.

Basically, the standard individual conceptual change model describes learning as the interaction that takes place between an individual's experiences and his or her current conceptions and ideas. These conceptions create a framework for understanding and interpreting information gathered through experience. Current conceptions held by the learner can result in problems from discrepancies between experience and current beliefs, but current conceptions also provide a framework for judging the validity and adequacy of solutions to these problems. Thus, a paradox exists for the learner; on the one hand, current conceptions potentially constitute momentum that resists conceptual change, but they also provide frameworks that the learner can use to interpret and understand new, potentially conflicting information.

The process of learning in a conceptual change model depends on the extent of the integration of the individual's conceptions with new information. If he or she knows little about the topic under study, new information is likely to be combined easily with his or her existing ideas; the process that accounts for this event is what Posner, Strike, Hewson and Gertzog (1982) refer to as assimilation. On the other hand, the individual may have well-developed concepts about the topic under study. Often, these concepts may conflict and be contrary to what is understood as true by experts in that domain; such individual ideas are often referred to as alternative frameworks, and studies have shown these to be highly resistant to change (Champagne, Gunstone and Klopfer, 1985; Nussbaum and Novick, 1982; Osborne and Freyberg, 1985). Overcoming these frameworks requires a more radical transformation of individual conceptions. This process is what Posner *et al.* (1982) refer to as accommodation. The processes of assimilation and accommodation are guided by the principle of equilibration whereby individuals seek a relatively stable homeostasis between internal conceptions and new information in the environment (cf. Chapman, 1988; Piaget, 1985)...

Clearly, the process of accommodation is critical for the continuing educational development of learners. Without the process of accommodation working on prior conceptions of content, little conceptual growth would occur. Not surprisingly, then, most work on conceptual change has focused on what processes encourage or drive accommodation. To explain how current conceptions influence how an individual will view new information, Posner *et al.* (1982) use the metaphor of a conceptual ecology...

The first condition is that of *dissatisfaction* with current conceptions. This suggests that, the less dissatisfied an individual is with his or her current understandings and ideas, the less likely he or she will be to consider a radical change of view. The second condition is that a new conception be *intelligible*. In order for an individual to consider a new concept as a better means of explaining experience than his or her current conception, he or she must be able to understand it. The third condition is that a new concept be *plausible.* While the learner might be able to understand the new concept, he or she may not see how it can be applied or may deem the new concept too inconsistent with other understandings to merit further consideration. Finally, the new concept must appear *fruitful*; that is, it must have explanatory power and/or suggest new areas for investigation.

This description of the four conditions necessary for conceptual change provides an interesting model of how learners might come to change their beliefs about academic subject matter. It presumes a very rational process of cognitive change, parallelling Brown, Bransford, Ferrara and Campione's (1983: 78) assertion that academic learning is 'cold and isolated' cognition. That is, it suggests that learners behave very much like scientists in that, when they become dissatisfied with an idea, they will then search out new intelligible, plausible and fruitful constructs which will balance their general conceptual model. However, there are both theoretical and empirical reasons to believe that academic learning is not cold and isolated. For example, there is empirical evidence that more affectively charged motivational beliefs, such as students' self-efficacy beliefs, and their goals for learning can influence their cognitive engagement in an academic task (see Pintrich and Schrauben's review, 1992). Accordingly, individual students' motivational beliefs may influence the process of conceptual change. In addition, there is a great deal of theoretical and empirical research to suggest that individual learning in classrooms is not isolated but greatly influenced by peer and teacher interactions (Blumenfeld, Soloway, Marx, Krajcik, Guzdial and Palincsar, 1991; Marx and Walsh, 1988; Palincsar and Brown, 1984; Resnick, Levine and Teasley, 1991; Tharp and Gallimore, 1988). Besides the influence of individual beliefs, then, the conceptual change process may be influenced by being situated within different classroom contexts and shaped dramatically by the nature of the interactions between students and the teacher.

The assumption that students approach their classroom learning with a rational goal of making sense of the information and coordinating it with their prior conceptions may not be accurate. Students may have many social goals in the classroom context besides learning – such as making friends, finding a boyfriend or girlfriend, or impressing their peers (see Wentzel, 1991) – which can short-circuit any in-depth intellectual engagement. In addition, even if the focus is on academic achievement, students may adopt different goals for or orientations to their learning. For example, it appears that a focus on mastery or learning goals can result in deeper cognitive processing on academic tasks than a focus on the self (ego-involved) or a focus on performance (grades, besting others), which seems to result in more surface processing and less overall cognitive engagement (Dweck and Leggett, 1988; Nolen, 1988; Pintrich and De Grout, 1990a, 1990b; Pintrich and Schrauben, 1992). . . . Accordingly, an individual student's goals for knowledge, learning, and for classroom life in general may have a significant impact on the conceptual change process.

In addition to this individual goal issue, the conceptual change model uses a metaphor of the individual student as scientist, engaging in rational enquiry and attempting to understand the natural and social world through the use of such devices as theories, models, experiments and data. Scientists attempt to make sense out of results from research studies and coordinate these results with their prior theoretical beliefs and conceptual models. At the same time, the individual scientist is part of a larger scientific community which emphasizes the search for meaning and understanding and the importance of coherence and consistency in theories, models and data. Although scientists may be members of a community that sets and enforces this norm of commitment to understanding and most scientists internalize this norm as a personal goal, it is doubtful that students in classrooms are members of a community that operates with this goal of understanding or that individual students will internalize this goal. . .

In our view, there are serious limitations to the power of existing conceptual change theory to explain learning in classrooms. We have shown that two of the greatest problems are the lack of theoretical reasoning about the way that: (a) individual motivational beliefs about the self as learner influence learning in classrooms and (b) the role of the individual in a learning community supports or resists instructionally guided conceptual change. . . Given these problems with the conceptual change model, there needs to be an integration of motivational constructs and an attention to classroom contextual factors in elaborating the model. The remainder of this chapter presents an argument for how motivational constructs like goals and beliefs may influence conceptual change in the classroom context and how the social and institutional characteristics of the classroom context may influence students' motivation and cognition.

Table 8.1 displays an overview of our analysis. We have displayed the factors by columns and broken them into cognitive, motivational and classroom factors (see Table 8.1), but we assume that the relations between these three general factors and the four conditions necessary for conceptual change are interactive and dynamic and that there is not necessarily a linear, one-to-one relation between the four columns. We assume that the four basic conditions of conceptual change (dissatisfaction, understanding, plausbility and fruitfulness) are dependent on a variety of cognitive factors (see Table 8.1). It seems likely that in order for students to engage in the type of cognitive accommodation for integrating their original beliefs with new ideas that is required by the conceptual change model they would have to be very active, generative learners and engage in a number of cognitive processes (Osborne and Wittrock, 1983). Although there are any number of different conceptualizations of the cognitive factors, there is beginning to be a remarkable consistency at a macro-level of analysis in that the cognitive factors that influence learning include knowledge, cognitive learning strategies, problem-solving or thinking strategies, and metacognitive and self-regulation strategies (see Bereiter, 1990; Perkins and Simmons, 1988; Pintrich, 1992; Snow and Swanson, 1992). In terms of linking these cognitive factors to conceptual change, there are a variety of paths a learner might follow. For example, selective attention to the new information would be required. If students are to become dissatisfied with their original ideas, they would have to attend to the discrepant information. If students have to encode the new concepts to make them understandable and plausible, then they might have to use various deeper processing cognitive strategies such as elaboration (paraphrasing, summarizing) and organizational strategies (concept mapping, networking) which have been shown to facilitate encoding and learning (Weinstein and Mayer, 1986). In the same manner, they would have to activate and utilize their prior knowledge in order to integrate it with the new information in a coherent and logical manner, rather than as just separate bits of new information to recall (Reif and Larkin, 1991). The conditions of dissatisfaction and fruitfulness also could depend on students' ability to find or become aware of problems (Arlin, 1986) as well as their actual problem-solving ability (Perkins and Simmons, 1988). As part of this problem-solving process, students would have to engage in metacognitive reflection, rethinking their old beliefs and comparing them with the new ideas in order to judge the new ideas as more plausible and fruitful. In addition, students would have to use various metacognitive strategies such as self-testing or self-questioning to determine if the new ideas are intelligible to them given their prior knowledge. Finally, all these types of cognitive engagement often require more effort and persistence on the learner's part, which can make volitional and self-control strategies important as students attempt to manage their effort in the face of challenging tasks (Corno, 1986, 1993; Corno and Kanfer, 1993).

A second assumption of our model is that these various cognitive processes can be influenced by students' motivational beliefs (see Table 8.1). This is not a new assumption. In fact, Piaget (1981) noted that cognition and affect were inseparable and proposed that affect – specifically, interest – was related to the energizing of all action, including cognitive activity, and that the speed of cognitive development would be facilitated by interest (Chapman, 1988). Besides interest, there are a number of other motivational beliefs that may influence the quality, not just the speed, of students' cognition. Our list of motivational beliefs is derived from a social cognitive perspective on motivation that highlights the important role that students' beliefs and interpretations of actual events play in motivational dynamics (Weiner, 1986). The discussion of motivational beliefs includes several different constructs that have been generated by different theoretical models (e.g., attribution theory, self-efficacy theory, goal theory, intrinsic motivation theory), but we have organized the beliefs around two general motivational factors. These two factors concern students' motivational beliefs about their reasons for choosing to do a task (value components that include goal orientation, interest

Table 8.1 Classroom contextual, motivational, and cognitive factors related to the process of conceptual change

Classroom contextual factors	Motivational factors	Cognitive factors	Conditions for conceptual change

Task structures
  Authentic
  Challenging
	Mastery goals	Selective attention	Dissatisfaction

	Epistemic beliefs	Activation of prior knowledge	Intelligibility

Authority structures
  Optimal choice
  Optimal challenge
	Personal interest	Deeper processing
		  Elaboration
			Plausibility

	Utility value	Organization	Fruitfulness

Evaluation structures
  Improvement-based
  Mistakes as positive
	Importance	Problem finding and solving	

Classroom management
  Use of time
  Norms for engagement
	Self-efficacy	Metacognitive evaluation and control	

	Control beliefs		

Teacher modelling
  Scientific thinking
  Scientific dispositions
		Volitional control and regulation	

Teacher scaffolding
  Cognition
  Motivation			

and importance) and their beliefs about their capability to perform a task (expectancy components that include self-efficacy, attributions and control beliefs). Finally, this social cognitive perspective on motivation assumes that students' motivational beliefs are more situation or context specific in contrast to older, traditional personality models of motivation that proposed that student motivation was a stable personality trait (e.g., students were high or low in need for achievement). Given this assumption, it is important to discuss how these motivational beliefs are created, shaped and constrained by various aspects of the classroom context (see Table 8.1).

GOAL ORIENTATION BELIEFS AND THE PROCESS OF CONCEPTUAL CHANGE

Goals are cognitive representations of the different purposes students may adopt in different achievement situations. Like general intentions and purposes, in motivational theory these goals are assumed to guide students' behaviour, cognition and affect as they engage in an academic task (Dweck and Elliott, 1983). . . Students who adopt a mastery goal orientation focused on learning and mastery should be more likely to engage in the type of cognitive processing necessary for conceptual change to occur.

Although the link between students' mastery goal orientation and their cognitive engagement seems to be relatively robust, it is important to note that most goal theorists assume that individuals' goal orientations are dependent on and situated within a classroom context (Ames, 1992; Blumenfeld, 1992). There seem to be several important dimensions of classrooms that can influence the adoption of a mastery goal orientation. First, the nature of the tasks that students are asked to accomplish can have an impact on students' goals. It appears that tasks that are more challenging, meaningful, and authentic in terms of actual activities that might be relevant to life outside school can facilitate the adoption of a mastery goal (Ames, 1992; Brophy, 1983; Lepper and Hodell, 1989; Meece, 1991). However, many, if not most classrooms, do not offer students the opportunity to work on authentic tasks (Gardner, 1991), thereby decreasing motivation and the opportunities for transfer of knowledge learned in school to other contexts. At the same time, the authority structures in classrooms often do not allow students much choice or control over their activities, which decreases the probability of a mastery orientation being developed in students (Ames, 1992; Ryan, Connell and Deci, 1985). Finally, evaluation procedures that focus on competition, social comparison and external rewards can foster a performance goal orientation where the learner focuses on besting others rather than gaining a conceptual understanding of the content (Ames, 1992; Elliott and Dweck, 1988; Grolnick and Ryan, 1987).

This research supports the assumption that the classroom context can influence the adoption of a mastery goal orientation, which in turn can influence the nature of students' cognitive processing and potential for conceptual change. It appears that teachers must consider how the instruction is embedded in the task, authority, and evaluation structures of their classrooms. If teachers use a conceptual change instructional model without changing the traditional task, authority, and evaluation structures of their classroom, then students still might adopt a performance goal orientation to the new instructional method. In turn, this performance goal orientation would tend to undermine the teacher's attempts to have the students engage the material in a deep and thoughtful manner. Accordingly, teachers may have to change not just their general instructional strategies for teaching for conceptual change but also their tasks, authority, and evaluation structures to focus the students on mastery and understanding goals (Blumenfeld, Mergendoller and Puro, 1992).

At the same time, the changing of these classroom structures creates additional demands on the classroom management system. For example, discovery and enquiry methods, which are suggested as potential ways to teach for conceptual change, often use *authentic* tasks (e.g., real science experiments), decrease the role of the teacher's authority, and change how students are evaluated, yet they can create many management problems. Science education reform efforts in the 1960s often failed because they were difficult to manage for many teachers in traditional classrooms (Blumenfeld *et al.*, 1991). As Doyle (1983) has pointed out, challenging and different tasks can create ambiguity and risk for both teachers and students. Students who are accustomed to tasks (e.g., worksheets) that require rather minimal or passive involvement may resist the teacher's attempts to engage them in more complicated and ambiguous tasks by negotiating the task downward to a rather simple level or by acting out when given more responsibility. Accordingly, the changes suggested by goal theorists (e.g., Ames, 1992) to the task, authority, and evaluation structures of the classroom must be considered in the light of both management and curriculum concerns (Blumenfeld, 1992). As McCaslin and Good (1992) have argued, it is important to develop authoritative management systems that help students become active, self-regulated learners who are engaged in problem-solving and meaningful learning, not just passive obedience as in an authoritarian system, or unfocused freedom as in a *laissez-faire* management system. In summary, the classroom contractual factors of task, authority, and evaluation structures as well as of the general management system can influence students' motivation and cognition and can either facilitate or hinder the potential for conceptual change.

Besides these goals for learning that focus on the self, Kruglanski (1989, 1990a, 1990b) has suggested that individuals might have different goals or motivations about knowledge as an object. He terms this motivation towards knowledge *epistemic motivation*. Most of the empirical work that supports his lay epistemic theory has been concerned with social cognitive issues such as attitude change, person perception and attributional beliefs. Nevertheless, the model assumes that individuals are active processors of information who develop and test hypotheses about their knowledge of themselves, other people, and the social world. This assumption of lay epistemic theory is identical to the assumption in conceptual change theory that individuals act as scientists as they try to understand the natural world. In contrast to conceptual change models, however, in Kruglanski's model this process of developing and testing hypotheses is explicitly a function of both cognitive and motivational processes. The cognitive factors that influence hypothesis generation and testing are the availability and accessibility of knowledge. *Availability* refers to all possible knowledge structures an individual can potentially access, and *accessibility* refers to the actual knowledge structures that the individual activates in the specific context. This general model is not unlike many cold cognitive models regarding the role of knowledge. However, Kruglanski argues further that individuals often do not test hypotheses all the time. Epistemic motivations provide the psychological mechanisms for the initiation, guidance, and cessation of the cognitive work involved in hypothesis development and testing.

In his lay epistemic theory, Kruglanski posits two general dimensions of epistemic motivation – seeking or avoiding closure, and specificity or nonspecificity. Kruglanski uses the metaphor of *freezing or unfreezing* of cognition to illustrate the potential influence of epistemic motivations. Freezing of cognition refers to the process where the individual does not attempt to develop or test new ideas or entertain new hypotheses. The individual basically does not seek out new information or discounts relevant information that might contradict already established beliefs or knowledge structures that are activated in that situation. In contrast, unfreezing refers to the individual actively seeking new information, questioning old beliefs, entertaining new ideas and hypotheses, and trying to solve problems or resolve discrepancies. It seems clear that Kruglanski's use of the term *unfreezing* shares many features with the cognitive processes that are assumed to go on when individuals have to accommodate new information in conceptual change models.

The epistemic motivation of seeking closure refers to an individual's attempts to obtain an answer to a question or resolution to a problem, thereby bringing to an end the hypothesis generation and testing process. In contrast, at the other end of the continuum, when operating under the avoiding closure goal, individuals will delay premature or early resolution of a problem in favour of continued information search and hypothesis generation and testing. The goal assumed to underlie this process of avoiding closure is assumed to be a need for accuracy which can then lead to the use of appropriate beliefs and strategies for reasoning (Kunda, 1990). These two aspects of the closure dimension can be combined with the other dimension which refers to the specificity of the answer. Specificity refers to the individual seeking one answer, whereas non-specificity refers to the individual being satisfied with any answer. The need for a specific answer also has been categorized as a directional goal which leads to the use of beliefs and strategies that will most likely produce the desired answer (Kunda, 1990). Individuals may seek non-specific closure where they will actively seek to end their cognitive activity by finding any answer to their question. Children in classrooms may be operating with this combination of epistemic motivations most frequently (i.e., find any answer as quickly as possible, Anderson, Brubaker, Alleman-Brooks and Duffy, 1985). In contrast, individuals seeking specific closure will engage in cognitive activity until they have obtained a particular answer. Kruglanski points out that cognitive activity is not only initiated and concluded by these epistemic motivations but that, when operating under a goal of specificity, an individual's processing of information will be guided in certain directions (i.e., towards the specific answer; cf. Kunda, 1990).

Besides these two-way interactions between closure and specificity, Kruglanski also predicts that the level of prior knowledge may influence cognition when combined with the epistemic motivations. For example, students who have low prior knowledge in an area and have a need to seek non-specific closure would engage in an intense cognitive search (unfreezing) for an answer, any answer. Once this answer is obtained, then the cognitive activity would be concluded. In the same way, a student who has a high level of knowledge in an area and has a need for non-specific closure would be unlikely to engage in further elaborate cognitive activity because he or she already has an answer based on prior knowledge. The process works basically the same way for students with a need to seek a specific closure in terms of the freezing or unfreezing of cognitive activity. However, the need for specific closure would influence the direction of the cognition by maintaining cognitive activity until a particular answer is found. Accordingly, students with low knowledge who are seeking specific closure might engage in cognitive activity longer than students with low knowledge who are seeking non-specific closure in order to obtain information that fits the specificity criteria.

Kruglanski (1989) also notes that the need to avoid closure might be particularly strong when there are costs associated with being wrong. Students with low prior knowledge would be unlikely to engage in cognitive activity when they are also trying to avoid closure. In this case of an ignorance-is-bliss orientation, students would not want to seek new knowledge that would lead to some type of answer. In contrast, students with high knowledge in a domain but also a need to avoid closure would be likely to engage in cognitive activity to seek out new information that might contradict or lead to change in their knowledge structures. In addition, given their relatively high level of knowledge, they might be less threatened by new information, and, because they are trying to avoid closure, they would be likely to engage in cognitive activity.

The four different epistemic motivations are assumed to be more situation specific than traits, although the need for closure may have some trait-like characteristics (Kruglanski, 1989, 1990a, 1990b). In his empirical work, Kruglanski has shown that all four of the different epistemic motivations can be activated by certain features of the environment. For example, setting time constraints and heightening the time pressure or instructions that stress the need for clear, definite answers usually lead to the seeking of closure. Stressing the costs of being wrong and the creation of evaluation apprehension by suggesting that responses will be compared to others seems to lead to fear of invalidity and the need to avoid closure (Kruglanski, 1989). These features seem readily applicable to many of the common aspects of the classroom context. Most classrooms have time constraints operating, but teachers can increase the time pressure by stressing the importance of finishing academic work within the allocated time period. This would tend to create a need for closure with the concomitant decrease in cognitive activity. Efforts at school reform that seek to increase the time available for students to work on extended projects would help set a classroom context whereby the motivational mechanism of need for closure would be lessened and cognitive activities such as hypothesis generation and testing increased. In the same way, if the teacher stresses that the products of student work (answers in a discussion, lab results) should have one correct answer, then a need for closure would be created, and students would be less likely to become cognitively engaged. In fact, in the science education literature there is evidence that many science labs are verification, not problem-solving, exercises and are seen as something to complete and to get the right answer on, rather than as a process by which one might learn something new (Hofstein and Lunetta, 1982; Walberg, 1991). Accordingly, classroom activities that are designed to be more open-ended and create a need to avoid closure in students may be more likely to facilitate cognitive activity and conceptual change. In addition, the issue of need to avoid closure may be less of a problem in classrooms, given their overwhelming press for closure.

In summary, classroom organization and the nature of many classroom academic tasks may encourage students to get it done, not think it through, so it may be important to create types of authentic tasks or projects (Blumenfeld *et al.*, 1991) without one right answer and with longer periods of time for completion in order to help stave off seeking closure and facilitate more cognitive activity and conceptual change. . .

INTEREST AND VALUE BELIEFS AND THE PROCESS OF CONCEPTUAL CHANGE

Although goals and goal orientation beliefs are related to students' choice of tasks and the quality of their engagement, there are other motivational constructs that also are related to students' reasons for engaging in tasks. These constructs are not the same as goals and goal orientations, albeit they also are related to the quality of students' engagement in tasks. These constructs include students' interest and value beliefs which are somewhat more affective or attitudinal in nature and which may be more stable and personal in comparison to the more cognitive and situational representations of goals. In this sense, interest and value beliefs may be at a different level of analysis than goals and goal orientations. It may be that students could have multiple goals operating due to differential interest and value beliefs. In fact, interest researchers (e.g., Krapp, Hidi and Renninger, 1992) have suggested that the effects of interest on learning may be generated by different interest and value beliefs that influence the types of motivational goal orientation that students adopt in classrooms and that then influence learning. For example, students may be intrinsically interested in a topic area, but they may also value it because of its importance for future career options. These differential interest and value beliefs could give rise to both mastery (intrinsic interest generating a mastery goal) and performance (importance generating a concern for grades) goal orientations. . . Accordingly, interest/value beliefs and goals may be operating at different theoretical levels of analysis (see Krapp *et al.*, 1992) but may be linked to one another in important ways as well as to students' cognitive engagement.

It is important to note that interest and value beliefs are assumed to be personal characteristics that students bring to different tasks, not features of the task itself. . . We will focus on the individual difference and the personal variables that are activated in the situation. Eccles (1983) has proposed that there are three general interest or value beliefs. Interest simply refers to the student's general attitude or preference for the content or task (e.g., some students just like and are interested in science). Utility value concerns the student's instrumental judgements about the potential usefulness of the content or task for helping him or her to achieve some goal (e.g., getting into college, getting a job). Finally, the importance of the task refers to the student's perception of the salience or significance of the content or task to the individual. In particular, the importance of a task seems to be related to the individual's self-worth or self-schema. If a student sees himself or herself as becoming a scientist – that is, a scientist is one of her possible selves (Markus and Nurius, 1986; Markus and Wurf, 1987) – then science content and tasks may be perceived as being more important, regardless of his or her mastery or performance orientation to learning.

Hidi (1990) has discussed issues related to the role of interest and its influence on learning. She summarizes the research on interest by concluding that both personal interest and situational interest have a 'profound effect on cognitive functioning and the facilitation of learning' (Hidi, 1990: 565). In particular, she suggests that personal interest influences students' selective attention, effort and willingness to persist at the task, and their activation and acquisition of knowledge. In addition, she notes that interest may not necessarily result in more time spent processing information – rather, depending on the nature of the task (complex vs. simple), students may take more or less time to perform the task. The difference lies in the quality of the processing, not the quantity of processing or time spent on the task (Hidi, Renninger and Krapp, 1992). . .

For example, Renninger and Wozniak (1985) demonstrated the effects of interest on the processes of attention, recognition and recall for young children. After first determining objects of interest for each of sixteen 3- to 4-year-olds through naturalistic observations, they showed in subsequent experimental studies significantly higher levels of both initial attentional fixation and numbers of attentional shifts toward objects of interest than toward comparison (control) items, all within a 3-second exposure period. Additionally, children were not only better able to both recognize and recall objects of interest but also more likely to recognize and recall objects of interest first, before comparison items. Not only were there strong and varied focuses of interest in children this young, but this interest, from initial attending on, influenced memory performance. More recently, Renninger (1992) has shown that fifth and sixth graders' reading and maths performance were influenced by individual interest. Tasks that included high interest or value contexts (e.g., interesting reading passages or maths word problems) resulted in more competent performance. It is important to note that this study showed that the high value context did not necessarily result in students' use of the prerequisite cognitive skills but that it did result in longer persistence at a task. In another study that assessed students' beliefs about value, Pokay and Blumenfeld (1990) found that high school students' beliefs about the value of geometry did not directly predict performance on tests but that value was predictive of use of general cognitive strategies, specific geometry strategies, metacognitive strategies and effort management strategies. These findings for task value support the view that perceptions of the value of a task do not have a direct influence on academic performance but they do relate to students' choice of becoming cognitively engaged in a task or course and to their willingness to persist at the task. Taken together, these studies suggest that personal interest and value beliefs are aspects of a self-generated context that interacts with the task features to support learning by increasing attention, persistence and the activation of appropriate knowledge and strategies (cf. Renninger, 1992). To the extent that conceptual change requires students to maintain their cognitive engagement in trying to understand alternative views, to accommodate to the new, conflicting information, these value beliefs may mediate the process.

Most of these studies have focused on students' personal beliefs and the interest that they bring with them to the task. Situational interest is influenced more by classroom, task and text features and is, therefore, more amenable to teacher control. At the classroom and task level, there are a number of features that could increase students' situational interest – such as challenge, choice, novelty, fantasy, and surprise (Malone and Lepper, 1987). . . Most of the work on challenge and intrinsic motivation (see Malone and Lepper, 1987) stresses the importance of optimal levels of challenge, keeping novelty, difficulty, and surprise within the capabilities of the student. Instruction that is designed to foster conceptual change but that goes beyond the students' range of knowledge and capability (or alternatively, zone of proximal development) will likely short-circuit the change process. In such a situation, assimilation processes are more likely to operate than accommodation processes, thus limiting the possibility that conceptual change will take place.

In contrast to the research on goal orientation, there is much less research on interest and value beliefs and students' cognition (see, however, Renninger, Hidi and Krapp, 1992). It is becoming clear that, although goals are important, interest and value beliefs might help shape goal adoption and that interest can be related to cognitive engagement independent of goals. . . There is a need for research on the links between interest and value and conceptual change. That is, are personal interest and value for a particular domain necessary for conceptual change in that domain? It may be that students can show conceptual change without being interested in or valuing the domain. . . In the same manner, classroom features (see Malone and Lepper, 1987) that increase interest may not lead directly to conceptual change unless students have the requisite prior knowledge and skills. There is a need for more research that examines the interactions of classroom features that heighten interest and students' cognitive capabilities.

SELF-EFFICACY BELIEFS AND THE PROCESS OF CONCEPTUAL CHANGE

Goals, interest and value beliefs represent students' reasons for engaging in different tasks. However, another important aspect of motivation is students' beliefs about their capability to accomplish the task. *Self-efficacy beliefs* have been defined as individuals' beliefs about their performance capabilities in a particular domain (Bandura, 1986). In an educational context, self-efficacy beliefs refer to students' judgements about their cognitive capabilities to accomplish a specific academic task or obtain specific goals (Schunk, 1985). Self-efficacy beliefs are assumed to be relatively situation-specific, not global personality traits or general self-concepts. In a conceptual change model of learning, self-efficacy beliefs could be construed in two ways. First, in the bulk of the research on self-efficacy, the construct is used to represent students' confidence in their ability to do a particular task. In applying this construct to conceptual change, this could translate into students' confidence in their own ideas and conceptions. In this case, higher levels of self-efficacy or confidence in one's own beliefs would be a hindrance to conceptual change. That is, the more confidence students have in their own beliefs, the more resistant they would be to new ideas and conceptions. In fact, much of the conceptual change literature is based on the notion of destabilizing students' confidence in their beliefs through the introduction of conflicting data, ideas or theories. A second way to conceive of the relation of self-efficacy to a conceptual change model is the confidence students have in their capabilities to change their ideas, to use the cognitive tools necessary to integrate and synthesize divergent ideas. . . In this sense, self-efficacy would refer to students' confidence in their own learning and thinking strategies.

There has been very little research on students' self-efficacy for thinking and using sophisticated strategies for problem-solving. . . However, there has been a variety of other studies linking students' self-efficacy beliefs for an academic task to their cognitive engagement in those tasks. . . Paris and Oka (1986) found that elementary school students' perceptions of competence were positively related to performance on a reading comprehension task, metacognitive knowledge about reading, and actual reading achievement. Pintrich and De Groot (1990a) also found that junior high school students' use of cognitive and metacognitive strategies was positively correlated with self-efficacy judgements. Shell, Murphy and Bruning (1989) found that college students' self-efficacy beliefs about their reading and writing skills were related to their performance on a reading comprehension task and an essay writing task. . .

Instructional strategies must be developed that increase students' efficacy in their capability to accomplish the tasks as well as their efficacy for using the appropriate cognitive and metacognitive strategies to facilitate understanding. In this sense, it is not useful for teachers to create tasks that increase the opportunities for cognitive conflict and then leave students entirely to their own devices to resolve the conflict. Students must be assisted in learning how to resolve cognitive conflict through both modelling and scaffolding. In his work on how to increase students' self-efficacy as well as cognitive skill, Schunk (1989) has suggested a number of instructional strategies that may be useful. Verbalization and modelling of appropriate strategies by both the teacher or other students seem to be helpful to students' efficacy and learning. In addition, there is experimental evidence that students observing a coping model, who initially has difficulty with a task and then eventually masters it, increase their efficacy and learning more than students who see a mastery-only model (Schunk and Hanson, 1985). In scaffolded instruction or other classroom instructional models that rely on a great deal of in-depth interaction between teachers and students, the possibility that students will see other students having difficulty is increased. This should then have positive effects on the observers efficacy and learning. Of course, this presupposes that the task is eventually mastered by some of the students in the instructional group. The complexity of classroom instruction and, in particular, the role of peer models as representations of successful learners highlight the need for conceptual change instruction to introduce tasks that may induce cognitive conflict but not at a level that is beyond the students' actual capabilities to master the task or beyond their efficacy beliefs about what they can master. . .

CONTROL BELIEFS AND THE PROCESS OF CONCEPTUAL CHANGE

Most social cognitive theories of motivation include some construct that refers to individuals' belief about how much control they have over their behaviour or the outcome of their performance. . . . Connell (1985) has proposed that there are three general control beliefs: internal control, external control and unknown control. He has shown that students who believe that they have internal control over their own learning and performance, in contrast to students high in external control or unknown control, perform better in school. . . Although there is an overwhelmingly large number of studies on the relations between control beliefs and just about any behaviour of interest (e.g., Baltes and Baltes, 1986; Lefcourt, 1976), including academic achievement (e.g., Findley and Cooper, 1983; Stipek and Weisz, 1981), research on its relation to students' cognitive engagement is fairly recent. . .

Students' perceptions of how much control they have over their own learning may have implications for the process of conceptual change. Bereiter (1990) has recently argued for a more global construct for the development of learning theory, which he labelled the *intentional learner*. This construct includes the idea that individuals assemble into modules the knowledge, skills, goals and affect (for both task and self-related factors) that are then used in a specific context for guiding and directing learning. In a conceptual change model, self-related beliefs about control over learning could direct the level of accommodation or assimilation to new information. If students did not see themselves as intentional learners with some control over their learning, they might be less willing to try actively to resolve discrepancies between their prior knowledge and the new information. Instead, they might regard the discrepancies as something beyond their understanding, something that takes place in the classroom but not under their control. In contrast, intentional learners who believe they do have some control over their learning may actively try to resolve the discrepancy in some fashion. This does not mean that it will be resolved in favour of the scientifically acceptable answer, only that students may be more willing to engage in thinking through some of the issues. Accordingly, control beliefs may be more related to the initiation of cognitive engagement, but they may not specifically influence the direction of thinking. This nondirectional effect is in contrast to the need for specificity in epistemic motivation which would direct the content of students' thinking.

Instruction designed to foster conceptual change is likely to take place over larger units of time than more conventional didactic instruction, thereby providing somewhat different opportunities for control. For example, project-based learning in science is often designed so that students investigate a significant problem with a specific question that serves to organize and drive activities. The pursuit of these activities results in a variety of products, such as analyses of water quality in the local watershed, that eventuate in a final product that answers the driving question of the project (Blumenfeld, Soloway, Marx, Krajcik, Guzdial and Palincsar, 1991). Conceptual change instruction, such as is implied by project-based learning, involves at least two venues for opportunities for student control.

First, students can exercise some control over what to work on, how to work, and what products to create in project-based learning. These features of project-based learning should increase students' perceptions of control. Given their choice over activities and how to do them, they should come to believe that they have some control over their own learning in project-based classrooms as suggested by intrinsic motivation researchers (Deci and Ryan,

1985; Malone and Lepper, 1987). This increase in control beliefs may lead to deeper levels of cognitive engagement. However, many research and instructional questions remain regarding the optimal degree of choice and control to be shared by teachers and students so that novices are not overwhelmed by the opportunities before they attain the requisite competence to use choice and control productively.

Second, a central feature of student control is the learning strategies they use to accomplish academic tasks. Control over learning strategies requires students to be metacognitive and self-regulating. Two aspects of metacognitive control are relevant to conceptual change instruction. One is tactical, relating to the moment-to-moment control of cognition; the other is strategic and pertains to more molar levels of control over larger units of thought. These two features of metacognitive control refer to different strategies for accomplishing academic tasks. Tactical control represents students' ability to monitor and fine-tune thought as they work through the details of particular tasks. This type of cognitive control enables students to remain focused on the goals of the activity while they struggle through the hard work required by conceptual change instruction. Learners with inadequate tactical control are likely to have difficulty sustaining mental effort in the moment-to-moment work of generating products in project-based learning. Strategic control represents the students' ability to engage in purposeful thought over what might seem to be disconnected elements of learning as they engage in a variety of different activities in project-based learning. Students need to be responsible for guiding and controlling their own activities and focusing their work over a long period of time in this type of instruction. The capability of students to organize their mental effort in the service of these more long-term purposes depends on strategic metacognitive control. In this sense, both tactical and strategic control beliefs are necessary for successful project-based learning and at the same time should be fostered by project-based instruction. . .

It may be that increasing students' control beliefs through various instructional changes leads them to spend more time on topics where they have more prior knowledge and interest, which could lead to more confidence in their own pre-existing beliefs and a discounting of new, more scientifically correct, information. Accordingly, research needs to look for both the potentially positive motivational effects of changing classrooms to give students more control, and the potential possibility that there could be some subtle negative effects. It may be that it is important to have instruction that encourages students' control over their learning and the various cognitive and self-regulatory strategies but does not relinquish control over the content of the instruction. . . Clearly, there is a need for more research on these various possibilities.

CONCLUSION

This chapter began with a brief review of the major theoretical features of conceptual change theory as it applies to learning in classrooms. As part of this review, we discussed a number of unresolved problems with the conceptual change model. In particular, we argued that two of the paramount problems are: (a) inadequate theoretical development of the way in which individual beliefs about the self as learner influence learning in classrooms and (b) how the role of the individual in a learning community sustains or hinders conceptual change through instruction. . . What remains to be developed is a programme of research that specifically investigates two critical features of the conceptual change model. These two features are the nature and functions of motivation and classroom contextual factors.

The structure of this chapter reflects our concerns and proposed remedies. The first major section outlined conceptual change theory and our critique of it. The second major section reviewed four areas of research on motivation and classroom learning that bear on issues of applying conceptual change models to classroom learning. Our intention was not to map particular motivational mechanisms uniquely to theoretical or instructional difficulties in using conceptual change models. Rather, we are proposing a range of theoretical entities in the field of motivational research that are possible candidates for incorporation in conceptual change theory and research. Our critique of the conceptual change model raised [several] issues.

First, prior knowledge plays a paradoxical role in conceptual change. This paradoxical role can be cast in at least two different ways. One is that prior knowledge can impede conceptual change. . . Yet prior knowledge also forms a framework for judging the validity of new information to be learned and thus forms a procrustean bed for the development of new knowledge. The second cast to this paradox is that the conceptual change model would suggest that students who possess little prior knowledge in an area would have few barriers to learning new concepts, yet the literature on learning shows clearly the value of prior knowledge. Thus, prior knowledge may impede learning through the alternative frameworks that students possess, or it may facilitate learning by providing a basis for understanding and judging the validity of solutions to problems. The conceptual change model assumes . . . that when faced with a discrepancy between a current framework and new, to-be-learned concepts, a student would undergo an unfreezing of his or her cognition in order to seek specific cognitive closure – that is, the resolution of the discrepancy. However, the learner's motivational beliefs about his or her current knowledge or about the knowledge to be learned texture the nature of the discrepancy in such a way that resolution might take on a very different form than is predicted by conceptual change theory. We have described motivational constructs such as goal orientation, values, efficacy beliefs and control beliefs that can serve as mediators of this process of conceptual change and are likely candidates for research on how assimilation and accommodation processes might operate in conjunction with student motivation in conceptual change instruction.

The second issue . . .[is that] learners do have intentions, goals, purposes and beliefs that drive and sustain their thinking. In addition, these motivational beliefs can influence the direction of thinking as the students attempt to adapt to the different constraints and demands placed on them by the tasks and activities they confront in classrooms.

Third, the model states four conditions for conceptual change (dissatisfaction, intelligibility, plausibility and fruitfulness). These four conditions are depicted as if they operated in a cold, rational manner that ignores the influence that motivational constructs might play regarding whether these conditions might be met. For example, both conceptual analysis and empirical research indicate that the condition of satisfaction will be influenced at least partly by affective variables and value beliefs. Students' personal interests as well as situational factors might determine whether they even attend to a discrepancy that could lead them to become dissatisfied with their conceptual understanding. The level of dissatisfaction might also be affected by the utility that the new concept would hold for them. Whether a new concept is intelligible or plausible is likely to be related to the depth of processing that students engage in; if they do not cognitively engage in the task, then it is unlikely that they will be able to understand the concept in an intelligent or plausible manner. In turn, depth of processing is related, at least in part, to motivational factors, such as whether learners have more of a mastery or a performance goal orientation, level of interest and efficacy beliefs with respect to the content area and the learning strategies to be used with the content.

Thus, school and classroom contexts might be designed and operated in a way that contradicts the way in which a community of purposeful scholars might act (Gardner, 1991). There is abundant anecdotal evidence that much of what happens in school is driven by need to maintain bureaucratic and institutional norms rather than scholarly norms. Much research literature documents this interpretation; it is likely that many students hold similar views of schools and the instructional activities that take place there. To the extent that this is true then, it is unlikely that individual conceptual change will take place without restructuring classrooms and schools along lines that will foster the development of a community of intentional, motivated and thoughtful learners.

REFERENCES

Alexander, P. A. and Judy, J. (1988) 'The interaction of domain-specific and strategic knowledge in academic performance', *Review of Educational Research*, 58: 375–404.

Alexander, P. A., Schallert, D. L. and Hare, V. C. (1991) 'Coming to terms: how researchers in learning and literacy talk about knowledge', *Review of Educational Research*, 61: 315–43.

Ames, C. (1992) Classrooms: goals, structures, and student motivation', *Journal of Educational Psychology*, 84: 261–71.

Anderson, L., Brubaker, N., Alleman-Brooks, J. and Duffy, G. (1985) 'A qualitative study of seatwork in first grade classrooms', *Elementary School Journal*, 86: 123–40.

Arlin, P. (1986) 'Problem finding and young adult cognition', in R. Mines and K. S. Kitchener (eds), *Adult Cognitive Development: Methods and Models*, New York: Praeger.

Baltes, M. and Baltes, P. (1986) *The Psychology of Control and Aging*, Hillsdale, NJ: Erlbaum.

Bandura, A. (1986) *Social Foundations of Thought and Action: A Social Cognitive Theory*, Englewood Cliffs, NJ: Prentice-Hall.

Bereiter, C. (1990) 'Aspects of an educational learning theory', *Review of Educational Research*, 60: 603–24.

Blumenfeld, P. C. (1992) 'Classroom learning and motivation: clarifying and expanding goal theory', *Journal of Educational Psychology*, 84: 272–81.

——, Mergendoller, J. and Puro, P. (1992) 'Translating motivation into thoughtfulness', in H. Marshall (ed.), *Redefining Learning*, Norwood, NJ: Ablex.

——, Mergendoller, J. and Swarthout, D. (1987) 'Task as a heuristic for understanding student learning and motivation', *Journal of Curriculum Studies*, 19: 135–48.

——, Pintrich, P. R., Meece, J. and Wessels, K. (1982) 'The formation and role of self-perceptions of ability in the elementary classroom', *Elementary School Journal* 82: 401–20.

——, Soloway, E., Marx, R. W., Krajcik, J. S., Guzdial, M. and Palincsar, A. (1991) 'Motivating project-based learning: sustaining the doing, supporting the learning', *Educational Psychologist*, 26: 369–98.

Brophy, J. (1983) 'Conceptualizing student motivation', *Educational Psychologist*, 18: 200–15.

Brown, A., Bransford, J., Ferrara, R. and Campione, J. (1983) 'Learning, remembering, and understanding', in J. H. Flavell and E. M. Markman (eds), *Handbook of Child Psychology: Vol. 3. Cognitive Development*, New York: Wiley.

Champagne, A. B., Gunstone, R. F. and Klopfer, L. E. (1985) 'Instructional consequences of students' knowledge about physical phenomena', in L. H. T. West and A. L. Pines (eds), *Cognitive Structure and Conceptual Change*, New York: Academic.

Chapman, M. (1988) *Constructive Evolution: Origins and Development of Piaget's Thought*, Cambridge: Cambridge University Press.

Connell, J. P. (1985) 'A new multidimensional measure of children's perceptions of control', *Child Development*, 56: 1018–41.

Corno, L. (1986) 'The metacognitive control components of self-regulated learning', *Contemporary Educational Psychology* 11: 333–46.

—— (1993) 'The best-laid plans. modern conceptions of volition and educational research,' *Educational Researcher*, 22(2): 14–22.

—— and Kanfer, R. (1993) 'The role of volition in learning and performance', in L. Darling-Hammond (ed.), *Review of Research in Education*, Washington, DC: American Educational Research Association.

Deci, E. L. and Ryan, R. (1985) *Intrinsic Motivation and Self-determination in Human Behavior*, New York: Plenum.

Doyle, W. (1983) 'Academic work', *Review of Educational Research*, 53: 159–200.

Dweck, C. S. and Elliott, E. S. (1983) 'Achievement motivation', in E. M. Heatherington (ed.), *Handbook of Child Psychology: Vol. 4. Socialization, Personality, and Social Development*, New York: Wiley.

Dweck, C. S. and Leggett, E. L. (1988) 'A social-cognitive approach to motivation and personality', *Psychological Review*, 95(2): 256–73.

Eccles, J. (1983) 'Expectancies, values and academic behaviors', in J. T. Spence (ed.), *Achievement and Achievement Motives*, San Francisco: Freeman.

Elliott, E. and Dweck, C. (1988) 'Goals: an approach to motivation and achievement', *Journal of Personality and Social Psychology*, 54: 5–12.

Findley, M. and Cooper, H. (1983) 'Locus of control and academic achievement: a review of the literature', *Journal of Personality and Social Psychology*, 44: 419–27.

Gardner, H. (1991) *The Unschooled Mind: How Children Think and how Schools Should Teach*, New York: Basic.

Garner, R. (1990) 'When children and adults do not use learning strategies: toward a theory of settings', *Review of Educational Research*, 60: 517–29.

Grolnick, W. and Ryan, R. (1987) 'Autonomy in children's learning: an experimental and individual difference investigation', *Journal of Personality and Social Psychology*, 52: 890–8.

Hidi, S. (1990) 'Interest and its contribution as a mental resource for learning', *Review of Educational Research*, 60: 549–71.

——, Renninger, K. A. and Krapp, A. (1992) 'The present state of interest research,' in K. A. Renninger, S. Hidi and A. Krapp (eds), *The Role of Interest in Learning and Development*, Hillsdale, NJ: Erlbaum.

Hofstein, A. and Lunetta, V. (1982) 'The role of the laboratory in science teaching: neglected aspects of research', *Review of Educational Research*, 52: 210–17.

Krapp, A., Hidi, S. and Renninger, K. A. (1992) 'Interest, learning, and development', in K. A. Renninger, S. Hidi and A. Krapp (eds), *The Role of Interest in Learning and Development*, Hillsdale, NJ: Erlbaum.

Kruglanski, A. W. (1989) *Lay Epistemics and Human Knowledge: Cognitive and Motivational Bases*, New York: Plenum.

—— (1990a) 'Lay epistemic theory in social-cognitive psychology', *Psychological Inquiry*, 1: 181–97.

—— (1990b) 'Motivations for judging and knowing: implications for causal attribution', in E. T. Higgins and R. M. Sorrentino (eds), *Handbook of Motivation and Cognition*, New York: Guilford.

Kunda, Z. (1990) 'The case for motivated reasoning', *Psychological Bulletin*, 108: 480–98.

Lave, J. (1989) *Cognition in Practice: Mind and Culture in Everyday Life*, Cambridge: Cambridge University Press.

Lefcourt, H. (1976) *Locus of Control: Current Trends in Theory and Research*, Hillsdale. NJ: Erlbaum.

Lepper, M. and Hodell, M. (1989) 'Intrinsic motivation in the classroom', in C. Ames and R. Ames (eds), *Research on Motivation in Education*, Vol. 3, New York: Academic.

McCaslin, M. and Good, T. (1992) 'Compliant cognition: the misalliance of management and instructional goals in current school reform', *Educational Researcher*, 21(3): 417.

Malone, T. and Lepper, M. (1987) 'Making learning fun: a taxonomy of intrinsic motivations for learning', in R. Snow and M. Farr (eds), *Aptitude, Learning, and Instruction: Vol. 3. Cognitive and Affective Process Analyses*, Hillsdale, NJ: Erlbaum.

Markus, H. and Nurius, P. (1986) 'Possible selves', *American Psychologist*, 41: 954–69.

Markus, H. and Wurf, E. (1987) 'The dynamic self-concept: a social psychological perspective', *Annual Review of Psychology*, 38: 299–337.

Marx, R. W. and Walsh, J. (1988) 'Learning from academic tasks', *Elementary School Journal*, 88: 207–20.

Meece, J. L. (1991) 'The classroom context and children's motivational goals', in M. Maehr and P. Pintrich (eds), *Advances in Motivation and Achievement*, Vol. 7, Greenwich, CT: JAI Press.

Newman, D., Griffin, P. and Cole, M. (1989) *The Construction Zone: Working for Cognitive Change in School*, Cambridge: Cambridge University Press.

Nolen, S. (1988) 'Reasons for studying: motivational orientations and study strategies', *Cognition and Instruction*, 5: 269–87.

Nussbaum, J. and Novick, S. (1982) 'Alternative frameworks, conceptual conflict, and accommodation: toward a principled teaching strategy', *Instructional Science*, 11: 183–200.

Osborne, R. and Freyberg, P. (1985) *Learning in Science: The Implications of Children's Science*, Auckland, New Zealand: Heinemann.

Osborne, R. and Wittrock, M. (1983) 'Learning science: a generative process', *Science Education*, 67: 489–508.

Palincsar, A. S. and Brown, A. L. (1984) 'Reciprocal teaching of comprehension-fostering and monitoring activities', *Cognition and Instruction*, 1: 117–75.

Paris, S. G. and Oka, E. (1986) 'Children's reading strategies, metacognition, and motivation', *Developmental Review*, 6: 25–56.

Perkins, D. and Simmons, R. (1988) 'An integrative model of misconceptions', *Review of Educational Research*, 58: 303–26.

Piaget, J. (1981) *Intelligence and Affectivity*, Palo Alto: Annual Reviews (original work published 1954).

—— (1985) *The Equilibration of Cognitive Structures*, Chicago: University of Chicago Press.

Pintrich, P. R. (1990) 'Implications of the psychological research on student learning and college teaching for teacher education', in R. Houston (ed.), *The Handbook of Research on Teacher Education*, New York: Macmillan.

—— (1992) 'Continuities and discontinuities: future directions for educational psychology', Paper presented at the convention of the American Psychological Association, Washington, DC, August.

——, Cross, D. R., Kozma, R. B., McKeachie, W. J. (1986), 'Instructional psychology', *Annual Review of Psychology*, 37: 611–51.

—— and De Groot, E. (1990a) 'Motivational and self-regulated learning components of classroom academic performance', *Journal of Educational Psychology*, 82: 33–40.

—— and —— (1990b) 'Quantitative and qualitative perspectives on student motivational beliefs and self-regulated learning', Paper presented at the Annual Meeting of the American Educational Research Association, Boston, April.

—— and Schrauben, B. (1992) 'Students' motivational beliefs and their cognitive engagement in classroom academic tasks', in D. Schunk and J. Meece (eds), *Student Perceptions in the Classroom: Causes and Consequences*, Hillsdale, NJ: Erlbaum.

Pokay, P. and Blumenfeld, P. C. (1990) 'Predicting achievement early and late in the semester: the role of motivation and use of learning strategies', *Journal of Educational Psychology*, 82: 41–50.

Posner, G., Strike, K., Hewson, P. and Gertzog, W. (1982) 'Accommodation of a scientific conception: toward a theory of conceptual change', *Science Education*, 66: 211–27.

Reif, F. and Larkin, J. (1991) 'Cognition in scientific and everyday domains: comparison and learning implications', *Journal of Research in Science Teaching*, 28: 733–60

Renninger, K. A. (1992) 'Individual interest and development: implications for theory and practice', in K. A. Renninger, S. Hidi and A. Krapp (eds), *The Role of Interest in Learning and Development*, Hillsdale, NJ: Erlbaum.

——, Hidi, S. and Krapp, A. (1992) *The Role of Interest in Learning and Development*, Hillsdale, NJ: Erlbaum.

—— and Wozniak, R. H. (1985) 'Effect of interest on attentional shift, recognition, and recall in young children', *Developmental Psychology*, 21: 624–32.

Resnick, L., Levine, J. and Teasley, S. (1991) *Perspectives on Socially Shared Cognition*, Washington, DC: American Psychological Association.

Ryan, R., Connell, J, and Deci, E. (1985) 'A motivational analysis of self-determination and self-regulation in education', in C. Ames and R. Ames (eds), *Research on Motivation in Education*, Vol. 2, New York: Academic.

Schunk, D. (1985) 'Self-efficacy and school learning', *Psychology in the Schools*, 22: 208–23.

—— (1989) 'Social cognitive theory and self-regulated learning', in B. Zimmerman and D. Schunk (eds), *Self-regulated Learning and Academic Achievement: Theory, Research, and Practice*, New York: Springer-Verlag.

—— and Hanson, A. R. (1985) 'Peer models: influence on children's self-efficacy and achievement', *Journal of Educational Psychology*, 77: 313–22.

Searle, J. (1992) *The Rediscovery of the Mind*, Cambridge, MA: MIT Press.

Shell, D., Murphy, C. and Bruning, R. (1989) 'Self-efficacy and outcome expectancy mechanisms in reading and writing achievement', *Journal of Educational Psychology*, 81: 91–100.

Singley, M. and Anderson, J. (1989) *The Transfer of Cognitive Skill*, Cambridge, MA: Harvard University Press.

Snow, R. and Swanson, J. (1992) 'Instructional psychology: aptitude, adaptation, and assessment', *Annual Review of Psychology*, 43: 583–626.

Spelke, E., Breinlinger, K., Macomber, J. and Jacobson, K. (1992) 'Origins of knowledge', *Psychological Review*, 99: 605–32.

Stipek, D. J. and Weisz, J. R. (1981) 'Perceived personal control and academic achievement', *Review of Educational Research*, 51: 101–37.

Stodolsky, S. (1988) *The Subject Matters*, Chicago: University of Chicago Press.

Tharp, R. and Gallimore, R. (1988) *Rousing Minds to Life: Teaching, Learning, and Schooling in Social Context*, Cambridge: Cambridge University Press.

Walberg, H. (1991) 'Improving school science in advanced and developing countries', *Review of Educational Research*, 61: 25–69.

Weiner, B. (1986) *An Attributional Theory of Motivation and Emotion*, New York: Springer-Verlag.

Weinstein, C. E. and Mayer, R. (1986) 'The teaching of learning strategies', in M. Wittrock (ed.), *Handbook of Research on Teaching*, New York: Macmillan.

Wentzel, K. (1991) 'Social and academic goals at school: motivation and achievement in context', in M. Maehr and P. R. Pintrich (eds), *Advances in Motivation and Achievement: Goals and Self-regulatory Processes*, Vol. 7, Greenwich, CT: JAI Press.

West, L. and Pines, A. (1985) *Cognitive Structure and Conceptual Change*, New York: Academic.

Winne, P. H. and Marx, R. W. (1982) 'Students' and teachers' views of thinking processes for classroom learning', *Elementary School Journal*, 82: 493–518.

—— and —— (1989) 'A cognitive-processing analysis of motivation with classroom tasks', in C. Ames and R. Ames (eds), *Research on Motivation in Education*, Vol. 3, New York: Academic.

Chapter 9

Learning as the social construction of meaning

Its implications for assessing and planning learning

Cesar Coll and Elena Martín
Translated from Spanish by Susan Mushin

Adopting a social constructivist understanding of how children learn has significant consequences for assessing their learning in the classroom. Written from the perspective of the Spanish education system, which is underpinned by constructivist learning principles, Cesar Coll and Elena Martin explore some of the practical implications of this increasingly popular theory of learning.* Note: Where the authors refer to evaluation, the meaning within the UK context is usually 'assessment'.

MEANING AND SENSE IN SCHOOLING: THE AFFECTIVE AND SOCIAL CONTEXTS IN EVALUATING LEARNING

The process of constructing meanings, which is carried out by pupils on the contents of schooling, cannot be separated from the process by which they make sense in one way or another of these contents. Pupils do not first of all make sense of the content of learning and then immediately proceed to construct meanings for it. Neither do they construct meanings first of all and then immediately make sense of what they have learnt. Pupils construct certain meanings on the contents in so far as they simultaneously make sense of it. However, the process by which pupils manage to make sense of what they learn is directly linked to the affective and social contexts of learning in schools. If this is true – and it has clear implications for the planning and development of specific teaching and learning activities, then it is even more true, if that is possible, for the planning and development of activities which it is hoped to use to evaluate how meaningful the learning that has taken place is. We have to be aware, when we plan and carry out an evaluation activity (whatever its nature and characteristics that may need to be taken into account), that pupils are also making sense of it, and that this, to a large extent, depends on how we approach the activity and how

* Translation of parts of 'La evaluación del aprendizaje en el currículum escolar: una perspectiva constructivista', in C. Coll *et al.* (1993), *El constructivismo en el aula*, Barcelona: Editorial Graó.

we behave as it develops. In other words, we have to be aware that the results of the evaluation depend as much on the meanings which pupils have constructed and which we can foster, as on the sense that they have made of the previous teaching and learning activities and the evaluation activity itself.

THE DEGREE TO WHICH LEARNING AND EVALUATION ACTIVITIES ARE MEANINGFUL

It is incorrect to consider whether learning in schools is in absolute terms meaningful or not. We rarely in practice come across learning that is purely mechanical and repetitive, lacking in any meaning. The maximum degree to which learning can be meaningful in theory is limitless: it is always, in principle, possible to add new meanings to the ones which have already been constructed, or to establish new and more complex connections between them. Meaningful learning is not a question of all or nothing, but of degree. Therefore, it is not possible to plan an evaluation activity to judge whether learning done by pupils is meaningful or not. The best approach is to discover the degree to which the learning that has taken place is meaningful, using activities and tasks which can be approached or solved in a way that allows children to draw on their understanding of contents to different degrees.

THE RELATIONSHIP BETWEEN MEANINGS AND THE INTRINSICALLY PARTIAL NATURE OF EVALUATION ACTIVITIES

Meanings which are constructed for the contents of schooling are stored in the memory and form complex networks of interrelated meanings. In fact, the degree to which learning is meaningful depends, on the one hand, largely on the breadth and complexity of the connections which are made between the meanings constructed, and, on the other, on the meanings which already exist in the cognitive structure. The richer, more extensive and more complex the connections are, the greater will be the degree to which meaning is achieved. However, the richer, more extensive and more complex these connections are, the more difficult it will be to try and explore them. In fact, even if they are not particularly rich and complex, one cannot be certain that they have been completely explored. This means that any evaluation activity is, in principle, partial [narrow] with respect to the nature and breadth of connections between meanings that it explores. Above all, it means that there is always the possibility that pupils have made connections which cannot be detected by the activities and instruments of evaluation that we use. In other words, it is highly likely that pupils always learn much more than we can discover from the evaluation activities that we give them.

THE DYNAMICS OF THE PROCESS OF CONSTRUCTING MEANINGS AND THE LIMITS OF EVALUATION

As the meanings constructed for the contents of schooling become part of wider and more complex networks, they undergo a virtually constant revision. Sometimes this revision happens when new meanings from learning done later are incorporated, and these new meanings broaden, enrich or contradict meanings that have previously been constructed. On other occasions, the revision is simply the result of new connections being established between meanings that already exist. This can lead to them being more or less reorganized. On yet other occasions, as the constructed meanings maintain somewhat tenuous and limited connections with the other elements in the cognitive structure, they become blurred in time until they are practically irretrievable and are completely forgotten. Memory, then, is constructive: it has both its own internal dynamic and meanings. Evaluation activities give us snapshots, which are by their nature static, of a process which is by definition dynamic. Of course, this process as such is not directly accessible to us, but we know that we shouldn't judge the whole process from one single snapshot. The range and depth of learning that has taken place sometimes does not become apparent until a certain period of time has passed. It is often interesting to determine, although in a partial and approximate way, how meaningful learning done by pupils at a given moment is. However, we should not lose sight of the fact that the true potential of learning only becomes apparent with time. Evaluation practices based on a single snapshot, (for example the 'qualifying' tests or exams) are therefore unreliable and they should be replaced, wherever possible, by others which take into account the dynamic nature of the process of constructing meanings and which pay attention to its temporal dimension.

THE IMPORTANCE OF THE CONTEXT IN CONSTRUCTING MEANINGS AND IN THE EVALUATION OF MEANINGS CONSTRUCTED

It is generally accepted that true learning produces meanings that can be generalized [transferred] and that are decontextualized. These meanings are no longer linked to the particular context in which they have been constructed and so, therefore, can be applied to different and varied situations. In fact, it continues to be a relatively common practice in some curriculum areas or school subjects to plan activities for evaluating learning which are as different as possible from the teaching and learning activities themselves. This is done with the aim of checking whether the pupils have 'really' learnt the content which has been covered. On extreme occasions, activities or tasks are even carefully avoided in classwork and are reserved for evaluation. This is done in order to check, once the corresponding topic or teaching unit has been completed, whether the pupils are able to 'generalize' what they have learnt. This way of proceeding does not take into account the fact that the context for learning a certain content always and inevitably influences the meanings which can be constructed around it. So the correct way of proceeding is to vary as much as possible the contexts in which learning takes place so that the meanings constructed are as rich as possible and don't become linked to only one context. The most powerful meaning is not the meaning that does not correspond to any particular context, but the meaning that corresponds to the widest range possible of particular contexts. When we consider evaluation, this supposes, on the one hand, that the particular context in which learning is being evaluated must not be considered as a simple characteristic which it is best to neutralize, but rather as a fundamental element of what is in effect being evaluated. On the other hand, it supposes that it is suitable, when proceeding to evaluate learning of determined content, to use the widest possible range of evaluation activities that place the content in specific contexts which vary.

TEACHING AS PROCESS AND THE REGULATORY FUNCTION OF THE EVALUATION OF PUPILS' LEARNING

If we see learning as a process of constructing meanings and making sense, a process with its own dynamic, progress and difficulties, with obstacles and even setbacks, it seems equally logical to conceive teaching as a process of helping in the construction that is done by pupils. Effective teaching, in a constructivist perspective, is teaching that manages to adjust the kind and intensity of help given to the difficulties of the process of constructing meanings carried out by pupils. Evaluation of teaching, therefore cannot, nor should be conceived as unimportant in the evaluation of learning. To ignore this principle is more or less equivalent to assigning the evaluation of teaching to being a formalized exercise. It also limits the uses of evaluation in feeding into decisions about teacher professionalism and promotion, and the appropriateness of particular forms of accreditation or qualification. When we evaluate the learning that our pupils have done, we are also evaluating, whether we want to or not, the teaching that we have done. Evaluation is never, in the strictest sense, evaluation of teaching or of learning, but rather of the processes of teaching and learning.

LEARNING AS PROCESS AND THE SELF-REGULATORY FUNCTION OF EVALUATION

The regulatory function of the results of evaluation does not apply to teaching. As we have discussed, evaluation of learning carried out by pupils gives the teacher irreplaceable information so that she/he can progressively adjust the help which she/he gives the pupils in the process of constructing meanings.

However, this evaluation can and must be used to give very useful information to the pupils themselves about the process of constructing that they are carrying out. Evaluation activities should pay more attention to this self-regulatory function which is possible and desirable, by making a clear and explicit presentation of what is being evaluated, the aims that are being pursued and the later analysis of the results obtained. In the last resort, the ideal would be that the pupils should be able to use the mechanisms of self-evaluation, which can provide them with relevant information for regulating their own process of constructing meanings. If 'learning how to learn' involves developing the ability to use the knowledge acquired in the whole of its instrumental capacity to acquire new knowledge, there is no doubt that the development and acquisition of procedures of self-regulation of the process of constructing meanings is an essential component of this educational goal.

Chapter 10

What school is really for
Revisiting values

Philip Gammage

In this chapter, Philip Gammage takes a wider look at what primary school is all about. He sets his analysis in the context of the values of the 1990s, where consumer concepts and language are applied to schools and hospitals, as well as businesses in the market-place. He urges us to remember that schools are simply one source of influence on children, among other equally or more powerful ones such as the family, peer groups and television. His analysis provides the context for his argument that primary schools should provide a learning environment which has genuine meaning and value for children. *

INTRODUCTION

Any chapter concerned with issues which preoccupy those one might term 'middle managers' should of necessity throw certain fundamental, recurring problems into relief. The prime one of these is that of achieving a balanced recognition by parents, teachers, governors and children that they are mutually interdependent in the exercise, that they must all know what school is really about, what it can be expected to achieve and what not. We must be careful about the wholesale adoption of the language of industry and commerce, since much is highly damaging to education and may subtly distort and misrepresent the processes, perhaps especially so at the levels of early childhood and primary education. For in the 1990s the language of education has been thoroughly taken over by the jargon of the market-place. Courses are 'delivered'; the quality of teaching is 'controlled'; there are enterprise 'initiatives' which make learning and creativity seem subservient to efficiency or 'standards'. Children are defined as 'products'. Schools and classes have 'outcomes'; teaching skills and subtleties are defined as 'competencies' to be defined on the job and rarely to be reflected upon in any professional manner! In particular,

* Originally published in C. Day, C. Hall, P. Gammage and M. Coles (1993) *Leadership and Curriculum in the Primary School*, London: Paul Chapman Publishing Ltd. (Slightly edited for this volume).

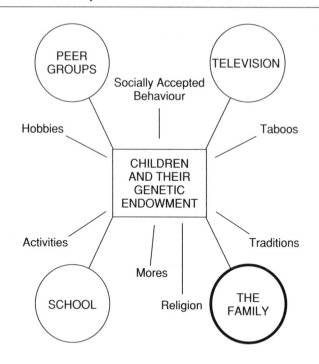

Figure 10.1 Influences on the growing child

pedagogical theory is derided and effective teacher training thought to consist solely of practice, with as little reflection or theory as possible.

The curriculum writer Berman has pointed to the danger of such language usage, saying, 'Within such a framework (of thinking) the products of education can be easily considered in quantifiable scores and the language of education becomes that of numbers' (Berman, 1987: 346). Thus, whilst we must as childhood educators be cognizant with the current vogue for images of accountability and product 'quality control' borrowed from industry (including the near deification of 'market forces' approaches to schooling), we must seek constantly to debate and emphasize other more important features.

Schooling and education are, of course, not necessarily synonymous. Education, one hopes, is a life-long process of humanizing and developing. Schooling is relatively short and, parents assume, reasonably systematic. We should remember too that many adolescents escape thankfully from school to an outside world often more meaningful and more stimulating. Moreover, we should remember the relative *position* of school in the scheme of socialization and the acquisition of values (see Figure 10.1), since we know from a variety of surveys that, for instance, other influences, such as television, are nowadays of paramount importance and may well preoccupy even the three-year-old for as much as twenty hours per week. Not only is it easy for us to confuse education and schooling, it is just as easy to confuse certification with it all. We may think that the measures of achievement add up to something altogether more significant than they really do, to think that marks and diplomas gained somehow equal the education itself! True they may overlap, but they are often painfully – almost irrelevantly – distinct.

Schools work in the real world, within the context of values expressed by or implicit in parents' and society's actions, critically mediated by the impressions and images of the consumer society. Such contexts may well generate messages of greater meaning for children than can school; and frequently those messages are presented in packages of such sophistication, attractiveness and slickness, that no mere schoolteacher can easily counter the fashion or the thought.

As 'leaders' at home and at school parents and teachers need to recognize the power of modern advertising, of images of great salience available at the touch of a button. They need to be aware that there are many factors affecting the socialization of our young. And of course, schooling *is* about socialization; it has to be about utility and social 'fit', but it must leave room for freedom and creativity, for both the measured and unmeasured curriculum.

RHETORIC AND REALITY IN EDUCATIONAL FASHION

Anyone who has been involved in education for more than ten years or so may well, at times, display a little cynicism about 'fashions' in education. Since education can always be improved, since we have all, in western societies, had some experience of school, lay person and professional alike may well regard themselves as experts. Such experience means that pronouncements about the purposes and processes of education abound. They form a rich leitmotif to every teacher's work. Topics are in; topics are out; testing is good; testing is bad. The list of assertions could be endless. A glance at the teacher's bookshelf might reveal comments from John Locke (1690) whose treatise against the 'over-indulgence' of children would still find agreement in some quarters today. Or one might note Crispus (1814) whose stern Calvinist views on depravity lying at the heart of childhood guided many a Victorian dominie. Continuing to browse across the shelves we might stray to a volume by Holmes in the early 1900s whose enthusiasm for freedom fuelled some of the 'progressive' thoughts which became fashionable with the middle classes of England in the 1920s. We might then turn to the writings of Susan Isaacs of the 1930s; and we could, in passing, note the way she used detailed observations of children to begin to frame curricula in a more carefully developmental mode. And so, as we range across the bookshelves, almost at random, we could come across Entwistle (1970) on child-centred education, or, more recently, Blyth (1984) on development and experience in the primary curriculum. Even if we ignored such 'academic' writings, we would be bound to stumble across the great reports and ministerial enquiries, from Hadow through Butler, to Plowden, or perhaps ponder on the polemics of the Black

Paper writers of the late 1960s and early 1970s, or those of Warnock or Lawlor today.

Everyone, it seems, has written about education, about its purposes, about the 'necessary' curriculum, about testing. Can you blame the class teacher, curriculum leader, Headteacher or teacher trainer for feeling just a little weary at times? All these enquiries; all these expert opinions. One can almost hear the tired response, 'Ah well, they should try it with little Mary Jones on a Friday afternoon', and so on.

If one returns to the browsing through reports and research, through opinion and legislation, one is immediately struck by the thought that *policy* does not appear logically consistent, articulated, or even particularly guided by research. Perhaps it is naive to expect the latter. One notes that belief, rather than substance, seems as much the power behind legislation for schooling (and curriculum change) as any cool rational enquiry. Indeed, our brief glance at the bookshelves of education could as well demonstrate how great changes occurred almost by whim. Worse perhaps, that powerful findings or pronouncements become overtaken by temporary need and that the latter has a more lastingly shaping effect than earlier defined intention. Did large-scale vertical grouping in British primary schools come about from conviction, or largely from the necessity of the falling rolls of the 1970s, one might ask? It is hard not to be cynical. Are we busy integrating 'special needs' children into the ordinary classroom (and closing down most special schools) only to wake up at some year in the future to find that special, focused, separate provision is once again the order of the day? (A feature already presaged in some parts of the United States.)

The history of education could so easily also be assembled in the form of a roll call of illustrious commissions and reports; most of which are now outmoded, superseded or ignored! The Plowden Report (CACE, 1967) is currently being derided and misrepresented in some quarters of government and the media. Indeed, whereas most of those at all familiar with primary teaching are aware that the tragedy was that Plowden never sufficiently *took hold*, we are now told that an over-reliance on Plowden 'methodology' is responsible for all ills and is the root cause of this or that failure. The principles of Plowden are distorted, more especially by some branches of the press, so as to appear synonymous with the language of sloppiness or of insufficient discipline. The careful marriage between process and content is ignored or, worse, declared null and void.

RECOGNIZING AUTONOMY AND RESPONSIBILITY

Perhaps one of the commonest 'mistakes' in thinking of schooling and the curriculum is to take the view that there is only one set of clients, the parents. If one does take such a view, then the implications for the curriculum are very serious indeed. First, the parents will often have a (necessarily) rather limited and subjective view of what they want for their children. Second, they may well have a view, somewhat glossily enhanced by the selective processes of human memory, that is embedded in the past, that implies stasis and tradition, rather than expansion and change. Third, most parents (and there is nothing intrinsically wrong with such a view) will want their children to succeed financially, or achieve status, or, perhaps, fulfil secret longings that they themselves had as children. There are other factors which must be taken into consideration. Briefly, they are as follows: the school curriculum is as much for the children *now*, as for their long-term future. It must be capable of expansion and relocation and not seen simply in terms of fixed content. It should reflect the whole society and not be viewed solely as the means of achieving greater economic progress. Above all, it should commit children to decisions about their part in it all. I can perhaps illustrate this best by referring to a story from a colleague I know well. In the late 1940s at about the age of ten years he began attending the Oxford High School for Boys; a school now defunct, but housed in a particularly fine building designed by Jackson. To his juvenile mind the school seemed immensely large. It wasn't; it held about 500 boys. The teachers (masters) seemed very old. He has since realized that they weren't, either! One meeting with the senior master, Mr R. W. Bodey, made a lasting impression. The new boys were gathered together to hear what science was about and how the curriculum should proceed. Mr Bodey stood before them and said something like this. 'My object, gentlemen, is not so much to teach you physics, as to bring you up as good Christian citizens, you worms. My views on education may not interest you, but they focus my attention and behaviour such that I intend you learn responsibility; responsibility for your thoughts and actions, but above all [and I fancy his voice softened] responsibility for each other; that is what education is about.' Mr Bodey is now dead, but his words, or my colleague's half-recalled approximation of them, have stayed with him for half a century. Incidentally, Mr Bodey rarely if ever had a 'failure', since he taught science with a mixture of humour and enquiry which would still be the envy of many.

Mr Bodey's view of the curriculum was not one which would have easily fitted into the current ten subjects of the National Curriculum. It *might* conceivably be partly encompassed by the 'cross-curricular themes', or something like Personal and Social Education. But primarily it was about recognizing autonomy and responsibility, about causal attributions both in the self and within the scientific method. For Mr Bodey I believe that the object of a good curriculum at any age was not so much to achieve a given mastery of content as to achieve a given mastery *over one's person*. Autonomy was a word he liked; responsibility another. Autonomy means the quality of and act of being self-governing and self-reliant (though not necessarily selfish) and most writers have thought of it in three main spheres: those of *emotions*, *behaviour* and *values*. To my mind the ideal school curriculum would not design situations in which children were expected to be passive, nor would government missives talk of its 'delivery', as though some crude parcel of knowledge was all that was required. Ideally, a curriculum values autonomy so that children can be responsible for their learning and their social behaviour from the start. In many respects, unfortunately, schools and their curricula run quite counter to this notion. They contain within them notions which can be best explained as 'not wanting children to depart from the way of truth', even if the 'truth' is a frozen mishmash of past tradition, rather than much related to current realities! Children are very much 'social products' of this time; that is, they are not re-creations of one's own childhood a generation earlier. As such, they are much more *in* the modern world, often more aware of contemporary influences, changes in knowledge, than are their parents (or, indeed, any adults). Thus, the balance in the curriculum is something which inevitably is quite delicate. Put this way, it is apparent that no national 'fixed' curriculum could ever succeed, because, as times change, so do the relative merits of some of what should or should not be included in the programme. Is there really much point in teaching quadratic equations, for instance? Does it really matter if we leave out some of the nineteenth-century narrative poems (grand though they are), because we now wish to incorporate some contemporary women's poetry? Surely, the answer must be *no*. If one takes Mr Bodey's avowed intentions one could teach self-responsibility and the wish to further one's own education as much through coracle-weaving as through kinetic energy!

Another aspect of the curriculum which is often left out is *how it appears to children* and how they attribute their success or otherwise. What too of responsibility? Its literal meaning is 'able to be called upon as a prime cause or agent, the quality of being held accountable'. In the educational context it more often has to do with the recognition of the role of one's own effort in the educational enterprise. If only schools could realistically present ways in which this could be achieved!

A CORE CURRICULUM AND INDIVIDUAL NEED

When talking of schooling, we should remember that there is no *single justification for even a core curriculum*. Currently, in England and Wales we follow the legislation of 1988 which provides for ten core and foundation subjects in the British National Curriculum. But there are a variety of arguments concerning core curricula, and some are complementary; some compete. At any age and stage, the types of core curricula arrived at are merely a reflection of the different emphases or criteria chosen. 'Educational Entitlements' seem to be the central components in the current British (and Australian) approaches; and we have seen from many discussions in the educational press (and from at least one official report: Alexander, Rose and Woodhead, 1992) that therein lie many tensions; most notably those between 'areas of experience' and modes of 'integration', between specialist content and looser poly-mathic generalism. The current British ethos is such that the 'developmentally appropriate practice' of the North American researchers is either misunder-stood as an educational principle, or, worse, is deliberately misrepresented. The current *official* British position seems to be one that could be deemed content rich and process thin; a strange situation for a country until recently admired for its apparent strengths in primary education!

At the heart of much of the theory and ideology of British primary and early years education, and we must acknowledge that theory and ideology are both confused and enmeshed, lies respect for each individual in school – and respect by him or her for each and all of the others. Schools which exhibit such central values can be seen positively to thrive on diversity such that mutuality and respect for persons become a major part of what the school is really about. Kirby, like many other primary educators, said that four key ideas had dominated early childhood education generally. These were:

1   Respect for children and what they do, particularly the recognition of each child's unique, unrepeatable identity.
2   The belief that human beings are different and that it is important for the educational process to acknowledge the individual character of each person and of the qualities and distinctions that he or she brings.
3   The recognition that experience (especially social experience) is a prime feature in learning and a vehicle for interpreting the world at large.
4   An awareness that the environment is vital and not only plays a major part in making that person unique, but can be used as a major vehicle in education.

(Kirby, 1981)

ARTICULATING THE VISION

For schools to be good, well-matched to the children's needs and abilities and able to function articulately in a minefield of conflicting goals represented as desirable in a modern society, no mere adherence to ill-defined and less-well-articulated principles can be enough. It is therefore especially important that teachers see themselves as professionals, able to describe, analyse and cogently place their practices in the context of research and common understandings. Unfortunately there is a tendency for many primary teachers (and Heads?) to know one hundred and one uses for old toilet rolls or plastic bottles without being able to articulate the principles that underpin their use! Professionalism means knowing, describing and defending one's views of education. It is not achieved simply through the in-group building of restric-tive practices and private languages. It is much more likely to be achieved through rational argument and constant explanation, through conviction and idealism, through continued study and reflection on practice. Richard

Peters was probably right when he suggested that a major contribution by early childhood educators (usually, but not always, the proponents what are loosely termed 'child-centred' approaches) was to emphasize important principles such as autonomy and respect for persons as *the* fundamentals in deciding how schooling should proceed. But how does a school exemplify these features within its organization and how does it justify them to the wider community? Answers to these questions are probably best culled from actual case studies of schools or from biography. But, in general, we believe it essential that leaders in primary schools should:

1 Try to establish fundamental agreement on what school is for, both with parents and among the staff: that is, recognize the very real tensions which exist between demands for utility and demands for personal fulfilment. These tensions should be discussed regularly and made *explicit*.

2 Acknowledge that *transaction frequently overrides content*: that is, that the relationship between teacher and pupil is the most important single factor in learning. This means reminding all concerned that we are dealing with pre-pubertal and (often) very adult-oriented children. It means emphasizing that definitions of content are not usually as important as defining the procedures whereby one hopes that content might be attained.

3 Emphasize that school ethos/climate is paramount. It is a major part of the hidden curriculum. Constantly ascertain the state of that ethos and reflect on ways of improving it.

4 Try to establish positions whereby interdependence and self-responsibility are encouraged and not allowed to slip into competition and blind loyalty.

5 Remember that 'all forms of play appear to be essential for the intellectual, imaginative and emotional development of the child and may well be necessary steps to a further stage of development' (Brierley, 1987: 111).

6 Recall (and celebrate the fact that) enjoyment plays an important part in influencing attitudes to study (APU, 1988: 6).

7 Note that children do not necessarily improve their achievement merely through being frequently tested. Agreed criteria for assessment do not of themselves improve either the curriculum or children's achievements. Put simply – weighing the pig is not the same as fattening it, nor does weighing tell you much about the quality of the preceding meals!

8 Emphasize the role of personal choice and ensure that children see the importance and consequences of certain choices made. As Peters once reminded us, the development of choice-making is something often denied to us, yet is, in many respects, crucial to our moral structure; surely a good education is in part the assisting of enthusiasms and the recognition of their own consequences and disciplines; the creation of the 'self as a passionate chooser' (Peters, 1973).

9 Note that in any school there will be occasional failures for children (and staff). Whilst failure and diminished self-esteem are rarely good

motivators, failure is inevitable in any human enterprise, from time to time. The important point to remember is 'that whilst failure is an inevitable process, negative criticism need not be. It is not failure which gives concern but the way we adults react to failure. *The ideal way to react would be to ensure first that the child was not being subject to a situation which was totally beyond his level of development*' (Lawrence, 1987: 72; emphasis added).

10 Try to establish an organization which illustrates a management 'style' which registers that attitude change (often necessary in children, staff *and* parents) comes best from reduced dissonances, not conflict, that in particular a happy staff who care for one another and enjoy their jobs are likely to have a happy, motivating school.

WHAT IS SCHOOL REALLY FOR?

Such generalizations as those above are broad, yet moderately practical. They stem in part from the burden of preceding chapters and from the research. They are the result of speculation and reflection tempered by observation and experience. There are few real absolutes. Schools, as units of analysis, are like people – infinitely different; and to generalize can be at times to trivialize and diminish. This chapter is intended to remind us of what has gone before and especially to rehearse first principles and directions. Such generalizations need detailed refinement, specific location and complex action plans. In the above form they may even appear somewhat daunting, reminding one of the great family house Victorian recipe and household management books which start particular culinary delights with such phrases as 'dice one large bullock'. So, mindful that such exhortations and conundrums concerning the purpose of school may be best expressed in the music of parables, we have included the following story.

The little boy

Once a little boy went to school. He was a little boy and it was a big school. But, when the little boy found that there was a way he could go straight to his classroom by walking in from the door outside, he was happy and the school didn't seem quite so big any more.

One morning, not long after the little boy had been in school, the teacher said, 'Today we are going to make a picture.' 'Good,' thought the little boy. He liked making pictures. He could make all kinds. Lions and tigers, chickens and cows, trains and boats – so he took out his box of crayons and started to draw with enthusiasm. But the teacher said, 'Wait! It is not time to begin!' And she waited until everyone looked ready.

'Now,' said the teacher, 'We are going to make flowers.' 'Good,' thought the little boy. He especially liked making flowers, and he began to make beautiful orange and blue and pink ones with his crayons. But the teacher said, 'Wait! I will show you how to make a flower,' and it was red with a green stem. 'There,' said the teacher. 'Now you may begin.'

The little boy looked at the teacher's flower and he looked at his. He liked his better than the teacher's, but didn't like to say so. He simply turned his paper over and began to make a flower like the teacher's – red, with a green stem. On another day, when the little boy had come into the classroom from the outside all by himself, the teacher said, 'Today we shall make something with clay.' 'Good,' thought the little boy. He loved using clay. He could make all sorts of things, and often did at home. Snakes and snowmen, elephants and mice, cars and trucks – and he took his clay and quickly began to pull and pinch it into shape. But the teacher said, 'Wait! It is not time to begin.' And she waited until everyone looked ready. 'Now,' said the teacher, 'We are going to make a dish.' 'Good,' thought the little boy. He liked making dishes and he began to make some which were of different shapes and sizes. Then the teacher said, 'Wait; and I'll show you how to make a proper dish. There! Now you may begin.' The little boy looked at the teacher's dish and he looked at his own. He liked his dishes better than the teacher's, but he didn't like to say so; and he rolled his clay into a fresh ball again and made a dish just like the teacher's – a plain, deep dish.

And pretty soon the little boy had learned to wait and to watch and to make things just like those of the teacher, and very soon he didn't make things of his own any more.

Then it happened. The little boy and his family were obliged to move to another house in another city; and the little boy had to go to another school. This school was even bigger than the previous one. Moreover, there were no doors from the play areas direct into the classroom. The boy had to go up some steps and walk down a long hall before he got to his room. But the first day that he was there the teacher said, 'Today we are going to make a picture.' 'Good,' thought the little boy and waited for the teacher to tell him exactly what to do. The teacher didn't say anything, however. She just walked around the room talking to each child. When she came to the little boy, she said, 'Don't you want to make a picture?' 'Oh yes,' said the little boy, 'What are we going to make?' 'I don't know until you make it,' said the teacher. 'But how shall I make it?' asked the little boy. 'Why, any way you like,' said the teacher. 'And any colour?' asked the little boy. 'Any colour you like,' said the teacher. 'Why, if everyone made the same picture and used the same colours, how would we know which was which and who made what?' 'I don't know,' said the little boy with a sigh – and he began to make a red flower with a green stem.

No doubt this is a very sentimental story. No doubt many have heard such parables before. But the point is apposite. All may recognize that certain things have been systematically removed from that child during his earlier experiences of school. What he underwent could hardly be distinguished by the term 'education'. His sense of personal responsibility, independence and self-reliance were (presumably) gradually eroded. Initiative, curiosity and creativity were stultified. Is that what school is really for? Many people have written about what school is for. Most are aware that it is a complex mixture of purposes which are not necessarily all *educative*. From use of 'busy work' with one group, whilst working with another, from social control to selection, from 'cooling out' to 'keeping children safe off the streets', from 'fellowship' to the creation of 'elites'; all have their place. Yet, throughout decades and across cultures, despite markedly different philosophical orientations, there is a fair consistency in opinions on what makes a school worthwhile and what school is really about at its central core of purposes. The recent South Australian document (Education Department of South Australia, 1988) set out principles for its primary schools which do not seem overly different from the Plowden Report in England some twenty years earlier. The British Columbian reforms clearly espouse a developmental and individually targeted view of appropriate learning (Province of British Columbia, 1990). Recently, the American Division for Early Childhood responded to the USA position statement 'America 2,000' and the latter's first goal which had been widely quoted in the run-up to the presidential election as 'All children will start school ready to learn'. The DEC make the points clearly. 'Schools should be ready to accept and educate all children. *Schooling will succeed or fail, not children.*' It is, perhaps, worth emphasizing some of their other points too, since they are addressing the education of children aged 3 to 9 years or so.

> Early educators must be schooled in and encouraged to use a wide variety of developmentally appropriate curricula, materials and procedures to maximise each child's growth and development.
>
> Achieving long-term academic goals does not imply that young children be drilled in English, science and math. These academic goals are best achieved when young children are provided with environments that encourage their eager participation, exploration and curiosity about the world.
>
> (DEC, 1992: 75)

Nearly twenty years ago Postman and Weingartner remarked that an effective school would seem to have the following characteristics:

1   When time and activity structuring were not arbitrary and could be tailored to the different rates, interests and developmental levels of the child; when children had the opportunity for choice and some organisation of their own time.
2   When it didn't make children unhappy.
3   When the children were involved, rather than passive.

4   When activities took place both within and without the school walls.
5   When school brought diversity to the fore, didn't denigrate difference and accepted other successes than the merely cognitive or 'academic' ones.
6   When school valued self-knowledge and emotional growth and evaluated positively rather than negatively.
7   When school has made its values clear and works in partnership with the community.
8   When school is oriented towards the future as well as to the past.

(Adapted from Postman and Weingartner, 1973)

CONCLUSION

... At the moment, in many Western societies there seems to be some mistrust, or at best some misunderstanding, between the partners who should be involved in the education of the child. Partly, this is due to genuine misunderstandings, partly it may be the fault of politicians (who, by and large, tend to look for the 'quick fix'), partly it is because primary and early childhood teachers are not known for their ability to articulate practices or principles. *All* of us have a responsibility to see that the values of the school are broadly congruent with the 'best' values of the society; and that these are constantly examined and exposed to the public gaze. But these outside exposures should not be determined or initiated by glib political statements. They need to take place in atmospheres which give teachers confidence; and this latter feature has surely been lacking in England for at least a decade or so. Moreover, outside agencies, whether they be industrial concerns, leaders of commerce or media gurus need to support schooling. They cannot on the one hand deplore the poor spelling exhibited by their recruits from schools whilst at the same time pursuing advertising standards which parade 'catchy' misspellings to influence the young. They cannot demand pro-social behaviour, whilst lauding the competition of the market-place or remarking that it is 'good for children to fail' (as one ministerial adviser did in 1990). They cannot ask for inventiveness and creativity in their children if they constantly demand return to old-fashioned or out-moded elements of basics.

True professionalism makes difficult demands on teachers, administrators and their colleagues. It would suggest that, whilst teachers must have time and dignity in the community and not merely be seen as 'delivering' someone else's ideas, they must remain educated, thoughtful, vigilant and reflective. They must be articulate, careful and sceptical. As Thomas Paine once remarked, 'The sleep of reason brings forth monsters.' Educational leaders have a mission; they need to know the job through and through, constantly to return to its reality, constantly to recall that their prime job is to provide a service. Schooling is not a factory process. It is about negotiation, understanding, quality and humanity. There is *no education 'business'*, since the 'products' are not inert, but creative, critical elements in the process.

Learning in schools is not static. An educational enterprise – if it is truly educational – is always 'in the building', never complete. To teach is to be aware that the country gets the schools it deserves. If people value education, enquiry, scholarship, creativity – they will get them. Whilst sharing the rhythms of continuity and change – or acknowledging the twin powers of content and process – we need to create value systems in which schools can grow, be valued and held dear.

Berman once said, 'To deal with aspirations, hopes and dilemmas, students [children] need a rich, invigorating and *problematic* curriculum. Such an unmeasured curriculum can help students deal better with the unmeasurable elements of life' (Berman, 1987: 350). The same might be said to apply to teachers and *their* learning. For their curriculum, too, needs dynamic leadership.

REFERENCES

Alexander, R., Rose, J. and Woodhead, C. (1992) *Curriculum Organisation and Classroom Practice in Primary Schools: A Discussion Paper*, London: DES.

APU (Assessment of Performance Unit) (1988) *Attitudes and Gender Differences*, Slough: NFER-Nelson.

Berman, L. M. (1987) 'Perception, paradox, and passion: curriculum for continuity', *Theory into Practice*, XXVI (special issue): 346–52.

Blyth, W. A. L. (1984) *Development, Experience and Curriculum in Primary Education*, London: Croom Helm.

Brierley, J. (1987) *Give Me a Child until He is Seven*, Lewes: Falmer Press.

CACE (1967) *Children and their Primary Schools* (Plowden Report) vol. 1, London: HMSO.

Crispus (Anon) (1814) 'On the education of children', in P. J. Greven (ed.) (1973) *Child-Rearing Concepts, 1628–1861*, Itasca, Ill.: Peacock Publishers, pp. 98–112.

DEC (Division for Early Childhood) (1992) 'DEC Position Statement on Goal One of America 2000', in *Young Children* (September): 75.

Education Department of South Australia (1988) *Children and Learning in the Primary Years*, Adelaide: EDSA, Publication Branch.

Entwistle, H. (1970) *Child-Centred Education*, London: Methuen.

Kirby, E. (1981) *Personal Values in Primary Education*, London: Harper & Row.

Lawrence, D. (1987) *Enhancing Self-Esteem in the Classroom*, London: Paul Chapman Publishing.

Locke, J. (1690) 'Some thoughts concerning education,' in P. J. Greven (ed.) (1973) *Child-Rearing Concepts, 1628–1861*, Itasca, Ill.: Peacock Publishers, pp. 18–41.

Peters, R. S. (1973) *Reason and Compassion*, London: Routledge & Kegan Paul.

Postman, N. and Weingartner, C. (1973) *How to Recognise a Good School*, Chicago: Phi Delta Kappa.

Province of British Columbia (1990) *Primary Program: Foundation Document*, Victoria, BC: Ministry of Education.

Chapter 11

Observing children choosing

Kurt Czerwenka

This chapter was written about changing pedagogy in German elementary schools where children's autonomy and free choice is increasingly encouraged. Czerwenka describes an action-research approach which involves systematic observation of individual pupils, at points in the day when they have free choice. The author's own observations raise questions of the extent to which enabling a child to choose is in fact empowering to them. His questions include the following. To what extent are children able to choose meaningfully (that is, in their own terms), and to what extent are they held back or inhibited? To what extent may free choice allow a child to regress? How important is the opportunity to refuse, and how significant is the chance to seek contact with others in a way that involves passivity in a potentially dynamic situation?*

TEACHING METHODS

Social freedom and economic mobility have now long since made their way into childhood. Even our small fry have already become individualists, not only because many children are now growing up as single children, but also because they have the opportunity to develop their special interests quite early. There are clothing, housing, leisure time, pets, toys, books, and media markets especially for children. Training of subjectivity begins earlier and earlier in our modern era.

Nor is the school immune to this drive toward freedom and individuality. Its response is individual learning and 'free' work. It is surely no coincidence that these long-known methods of pedagogical reform (see Maria Montessori, Hugo Gaudig) are finding application in the public school system at this very time. But are our children really more independent, more self-aware, and also more self-controlled so that they are able to make meaningful use of the

* Originally published as: 'How learning-effective is "free work"? Ways to observe the effects and results of open classroom situations', in *European Education: A Journal of Translations* (Summer 1994), New York: M.E. Sharpe. German text © 1991 by *Pädagogische Welt*. 'Wie lernwerksam ist "freie Arbeit"?', *Pädagogische Welt*, no. 9: 395–9 (edited for this volume).

measure of freedom granted to them? Or are we merely projecting our own expectations on to children, thus placing too great demands on them? Or are 'open classrooms' or 'free work' just one more of those pedagogical fashions to which pedagogy has always been susceptible?

Pedagogy and hence the school are suffering under an explanation and justification gap *sui generis*. They are continually called upon to demonstrate anew their function and hence their effects. Educational establishments should also be required to pass muster, especially in a time in which the future seems to lie primarily in the realm of economics.

But these queries must remain for the most part unanswered. Neither culture nor a mature personality nor upbringing nor learning can be described and assessed in terms of demonstrable facts. Even in such areas as learning and performance, behaviourist hopes have disappointed us. We have had to see that here too only the more unimportant data can be quantified – for example, good spelling, the number of vowels learned, the number of arithmetic problems solved – whereas the actual objectives such as flexibility and creativity, independent activity, linguistic skill, scientific ingenuity, and responsibility can never be properly demonstrated. We often do not know not only to what extent we have reached the targeted objectives, but even whether they are at all achievable after long and arduous educational work. Thus, for centuries the only guideline the educator has actually had to go by was his own optimism that all his efforts would lead to success, even if not necessarily visible success. Only the utopian hope that the new generation would be better human beings (Kant) enables educators to resume the burden of the work of education.

But educators also cannot continue endlessly to produce hopes without endeavouring to anchor them on the bedrock of real events or realistic ideas. Educational theories experienced a boom in the last few years, and are being further developed even if they do run the risk of going beyond the bounds of their reflective capacities (see Tenorth, 1983: 351ff.). The hope that subsequent generations will learn more, act better, take more moral decisions and, in short, will live in a more responsible way is however very difficult to anchor in human nature. After all, why should people suddenly become different from what they already are? Belief in science and in the progress of the human spirit does not just stop with pedagogy. This progress of the human spirit, however, should be reflected in teaching procedures, teaching methods, new and better visual aids, more skilful learning techniques, deeper motivational capacities and further experiential opportunities. Only then can education keep pace with advances in the other scientific disciplines, and only then can research activities be legitimated. If, even so, the gap between hopes and abilities cannot be closed, this is a question of pedagogy, for not everything in pedagogy can be scientifically grounded or even scientifically derived (Spranger, 1953: 350).

We cannot pursue this theoretical notion further here; rather we shall turn our attention to legitimation. The momentary hope that is presently being placed in open classrooms or 'free work' seems to me to be grounded only in part in the actual method; the other part is grounded in the dream that there must be a way in which learning can become enjoyable and education can become a self-evident matter. If childhood interests and differentiated school programmes coincided, teachers would actually be superfluous, for learning and the challenges of education would then be a matter of course. What is not taken into account is today's media world of children, which is still more exciting than the most attractive school; there are the children, with their fears of failure, who come to school already discouraged; there is the necessity that cultural techniques which are not fun must also be learned; and there is the sociological observation that children who have also been encouraged and motivated in the home especially profit from the new learning techniques.

Our purpose with these reflections is not to make the methods of reform pedagogy now finally coming into public schools more fashionable or to polemicize against the differentiating, individualizing forms of learning currently so popular; we wish, rather, only to warn against a new euphoria. After the behaviourist mania over learning objectives, and the educational technology of the social sciences; after the antipedagogical overestimation of the child and the unbounded belief in the expansion of education, we should be more cautious today with our pedagogical expectations.

The greatest chances of protecting ourselves against unfounded euphoria seem to lie in a sober comparison of the ideal picture with realities. The limits, but also the possibilities, of new directions can be made evident only if the facts are determined *sine ira et studio*, and we are thoroughly aware of the actual relativity of knowledge.

Thus we have designed an integration project for assimilating handicapped children into normal elementary school. In this project the open classroom was the inevitable method of choice (Czerwenka, Schmidt and Arlt, 1990). Our purpose was to develop instruments of observation with which we then attempted to map the course and record the results of open work and the individualization of learning. We focused our attention especially on the question of when children begin to wander or retreat from the task at hand in a learning process they themselves have initiated and for which they themselves feel responsible, or how long an activity which has been selected freely by the children actually remains meaningful from the standpoint of a structured learning process.

There are, of course, a number of imponderables in this decision-making process, but these certainly cannot be diminished by leaving them out of consideration. Nor is it our purpose to settle the argument as to which is more successful – traditional or open instruction; rather, after making the value judgement that open instruction and free work are meaningful and called for in specific school situations, we attempted to shed closer light on their capacities and their limits. We assume that free work can or even should occur also in individual phases of instruction, and that it need not dominate instruction.

Observations

Observation of individual pupils in classroom hours offering open instruction

Many individual observations preceded the filling out of the observational questionnaire, without a specific structure being provided beforehand for our perceptions. Once again it became clear that classroom instruction was a complex process that had to be precisely understood before any basic decisions could be taken.

- Do I want to observe the entire class in general or one pupil more precisely?
- Do I want to convey an impression through the actions of this pupil, or do I want to get a clearer idea of individual characteristics?
- Do I want to get just an overall and general picture of the classroom situation, or do I want to view it only as a horizon within which the individual pupil can be stimulated?
- Do I set down a few categories for observation and attempt to classify the relevant characteristics as accurately as possible during instruction, or do I gather 'results'; that is, newly recurrent characteristics during the period of observation?

We decided to observe a single pupil over the entire course of a classroom hour with reference to a few preselected characteristics. We assumed a 'normal' teacher-led instruction for these characteristics. We distinguished between active – that is, visibly engaged cooperation – and a receptive – that is, actual or presumed – listening or onlooking by the pupil. Of course, we could not determine the particular thoughts of the pupils, so we had to presume the observers' benevolent attention in this phase. Nor was it important for us in this case to be the meticulous detective, since we were interested first and foremost in free, self-chosen activity.

1st Feature: Cooperation with teacher-led classroom instruction
- Active (discernible from behaviour; e.g., reporting, writing, singing, speaking)
- Receptive (visible or implied; e.g., by the direction of the gaze, seeming concentration, sitting alongside, listening in)

The first thing to be observed was individual work, although it still was initiated by the teacher.

Concentrated work alone without help or without the direct presence of a teacher can be seen as a preliminary stage of a self-chosen activity. To that extent, a child's ability to concentrate can be assessed from his or her independent work initiated by the teacher. But this ability is an indispensable precondition for effective free work. The extent of help still required from the teacher in independent work sets limits on the preconditions for self-chosen activities.

2nd Feature: Working alone on a teacher assignment

- With the help or presence of the teacher (sitting alongside)
- Without teacher (with concentration)

At this point the actual observation of self-activity begins. The initial situation was based on the presumption that the teachers were working with several learning materials, play or work materials, opportunities for employment, or differentiations of tasks, or that these are already present, and that the teacher signals that the pupils may now choose freely. It seemed important to us that the children should also be allowed to choose activities – for example, from the classroom's play corner or activity corner – which were not a direct part of the teacher's expectations.

3rd Feature: Self-chosen activities (in the free work phases or even when material is offered for differentiation during the course orientation)

- Subject-related, concentrated (in so far as that can be outwardly determined or assumed)
- Sporadic, fluctuating (e.g., frequent change of activities, rapid leafing through a book, throwing work and play objects around)

The criterion at issue was: can a pupil's activity, having anything at all to do with something not initially intended in classroom instruction – for example, looking at a picture book, testing a game, strumming on a musical instrument – be nonetheless regarded as consciously chosen and undertaken, as something that is able formally to shape the forces of the ego independently of that activity, or specifically to strengthen decision-making abilities, or does attention wander and action become a preconscious motor activity, or an accompaniment of deep and ponderous reflection, or simply an indecisive transitional act? These functions, too, have their roles, if no longer that of strengthening the ego or cultivating the mind but now rather a compensating or repressing role.

The relative significance of open instruction or free work seems to divide on this point. If the offering of free choice can become a conscious act of decision, the individual's own planning of a future action, an experience that one's behaviour is independent of the environment, a retroactive relating of an action to one's own decision, a sensorimotor and cognitive knowledge of things and contexts, or a cognitive, volitional, and emotional interplay between decision and satisfaction, then that offering has achieved its objective – initially independent, moreover, of the content of activity.

If, on the other hand, an unstructured situation allows the child to revert to inhibition, self-absorption, 'learned helplessness' (Seligman), the regressive thrill of mere functioning, a definite inability to decide, resigned conflictual decisions, and emotive-motor relief, then those processes which in fact the free-choice offering should overcome, are in fact reinforced. These points should be given meticulous consideration – which, moreover, should also be the task of a teacher who has been freed from the task of steering the classroom. These features, reflected upon and discussed thoroughly, helped us in these observations.

But what happens when the individual pupil begins to wander or regress? The pupil is then usually encouraged by the teacher (in our case by the educator, if one is present) to get busy or to take a decision. This can be done in a polite and understanding way, for the teacher is after all relieved of the task of steering the general conversation in this phase. A pupil can either accept or reject this encouragement.

4th Feature: Encouragement to get busy or take a decision

- Accepted (the pupil chooses a meaningful activity or again takes part in group activities)
- Refused (the pupil refuses, mumbles, and continues with an easy activity, or does not react at all)

It is very important that the opportunity to refuse is generally left open, for decision is nurtured by alternatives. If there is no possibility to decide against a meaningful activity, decision is no longer of any value. There will always be children who want to test this space of freedom.

We found that many pupils seek contact with others when they are uncertain, in order to acquire models or even stimulation for their behaviour. These contacts can relate to matters that are relevant to instruction, to observations, or to actions, or they can also be an attempt to divert one's schoolmates' attention or to draw them into one's own undertakings. If the teacher's previous demands were vexatious, or if the pupil himself suffers from a growing indecision and hence is under pressure to take a decision, he may also attempt to pass his annoyance on to his schoolmates, or to let off steam by means of aggression. In this case, we scored this non-classroom-related social contact as negative.

But it may also happen that undecided or cross children will turn to the teacher (or to some other adult present), expecting him or her to come to assistance or to structure the situation. It then makes a difference whether the child takes contact himself or whether it is the teacher who turns her attention to the obviously perplexed child. This feature of passive pupil contact with the teacher often overlaps with the feature 'encouragement to get busy'.

5th Feature: Social contact with children

- Instruction-related
- Not instruction-related
- Positive (friendly, communicative, playful)
- Negative (irritating, aggressive, disruptive)

This observation of social contact seems to be important, especially in open instruction or free work, since the forms of individualization of learning always present the risk of social isolation. A pupil can work with intense concentration, but he may also forget all the others. If, then, only contact with adults is left, countermeasures should be considered (joint games, group work, conversations, learning circles, etc.).

6th Feature: Social contact with adults

- Active (pupil makes contact himself)
- Passive (pupil is spoken to by the teacher)

The opposite to the pupil who works calmly in a corner is the extroverted pupil who first makes a visit to all his 'schoolmates' during the open phases. However, this running around loses this function of social reassurance if it lasts too long. It then once again becomes a compensatory surrogate action.

7th Feature: Running about in the classroom

The observation sheet (see Table 11.1)

The classroom background to all these features should be mentioned, for it is not unimportant to know during what themes, what times, and what subjects, and in the presence of what teacher a pupil shows a specific behaviour. Therefore, we have always noted down on separate lines the date, the time, the discipline, the teacher, the theme and the special teaching methods being used. In special cases we also noted down the work material used and/or the way the particular student made use of space. The product of this is the following observation sheet (see Table 11.1: observation sheet).

Application

The most favourable situation for observation is when a person can concentrate on one pupil. In a normal school day this person might be a guest, a

Table 11.1 Observation sheet

		5	10	15	20	25	30	35	40	45
Time collaboration in classroom instruction	Active Receptive									
Working alone	With teacher Without teacher									
Encouragement to work (by an adult)	Accepted Refused									
Self-chosen activity	Object-related concentrated Sporadic fluctuating									
Social contact with other children	Instruction-related Not instruction-related									
Social contact with adults	Active Passive									
Running about										
Name, date, time										

student teacher, another colleague or the counsellor. Under these optimum conditions, the features may be recorded every minute throughout the entire classroom hour. After a few practice sessions, two pupils sitting next to each other can even be observed at the same time.

But often the teacher has no observer available. Then she herself may note all features displayed by one pupil over the course of several phases, or one feature over a longer period. But perhaps the teacher is also interested (especially in the transitional phase after open work begins) in the concentrated self-activity of a few pupils. She can then note the state of the features under observation once more before the beginning of the classroom hour, and observe the critical phases precisely, and then, after this period, write down random notes about what she has particularly noticed. In this case the teacher need not follow the observation sheet exactly.

The observation sheet should not be standardized and objectified; it should be used to sensitize and stimulate experience in critical phases of open work, especially when the pupils differ in their initial learning conditions. Nor can it be used to arrive at a judgement for or against open instruction; at most it can provide the conditions for making a decision on whether the different student populations are suited or not suited for such work. It might even be found that after a long observation period poor learners or diffident pupils will become irritated by the unstructured situations (see Bennett, 1979). The evaluation of, for example, social contact with schoolmates or adults and of active or receptive collaboration in classroom instruction, can never take place outside the classroom situation. The observation sheet cannot replace reflection over and evaluation of one's own instruction; at best it can only be a preliminary aid.

REFERENCES

Bennett, N. (1979) *Unterrichtsstil und Schulleistung*, Stuttgart.
Czerwenka, K., Schmidt, H. and Arlt, D. (1990) *Schlussbericht über die wissenschaftliche Begleitung des Schulversuchs 'Gemeinsamer Unterrricht von behinderten und nichtbehinderten Schüler'*, Lüneburg.
Einsiedler, W. (1979) *Konzeptionen des Grundschulunterrichts*, Bad Heilbrunn.
Flitner, W. (1966) *Das Selbstverständnis de Erziehungswissenschaft in der Gegenwart*, Heidelberg.
Hanke, B., Mandl, H. and Prell, S. (1973) *Soziale Interaktion im Untericht*, Munich.
Neumann, D. (1985) *Tradition und Fortschritt in der Lehrerausbildung*, Bad Heilbrunn.
Spranger, E. (1973) 'Ist Pädagogik eine Wissenschaft? (1953)', in E. Spranger, *Gesammelte Schriften*, vol. 2, ed. O. f. Bollnow and G. Bräuer, Heidelberg, pp. 341–50.
Tenorth, H. E. (1983) 'die Krisen der Theoretiker sind nicht die Krisen der Theorie', in *Zeitschrift f. Pädagogik*, 3: 347–58.
Terhart, E. (1978) *Interpretative Unterrichstforschung*, Stuttgart.

Chapter 12

Classroom practice in England and France

Patricia Broadfoot and Marilyn Osborn, with Michel Gilly and Arlette Bucher

*Drawn from a comparative study of primary schools in England and France, the authors document different aspects of school and classroom practice in the schools observed in the two countries.**

What are the characteristics of the schools in which the primary school teachers in France and England work? How similar are the buildings and their layout, and the individual classrooms? Does their use reflect similar working habits? Do teachers in each country work with similar class sizes and types of pupils? How do the teachers differ in their classroom practice, their organization and management? These are the questions with which this chapter attempts to deal on the basis both of the observations made during the authors' many classroom visits and of the quantitative information given by the teachers themselves.

THE SCHOOLS

The buildings

There are many similarities in the exterior of the school buildings visited in both countries. Both reflect a succession of new ideas in architecture from the turn of the century onwards, and it is noticeable that the differences between school buildings within one country are as great as the differences between the countries.

There are, however, clear differences in the internal organization of the buildings. In England, schools have more rooms allocated to uses other than standard classroom activities. All English schools have staffrooms and most have school halls which are used for assemblies and school gatherings as well as for physical education activities. In French schools there is at the most only one spare room, often small (described as multi-purpose), for all

* Originally published in P. Broadfoot and M. Osbourne, with M. Gilly and A. Bucher (1993), *Perceptions of Teaching: Primary School Teachers in England and France*, London and New York: Cassell.

non-standard activities. These differences are an indicator of the much greater significance of collaboration and interchange of teachers and pupils in England as compared with France. Also, English classrooms and external areas such as corridors and entrance halls present a warmer, more friendly appearance because of the many decorations and exhibits of pupils' work. Schools in both countries have outdoor play areas, but in France a section of these, known as the *préau*, is often covered so that pupils can play games outside even in wet weather.

School size

In both cohorts the number of pupils on the school roll varied considerably. At one extreme were schools with fewer than 25 pupils, and at other schools with more than 300. It will come as no great surprise that the small schools were in the majority of cases rural schools, which accounted for 77 per cent (France) and 70 per cent (England) of schools with fewer than 125 pupils; the large urban schools accounted for 100 per cent (France) and 95 per cent (England) of the schools involved in our study with more than 200 pupils.

Table 12.1, however, shows that very large schools were much more common in England than they were in France: in the county of Avon 11 schools out of the 105 studied had more than 300 pupils, whilst there was only one such school out of the 95 studied in the Académie d'Aix-Marseille.

Table 12.1 Number of pupils on roll

Population	No. of pupils	No. of schools				
		Zone 1: rural	Zone 2: working-class	Zone 3: inner city	Zone 4: middle-class	Total
French	<25	11				11
	26–125	22	5	1	4	32
	126–200	7	7	9	8	31
	201–250		5	3	6	14
	251–300		2	2	2	6
	>300			1		
		40	19	16	20	94
English	<25	2				2
	26–125	21	1	6	3	31
	126–200	8	7	13	7	35
	201–250	2	6	2	5	15
	251–300		3	4	4	11
	>300			4	7	11
		33	17	29	26	105

Conversely, very small schools (fewer than 25 pupils) were much more common in France than they were in England, accounting for 27.5 per cent of rural schools in France, but only 6 per cent of rural schools in England.

THE CLASSES

General overview

The classes involved in our study reflect exactly the general differences observed between the two countries. In the French classes that we visited, almost invariably the layout of the desks followed the classical pattern of the teacher's desk facing neat parallel rows of pupils' desks. We very rarely found the layout which is characteristic of the vast majority of English primary schools: desks or tables grouped together in a number of areas corresponding to different themes or activities, with the pupils sitting around the areas defined in this way, and the teacher often moving between the groups. In the French cohort, the very few classes which had that layout were most often classes run by a teacher who had adopted a different pedagogical philosophy (Freinet's, for instance), or classes with a special purpose (remedial classes for pupils from underprivileged areas in a 'ZEP' – *zone d'éducation prioritaire* – for instance). The choice of different working methods, which affects both the objectives and the running of the class, here leads the teacher to adopt a layout that is different from the standard one.

Class size

General remarks

A comparison between French and English classes reveals so many important differences that it hardly needs a commentary. A quick glance at Table 12.2 will reveal that, whatever the geographic zone, the numbers of pupils per class were much higher in English schools than in French schools. The average for both of our cohorts was 22.3 pupils per class in France and 27.5 in England, which means, on average, 4.2 more pupils in English classrooms.

The difference is even more striking if we consider the spread of classes according to their size. Whatever the zone considered, there were many more small classes, and fewer large classes, in the French cohort. Thirty per cent of French classes had a maximum of 20 pupils, as opposed to only 13 per cent in the English cohort. Also, only 24 per cent of French classes (as opposed to 71 per cent of the English classes in our study) had more than 25 pupils. If we consider only the very large classes, the difference was even more striking: there were more than 30 pupils in at least one in three English classes (36 per cent), whilst in France this was exceptional (fewer than 2 per cent of classes). It is ironic that, in England, teachers are attempting to practise

Table 12.2 Class sizes

Population	No. of pupils	Percentage of classes				
		Zone 1: rural	*Zone 2: working-class*	*Zone 3: inner city*	*Zone 4: middle-class*	*Mean (%)*
French	<15	15.8	4.8	6.1	1.0	6.9
	16–20	22.5	23.3	38.3	9.1	23.3
	21–25	41.5	46.7	42.4	52.5	45.8
	26–30	18.0	22.3	12.1	36.4	22.2
	>30	2.2	2.9	1.1	1.0	1.8
		100	100	100	100	100
English	<15	8.7	9.2	10.5	1.3	7.5
	16–20	10.0	2.6	10.5	–	5.8
	21–25	21.3	14.5	22.4	3.9	15.5
	26–30	37.5	35.5	35.5	34.3	35.7
	>30	22.5	38.2	21.1	60.5	35.5
		100	100	100	100	100

an individualized pedagogy with class sizes far larger than those with which the French teacher works in a formal, didactic way. Clearly, the situation is likely to be easier for the teacher in France, where since 1975 a number of governmental measures have led to a decrease in class size.

The role played by the location of the schools

In both countries, it was in the affluent middle-class zones (Zone 4) where the largest classes were to be found. In Aix-Marseille 37 per cent of classes in the middle-class areas had more than 25 pupils, whilst only one in ten (10 per cent) had 20 or less. The very same phenomenon can be observed in the English cohort. In the county of Avon it was also in the affluent middle-class areas that the classes were the largest, to such an extent that 95 per cent of classes had more than 25 pupils, and 60 per cent more than 30. And in those areas only one class in 100 (1 per cent) had 20 pupils or less.

In both countries, it is in the inner city that there are proportionately more moderately sized classes and fewer large classes. In both countries too the greatest contrast is between the affluent middle-class areas and the inner city, while the greatest similarity is between rural areas (Zone 1) and inner-city areas (Zone 3).

The contrast between the affluent middle-class areas and the inner-city areas in both countries may be explained in similar ways. The attractive nature of schools in affluent middle-class areas leads a certain number of parents living on the periphery of those areas to try to get their children into those schools. Their success in this depends on whether the regulations (official or not) relating to the location of the residence carry much weight or are respected to the letter. In the county of Avon, where there were few geographical restrictions regarding the choice of school at the time of the study, this phenomenon reached maximum proportions. And it is still very much apparent in the region around Marseilles, despite a fairly strict allocation of school places according to residence. Parental pressure leads to exceptions being made.

The relatively small size of classes in the less well-off inner-city areas (Zone 3) can also be explained by the educational policies in both countries. An undeniable effort has been made during the past two decades to improve teaching conditions in this respect. In England there has been a particularly marked policy of allocating a more favourable teacher–pupil ratio to such schools.

The scholastic progress of the pupils

The progress of the pupils

Table 12.3 gives very general information on the way in which the schoolchildren from both our cohorts progress through school. The differences emphasize the extent to which educational policies differ in the two countries. In France, at the time of the study, the policy of *redoublement* (repeating the year) was still being implemented for pupils judged not to have reached the required level. This was despite often-voiced reservations and criticisms, both in educational and in psychological circles (see, for instance, Gilly, 1967),

Table 12.3 Percentage of pupils in advance, at the legal age, and behind by one or two years

Population	Relative progress	Percentage of pupils				
		Zone 1: rural	Zone 2: working-class	Zone 3: inner city	Zone 4: middle-class	Mean (%)
French	In advance	2.1	1.8	1.9	4.4	2.6
	Legal age	75.6	66.7	47.8	80.9	68.0
	1 yr behind	15.6	21.2	28.7	11.1	19.1
	2 yrs behind	6.7	10.3	21.6	3.6	10.3
		100	100	100	100	100
English	In advance	5.3	3.5	3.7	4.1	3.9
	Legal age	87.6	92.9	92.6	93.0	91.5
	1 yr behind	4.5	3.1	2.7	2.4	3.1
	2 yrs behind	2.4	1.0	1.0	1.0	1.3
		100	100	100	100	100

and the wishes of the educational authorities since the Haby reform in 1975. Twenty-nine per cent of all primary school pupils in our study had repeated at least a year. Nineteen per cent had repeated one year (thus being one year behind their age mates) and 10 per cent had repeated two years (being therefore two years behind). For a French pupil, progress in school is rather like running an obstacle course: the first obstacle has to be tackled successfully before the pupil is allowed to tackle the next one. Being allowed into the next higher class is usually possible only if the pupil has reached the level corresponding to the norm-referenced objectives for the class in which he has just spent a year.

In England, the situation is quite different in that pupils never repeat a year. They all move on to secondary school at age 11, whilst in France the *redoublement* system means that it is possible for pupils to be entering secondary school at 12, 13 or, exceptionally, 14 years old.

Where our data indicate a small proportion (4.4 per cent) of English pupils who were 'behind' by a year, this is very often because they were in small rural schools where mixed-age groups of pupils were kept together in one class owing to the small numbers of pupils in each age group. Sometimes with such mixed-age groupings 'vertical age groupings' are also set up for pedagogical reasons.

If the difference between French and English schools is so dramatic, it is quite simply because the underlying pedagogical principles are very different. In England, at the time of our study, progress at school was not dependent, at every stage, on norm-referenced criteria relating to knowledge, and defined by an official National Curriculum imposed by an outside body. Every year each school established and adjusted, on its own initiative, its own curriculum and progression. It follows that the objectives defined were established much more on the basis of the true level of the pupils than on the basis of theoretical levels which are assumed to be typical of average pupils for the different ages, as is the case in France. It seems therefore reasonable to assume that there was less discrepancy in England between the objectives proposed and the average abilities of the pupils than is the case in France, where a considerable body of research has over a period of years stressed the unreasonable nature of the expected learning objectives (see, for instance, Gilly, 1967). Will this still be the case in the years to come? Will there still be no repeating of years in English primary schools? The question arises because the introduction of the National Curriculum, as a result of the 1988 Education Reform Act, may eventually lead to such a measure being necessary for those pupils who fail to reach the nationally imposed objectives.

Estimated level of the pupils

The consequences for pupils' progress of the different educational policies practised in the two countries naturally go hand in hand with differences in

Table 12.4 Teachers' assessment of pupils' academic level

Population	Academic level	Percentage of teachers				
		Zone 1: rural	Zone 2: working-class	Zone 3: inner city	Zone 4: middle-class	Mean (%)
French	Above ave	16.5	16.9	7.8	24.9	16.8
	Average	61.5	58.1	48.2	58.8	56.8
	Below ave	22.0	25.0	44.0	16.3	26.4
		100	100	100	100	100
English	Above ave	24.8	17.9	10.3	35.7	22.3
	Average	53.9	46.5	37.3	45.1	45.7
	Below ave	21.5	35.6	52.4	19.2	31.9
		100	100	100	100	100

the working conditions of the teachers, and the way in which they manage their classes. We saw (Table 12.2) that the teacher in England normally has much larger classes than her French counterpart. In the absence of a policy of systematic elimination of the weaker pupils at the end of the school year, classes in England are certainly much more heterogeneous regarding level. At least, this seems to be the conclusion that should be drawn from Table 12.4, which presents a subjective evaluation by the teachers of the levels attained by their pupils in relation to the teachers' assessment of the general 'average' level of pupils for that particular year.

First of all, it is clear from the last column of Table 12.4 that, on the whole, both English and French teachers were pleased with the level of their pupils. When they gave an opinion on the average level of their class, the English teachers were even slightly more satisfied than the French teachers, but the difference was so small as to be negligible. However, if the difference is negligible when talking of averages, this was definitely not the case when considering the spread of the assessments. Whatever the zone considered, this spread was much bigger for the English cohort than it was for the French cohort. If the assessments made are a true reflection of the real level of the pupils, then the heterogeneity of English classes is considerably greater. This has clear implications for the management of the classes. It would be far less easy for the English teacher to treat the class as a homogeneous group for all teaching purposes. Certainly the format of the formal presentation by the teacher followed by practical exercises is not a commonly used practice in English schools as it is in French schools. English teachers are much more likely to practise small-group teaching than their French counterparts, as we shall see later on in this chapter.

Not surprisingly, in both countries it is in the affluent middle-class areas where teachers feel most satisfied with the level attained by their pupils, and in the inner city where the estimated level is lowest. This is despite the existence of larger class sizes, particularly in English middle-class areas.

CLASSROOM PRACTICE

The different institutional characteristics reported in the preceding sections are closely related to the striking differences in classroom organization and management which we report here. The observations which follow are based upon the shadowing of 16 teachers in each country for up to a week at a time, using field notes and a systematic observation schedule.

This investigation revealed striking differences in pedagogy, in classroom organization and in teacher–pupil relations, which were far greater between the two countries than any of the differences observed *within* one country (for example in schools located in different socio-economic catchment areas).

Pedagogy

Particularly evident were different practices of differentiation and grouping, a differing emphasis in the two countries on the acquisition of principles and concepts compared with an emphasis on knowledge acquired through rote learning, and a different value placed on the product of learning as opposed to the process.

In most English classrooms there were typically three or four different activities going on at the same time; in France this was very rarely seen, much of the teaching being didactic and centred on one activity for the whole class. English teachers were also more likely to divide the class into groups and to use attainment level as a basis for this division and for differentiated approaches in their teaching. A much greater tendency to relate teaching to perceived pupil and group need was apparent in English classrooms than in French ones because, for the most part, French pupils were typically engaged in the same task for most of the time. Nevertheless, even in England teachers often maintained a high degree of control over the pacing of children's tasks.

Teachers in England, because of their greater need to maintain individual contact and to supervise groups, were much more likely to move around the class looking at children's work, helping and giving instruction and direction, whereas French teachers were typically on the platform or on a stool at the front of the class, as might be expected for a more 'whole-class' pedagogy. Reading provides another example of these differences. Whilst English teachers, typically, heard children read individually, French teachers commonly had children read around the class. In England the whole approach was typically found to be much more active and emphasized discovery-based learning. The teacher often appeared to be encouraging creative thinking, whereas in

France the effort was more likely to be directed towards leading children to the correct answer.

Thus teachers in England were more likely to use questions in a way that built upon children's responses until the desired result was achieved, whilst French teachers would typically reject a child's response if it was not exactly what they wanted.

For example, one teacher in England, doing language work with a small group, asked 'What are sentences?' The children made various attempts at an answer, including 'bits of writing' and 'writing put together'.

TEACHER: 'So it's a piece of writing, isn't it? Strings of what?'
CHILDREN: 'Words.'
TEACHER: 'A string of words that makes sense. If I said to you "In the sky", is that a sentence?'
CHILDREN: 'No.'
TEACHER: ' "There's a bird in the sky" is a sentence, isn't it? What does it end with?'
CHILDREN: 'A full stop.'

In one school in France, the teacher took in children's books where the children had been asked to write a complete sentence.

TEACHER (looking through books):   'This is not a sentence, this is not a sentence either, neither is this. This looks, smells and tastes like a sentence, but it is not one. It's wrong. A sentence has to use existing words and in the right order. Marc, read us your sentence using "champignons".'
MARC: 'J'ai mangé des champignons.'
TEACHER: 'It's not wrong, in fact it's correct, but it's boring.'

The teacher then gave more examples of sentences, and went on to analyse the objects of each sentence.

On balance, English teachers appeared to be concerned to encourage creativity and inventiveness, giving clear priority to the understanding of principles and concepts. French teachers in contrast placed a strong emphasis on acquiring knowledge through rote learning and were more concerned to achieve pupils' conformity to a common goal. Suggestions from pupils in some cases were not often welcomed or used, and typically much less sought after than in England. Creative writing was consequently an important feature in English schools, whilst in French schools there was more emphasis on grammar and analysis of sentence structure as well as on poetry recitation skills. Children often worked extensively with dictionaries, concentrating on definitions of words. However, evidence of genuine open-ended discussion was rare in both countries.

In summary, the pedagogy of many primary classrooms in France seemed to be characterized by an emphasis on the product rather than the process of learning. There was a strong emphasis on reaching the correct answer as quickly as possible, and neatness and attractive, well-set-out exercise books and impressive pieces of finished work were highly valued. In England generally, more stress was laid on the learning process and less on the finished product, with teachers differentiating work according to level and breadth to meet pupils' perceived capabilities.

By contrast, the main aim of virtually all the French teachers observed was for all pupils to achieve the same basic standard in order to meet the objectives set by the end of the year. Work was paced to conform to the level of the middle group. Those who could proceed faster were unlikely to be permitted to undertake work at a higher level.

Classroom organization and teacher–pupil relations

Because of the variety of activities and the individualized pedagogy, queuing at the teacher's desk was a constant feature of many English classrooms, whilst it occurred rarely, if at all, in France. Consequently there was more apparent time-wasting of children in England and less apparent application to work. Although some teachers in England showed great awareness of queuing as a problem and used strategies to cut it down, there were obvious limitations to such possibilities. Thus whilst English pupils experienced considerably more feedback of a concurrent kind than their French counterparts, the corollary of this was frequently delay and some pupils getting more help than others.

In France the level of participation of pupils was generally very high, and here too we observed more constant pressure on the part of teachers to secure pupils' work and effort, whilst there were far more instances in England of lapses of concentration and lack of pupil effort being unchallenged by the teacher.

The typical approach in French classrooms was to encourage pupils to work on their own without helping each other. Sometimes children were told to work with satchel on the desk between them to hide their work from other children. Occasionally slates were used so that children could write the correct answer on them and then hold them up to show the teacher. In one classroom, a boy was called to the front of the class to recite his five times table all the way through. The teacher insisted that he do this alone without help from other children, and when he got stuck the teacher became angry at the number of children calling out answers, saying that the first who spoke would be punished. The boy was sent back to his place and told that he would have to repeat the task the next day.

In contrast, most English teachers encouraged children to work cooperatively for much of the time. This meant that children were likely to be free to move around the room, and to seek other pupils and resources, even outside the classroom, whilst in France pupils were often rooted to their desks. Consequently the English classrooms were often characterized by children talking much of the time while French classrooms were likely to be relatively quiet and undisturbed.

Both groups of teachers showed considerable pleasure in the act of teaching, with many in both countries showing sympathetic interest in pupils and enthusiasm in their teaching. However, teachers in England had to work much harder at maintaining discipline, whilst in France, where teacher–pupil relations were more formal and the level of control generally stricter, teachers appeared to need to exercise that control far less frequently. Often a mere glance was enough to quell deviant behaviour.

In English classrooms relations between teacher and pupil were warmer and more informal. There was also considerable evidence of teachers striving to protect and encourage pupils' self-esteem by using praise both of pupils and their work. Criticism of children's work and even calling them names was very noticeable in France, with most positive reinforcement being used in the inner-city areas. It was also common in England for children to be discouraged from commenting on each other's mistakes, while in France this sometimes appeared to be encouraged implicitly by teachers. In one class we observed the teacher went from desk to desk commenting to the whole class, 'C'est bon', 'C'est mauvais', about children's work, with accompanying gasps from the rest of the class. One boy was told in front of others that he had made serious mistakes and that he would probably have to *redouble* (repeat the year).

In practice, teachers in France appeared to take one of two roles, either that of parent or that of dictator. In England there was typically a third dimension: teacher as colleague or facilitator, allowing children to make their own decisions and supporting their learning.

Summary of classroom practice

Thus in summary it may be said that a number of the factors which research suggests to be positive features in teaching, such as teacher warmth, sensitivity to pupils, an emphasis on pupils' positive achievements, working towards pupils' achievement of self-control and autonomy, were all more often observed in England than in France. In England also there was a greater variety of activities going on in the classroom, more variation of treatment according to pupil needs, more emphasis on teaching for understanding and more concurrent feedback to pupils.

However, these features, which would appear to most English teachers as desirable, seemed sometimes to be achieved at the expense of an orderly, calm classroom and perhaps of a good working environment. We have reported more evidence in England of pupils avoiding work and of teachers being unaware of what was going on in the class as a whole. There was also more evidence of teacher anxiety and tension. Whereas in France most of the teachers observed controlled the class easily and effectively, this was less true in England, although, as noted above, these observations need to be seen in the context of an average class size in the English classrooms of 30 and in France of 22. Thus, ironically, English teachers are typically working with an ideology of child-centredness and attention to the individual in the context of a class size much larger than that of the French teacher, who is aiming at whole-class teaching and an undifferentiated pedagogy in which the size of the class is much less significant.

It is important to emphasize that French teachers believe strongly in the need for a National Curriculum as the basis for equality and unity in their society. More immediately, however, they feel an overwhelming pressure to meet the attainment targets laid down for children by the end of the year. That strong sense of obligation to equip children with the skills and knowledge expected from a particular year grade so that they will not be forced to *redouble* is the source of much of the conformity, the emphasis on rote learning, the didactic teaching methods and the lack of response to perceived variations in pupil needs identified in our observations.

OVERVIEW AND SUMMARY

The data analysed in this chapter showed that there are clear differences in the way school buildings and classrooms are organized in France and England. The English schools we studied have more rooms reserved for special purposes such as staffrooms and assembly halls, and the layout of their classrooms favours group work around specific themes.

The quantitative data analysed also revealed important differences. In England, large schools are more numerous, and the average class size is much bigger. Finally, whilst in England entry into the next higher class at the beginning of a new school year is automatic, regardless of the location of the school, the progress of French schoolchildren is often (for almost 30 per cent of the cohort) halted by the repeating of at least one year, this being the case particularly for children from disadvantaged areas. The lack of elimination in English schools of the 'less able' children from one school year to the next leads to a greater spread of levels (as judged by the teachers). However, this greater spread does not mean that the English teachers are less satisfied with the average level of their pupils than their French counterparts.

It would certainly seem to the outside observer looking afresh at both systems that working conditions in English schools are rather less good than they are in French schools: larger schools, larger classes and a greater spread of levels. At the same time, English teachers are attempting to deliver an individualized and child-centred pedagogy.

However, it is important to bear in mind that, at the time of the study, the English primary school teachers did not share with their French counterparts a fear of pupils' not reaching the prescribed objectives, and of being held responsible for the failure of those pupils. This fundamental difference between the two systems, which resides in the freedom of the teacher to determine the nature of the objectives to be reached, is essential to an understanding of teachers' responses. It is clear that reasons of economy rather than educational policy are the determining factors in the size of the classes, but it is hard to see how the English teacher could handle satisfactorily the numbers and the varied levels of her pupils if she did not have a certain degree of freedom in the exact details of the curriculum to be followed. A system which on the whole does not have official norm-referenced stages allows for a better handling of individual differences, and quite naturally leads to a pupil-targeted approach on the part of the teachers. On the other hand, the focusing on norm-referenced objectives chosen by an outside body leads to set teaching methods, based on the formal lesson directed at the whole class. This is what happens in France, despite real efforts to get the teachers to take into account individual pupils instead of treating their class as a mono-lithic entity. There is in fact an incompatibility between norm-referenced objectives imposed by an outside body, and the possibility of adopting truly pupil-oriented teaching methods. This latter type of approach is possible within a class only if the principle of different levels for different pupils at the end of the school year is accepted. However, such a principle is funda-mentally in disagreement with the norm-referenced objectives prescribed by the official programmes. There would seem to be a strong argument for taking into account the differences between individual pupils from the outset, rather than becoming obsessed by the awesome task of having to get all the pupils to learn the same thing. With such a system, it ought to be possible to orga-nize the class in such a way that each pupil can learn at his own speed, and make the most of the objectives proposed; as a consequence, the pupils' new knowledge will be acquired on a more solid basis than if the same speed of acquisition, and the same testing requirements, had been imposed on all pupils.

One of the problems associated with the introduction of the National Curriculum in England without an accompanying reduction in class size is clear. How will teachers be able to carry on with such varied attainment levels in their class unless, eventually, a system of repeating the year is introduced?

An analysis of the teachers' assessment of the level of their pupils shows that both French and English teachers make a close link between social class and scholastic achievement. Moreover, our data confirm that in both coun-tries the educational authorities aim for smaller classes in disadvantaged areas. It would be interesting to carry the comparison further. How do schools tackle inequalities caused by social class in a system where repeating a year is standard practice and in a system where it isn't, and what are the compar-ative consequences of the measures taken to that effect?

REFERENCE

Gilly, M. (1967) 'Influence du milieu social et de l'âge sur la progression scolaire à l'école primaire', *Bulletin de Psychologie*, 20: 797–810.

Part III

Policy development in assessing and planning learning

Chapter 13

Discussion points for primary schools

Anna Craft

This chapter summarizes the issues which OFSTED identified in their discussion document Primary Matters, *published in 1994.* *It is the most recent in a series of discussion papers on primary practice (of which the first was published in 1992), in which inspection findings on the implementation of statutory curriculum and assessment were combined with the development of an agenda for developing primary practice.*

Details of how to obtain the original publication, free of charge, are given at the end of the chapter. What follows is a summary of the main discussion points raised in Primary Matters.

Four areas in which primary schools need to modify their policy and practice have been identified by the Inspectorate since the introduction of the National Curriculum in 1988. These are:

- curriculum management;
- subject expertise;
- curriculum organization, subject work and topic work;
- teaching the basics of learning.

The introduction of streamlined curriculum and assessment arrangements, and the start of an inspection cycle for primary schools, are seen in the report as providing 'an appropriate context' for responding to these four sets of issues.

CURRICULUM MANAGEMENT

The Head Teacher's role in curriculum management is outlined in detail, as follows:

---

* OFSTED Inspectorate (1994), *Primary Matters: A Discussion on Teaching and Learning in Primary Schools*, London: Office for Standards in Education.

Coordination: this includes

- facilitating and developing the school's agreed definition of the curriculum, and clarifying its relationship to the National Curriculum;
- identifying the principles and procedures by which the parts of the curriculum are combined;
- clarifying principles and procedures for making and implementing curriculum decisions;
- establishing roles and responsibilities of curriculum decision-makers;
- organizing the school curriculum so that it supports the school's aims, enables coverage of the statutory curriculum, and fosters pupil achievement.

Monitoring: this includes

- monitoring the planning and preparation of each teacher, to ensure coverage of the statutory curriculum and also the school's agreed curriculum;
- monitoring classroom practice, to see how the teaching and assessment relates to the planning and preparation.

Evaluation: this includes

Using various sources for evaluation, including the OFSTED Framework for Inspection,

- evaluating the whole curriculum for breadth, balance, continuity, progression, coherence and compliance with National Curriculum requirements;
- evaluating teaching and organizational strategies, looking at fitness for purpose;
- evaluating the achievement and progress of individual children and groups, seeking trends and patterns of achievement;
- evaluating the overall quality of educational provision (including extra-curricular activities);
- evaluating the standards achieved.

Clearly, the Head Teacher's task is onerous. The processes which Head Teachers will need to undertake in order to discharge these responsibilities will, OFSTED says, include: 'a great deal of focused discussion about the curriculum with colleagues; leading and contributing to staff and team meetings; developing and reviewing policies; analysing assessment data and children's work; observing teachers and children at work; consulting members of the governing body and others with a concern for the work of the school; keeping up to date with local and National Curriculum documentation; and, very importantly, finding time to reflect upon progress and the direction of the work' (*Primary Matters*: 9).

As well as the Head Teacher's overview and coordinating role in managing the curriculum, OFSTED stresses the importance and, except in the very smallest primary schools, the feasibility of teachers who act as 'subject managers' for the whole school – to whom the Head Teacher can delegate. The subject manager has a wider role than the 'subject coordinator'; and the areas of responsibility include: developing a clear view of the nature of their subject, and its contribution to the wider school curriculum; providing advice and documentation to help teachers to teach the subject, integrating all aspects of it; and playing a major role in organizing the teaching and the resources of the subject to ensure statutory requirements are covered. The subject manager's role requires 'a considerable investment of time and energy', and although many aspects of the role can be done outside school hours, there are essential aspects of the subject manager's role, such as monitoring of teaching, learning and assessment practices, and also the evaluation of work in the subject against agreed criteria, which require 'non-contact' time during the teaching day.

SUBJECT EXPERTISE

Despite the reduction in the statutory curriculum to be implemented from 1995, OFSTED nevertheless predicts that 'The National Curriculum will, however, continue to be demanding. Reconstituted programmes of study, however detailed, will continue to require subject knowledge which some (perhaps many) primary schoolteachers do not yet possess' (*Primary Matters*: 9). In particular, stretching and challenging children at the top end of the primary school in all subjects will involve 'considerable knowledge, not only of the children themselves, but also of the subject matter which they are learning' (ibid.). In addition, the restructuring of the curriculum now provides schools with 'discretionary' time for teaching one or more National Curriculum subjects to a greater depth, and consequently will demand greater subject expertise of teachers.

Therefore, a key task for primary schools will be to locate amongst the staff current subject expertise, which may be due to teachers' professional development activities in higher education or at local non-accredited level, or the result of long-term enthusiasms. The expertise, which is required in three forms – knowledge of subject content, knowledge of National Curriculum requirements, and knowledge of how to apply the subject in teaching pupils in primary schools – is often hidden. So 'auditing' the subject expertise of all teaching staff and also the Head Teacher is a priority, followed by supporting teachers in developing and sharing their subject expertise, regardless of whether they have formal responsibilities for a particular subject. OFSTED recommends that, in the course of time, the formal responsibilities for each subject should reflect the subject expertise of individual teachers.

In addition, they recommend that schools consider how best to deploy staff to give children access to subject specialism. For example:

1 a class teacher acts as a specialist when they teach a subject in which they have particular expertise to their own class. The main issue is not whether this kind of specialist teaching should take place – it inevitably will! – but how far it should be capitalized upon and made an explicit feature of school policy;

2 a teacher acts as a specialist when they teach a subject to the class of a colleague on an exchange basis. A key issue here is how far the exchange provides the subject specialist teaching for both of the classes involved or whether only one class receives such teaching;

3 an individual teacher may teach a particular subject to a variety of classes while retaining overall responsibility for the work of their own class. This already occurs in some schools in subjects such as music, science or art;

4 an individual teacher may be deployed to teach one subject exclusively. It is fairly rare for maintained primary schools to employ full-time staff in this way; but many smaller schools employ part-time teachers for all of their teaching time on aspects such as music or special needs.

(ibid.: 10)

Primary schools are urged to consider all possible options for offering children full access to the curriculum appropriate to their developing capabilities, and to monitor and evaluate the effectiveness of different approaches tried out.

The use of time needs to be better monitored. Because the prescribed timetable approach tends to be less commonly used in primary schools than in secondary schools, primary teachers rarely audit the time they actually spend on specific subjects. The integration of the curriculum, and the dominance of the class-teacher system contribute to the lack of effective and systematic audits of time spent teaching each subject. However, OFSTED notes that inspection findings reveal considerable variation in the time spent on different parts of the curriculum, and recommend that schools should estimate how much time should be spent on each subject in each class, and for the Head Teacher, aided by subject managers, to monitor this. The overview should include analysis of 'start-up time' and any slippage of time at the beginning or end of activities (including time spent on registration and moving to and from the playground, dinner hall or specialist teaching areas), the pace of work, resourcing and 'time on task', as well as the length of the taught week, since, according to OFSTED, 'in primary schools with shorter taught weeks, the time allocation for some subjects is often too short to give the National Curriculum the necessary coverage to pave the way for pupils to achieve higher standards' (ibid.: 11).

The use of time should be seen as flexible, and needs to be skilfully manipulated to include a balance between direct teaching and intensive but indirect study, so that 'the time the pupils spend learning includes but overruns the time in which they are [directly] taught by the teacher' (ibid.); this may include planning homework, which does not tie all learning to the hours a child spends in school.

CURRICULUM ORGANIZATION

Primary schools are urged to consider carefully the balance between subject teaching and topic work, in meeting the requirements of the National Curriculum; and to adopt an appropriate range of topic foci and time frames which allow children's interests to be fostered and followed up, but which also offer scope for progression in subject areas and cumulative understanding of the National Curriculum subjects. Subject-focused topics, now emerging in many schools, offer one way of doing this. However, topic work needs to be 'complemented by alternative modes of curriculum organisation, including separate subject work' (ibid.: 12). OFSTED urges teachers to consider the balance of time given to different subjects within topic or separate subject teaching, and the implications of time allocation for meeting National Curriculum requirements: for example:

> A subject such as mathematics is taught for a considerable period of time daily or almost daily; this is likely to go far in meeting many National Curriculum requirements but cannot be offered for more than two or three subjects because of time constraints. Some subjects such as music or physical education are taught once or twice a week in short time slots; this approach is likely to help pupils meet some curriculum requirements but not all.
>
> (ibid.)

TEACHING THE BASICS OF LEARNING

The paper suggests that the 'basics of learning' for effective functioning in the twenty-first century will include literacy, oracy, numeracy and basic competence in the use of information technology. OFSTED draws attention to advice given in the Dearing Report that schools should seriously consider using discretionary time to support work in these aspects of basic learning.

There is a need for teachers and parents to clarify and gain a deeper understanding of what 'the basics of learning' actually involve, and it is for schools to define 'the thresholds of that basic learning, particularly at ages 7 and 11, in terms which are readily understandable to parents' (ibid.: 13) since this will help parents to form realistic expectations of both their child's progress, and the school's performance.

The paper calls for each school to take a lead in defining and spelling out the basics of learning 'which should be secure by all pupils by the end of Key Stage 2' (ibid.), giving particular attention to keeping pace with the rising criteria which our society demands.

Finally, teachers and schools are urged to prioritize the management and evaluation of the primary curriculum and its teaching and assessment.

REFERENCE

OFSTED (1994) *Primary Matters: A Discussion on Teaching and Learning in Primary Schools*, London: Office for Standards in Education.

The original document can be obtained, free of charge, from OFSTED Publications Centre, PO Box 6927, London E3 3NZ, tel. 0171-510 0180.

Chapter 14

International developments in assessment

Keith Morrison

Morrison's chapter traces a number of similar trends in assessment across countries as geographically widespread as the USA, UK and New Zealand, and as culturally disparate as Germany, Saudi Arabia, Italy, Bulgaria, Ethiopia, Lesotho, Malawi, Swaziland and Zambia. Based on the increasing importance being placed on assessment, its practice and purposes, he puts forward an international agenda for debate in the field.*

INTRODUCTION

Nearly two decades ago Dore (1976) remarked on the increasing credentialist spiral which was gripping nations across the world. He observed the systematic sacrifice of creativity, curiosity and the development of the whole person to a ritualistic, tedious, anti-educational reduction of education to mere qualification-earning. The scene has changed little since then: not only has the significance of assessment risen on the international scene but the anxieties voiced by Dore seem not to have been heeded. The message of this paper reaffirms Dore's concern and argues that, though there is a uniformity of concern about and practices in assessment across nations, there is considerable room for diversity to be introduced. Further, this diversity will enable assessment to become more differentiated and thereby redress the problems of validity and reliability in assessments which appear to be increasing on an international level. Diversity in assessment provides an agenda for developing assessment which can replace Dore's stark pessimism with an optimism of opportunity.

Optimism springs from the recognition that assessment can serve the purposes of: (a) educational improvement: (b) increased school effectiveness; (c) curriculum reform.

Anxiety stems from the observable international trends of using assessment for the purposes of: (a) political control of teachers, students and curricula

* Originally published as 'Uniformity and diversity in assessment: an international perspective and agenda', *Compare* (1994) 24 (1), Oxford: Carfax Publishing Ltd.

(e.g. McLean, 1988; Harnisch and Mabry, 1993); (b) centralized policy-making (ibid.); (c) narrow accountability (e.g. Gipps, 1988; Noah and Eckstein, 1988); (d) credentialism (e.g. Singh *et al.*, 1988); (e) educational selection (e.g. Halsey, 1992); (f) the determination of life chances in competitive markets (e.g. Okano, 1993).

Furthermore assessment is becoming redefined internationally as testing (Harnisch and Mabry, 1993), diagnostic and formative assessment are being overtaken by summative examinations. The message deriving from an international analysis of assessment is as promising as it is salutary: to change assessment is to enhance its validity and broaden its purposes, contents, formats and uses in educational, political and economic contexts. From an international perspective this paper demonstrates that many nations, regardless of location or stage of development, appear to be treading a similar path in developing assessment, the differences between them being only in the time they take to reach the same end. The single path is to an increasing national control of assessment, an increasing uniformity of styles and practices of assessment, an increasing importance of assessment, an increasing amount of assessment activity, an increasing scope of assessment, and a uniformity of purposes of assessment.

Two stages on this path can be identified. Stage one sees the development of extensive centralized systems and frameworks of testing and assessment which are administered institutionally, which are characterized by detailed assessment foci and criteria and which constitute a return to the behavioural objectives movement. This stage also accords a role to teachers' assessments of students. Stage two includes national and teacher-derived assessments which, though different from stage one in the widening of the foci beyond the academic and vocational to include a range of non-cognitive qualities and extra-curricular achievements, nevertheless indicate a sympathy withbehaviourism.

This uniformity is scarcely surprising for one can detect a common set of features of societies. Parkes (1990) suggests that across all countries, regardless of whether they are first, second or third world, the following characteristics obtain: (a) centralization and decentralization are occurring simultaneously; (b) privatization and soft-money schemes are a feature of all systems; (c) a market ideology exists with emphasis placed on competition and employers' interests; (d) the location of decision-making is in corporate institutions.

This diminishes the resources available to the public sector and, in its wake, brings extensive accountability, quality control measures and performance indicators. The educational instrument in which all of these features find a focus is assessment. It is little wonder, then, that assessment has aroused international attention for its putative educational and economic benefits. However, the message of this paper is unsettling. It suggests not only an inexorability of the development and usage of assessments which patterns itself across nations, but that this very patterning represents a uniformity of development at a time when the potential for a differentiated response to similar situations is possible. In this context developing countries are emulating the practices of the developed countries, indeed they can become better at playing the western system than countries in the west (e.g. Goodman's, 1992, account of Japanese education). This paper identifies the realms in which uniformity and diversity of assessment exist and, from an analysis of international trends, indicates how diversity and uniformity might coexist in the interests of educational development.

There are two key questions which stem from an analysis of practices in several nations:

- How can a balance be struck between uniformity and diversity of assessment purposes and practices?
- How can the striking of this balance serve a view of education as an opening rather than closing of doors to opportunity?

This paper addresses these questions by setting out four areas (sets of practices) in which uniformity exists but in which diversity could be introduced. For each area the paper provides an agenda for debate about assessment in form and function. The suggestion here is that a uniform attention to purposes of assessment does not require a uniformity of response and that a diversity of responses might be more fitting for assessment to serve diverse purposes of education.

THE LOCUS OF CONTROL OF ASSESSMENT

One can observe on an international level an overt and developed centralization of control of assessment, with a direct relationship existing between the significance accorded to assessment and the degree of centralized control of assessment.

At the extreme of uniformity is the *sole* use of national examinations (for example in China – Singer, 1990a) and the *extensive* use of national examinations, for example in the US (Harnisch and Mabry, 1993), the UK and New Zealand – where the Minister of Education publishes national achievement standards (Lee, 1992).

At the extreme of devolution is the practice in Austria (Gruber, 1992) where transition to secondary school is contingent upon successful grades which primary school teachers award subjectively, with no moderation across the country. Gruber draws attention to the low incidence of low grades and the high incidence of high grades in Austria, a feature matched in kind in the UK by the central tendency in using Likert scales to record achievements which has been observed in teachers' rating of students (Nixon, 1990). Further, in Italy an anomalous feature exists where national examinations are prescribed but no national criteria are available for marking (Ferraris and

Persico, 1990). The extent of decentralization and centralization of assessment is phase-specific; typically the older the student is the more formal and centralized is the assessment system, culminating in the national examinations at the end of a student's secondary school career.

The issue of control, however, is capable of different interpretations. In the example of China, control of the contents of examinations, their marking and consequent determination of results is undertaken at a national level. Control here is extensive. A similar practice exists in the US, where tests are developed, disseminated and marked by commercial companies (Harnisch and Mabry, 1993). In some countries this is attenuated in two ways, either by providing a national framework within which teachers' assessments are undertaken, or by combining national and teacher assessments.

Examples of the former are the many continuous assessment schemes which provide (a) national criteria for teachers to use; and (b) the grades and scores to be awarded for performance using these criteria. If national awards or transition from one school to another or to higher education are to be based on continuous assessment (through staged examinations or course work) then this requires extensive preparation of teachers in order to control the assessment process itself (cf. Pennycuick, 1991).

Examples of the latter are the attempts which have been made to combine national examinations with teachers' assessments of students (e.g. Sweden, the UK, Germany, New Zealand). In the UK students are compulsorily examined at four points in their school careers – at ages 7, 11, 14 and 16 – with the examination being a composite of national tests and teachers' assessments. In this context procedures for moderation are vital (Pennycuick, 1991) if parity across teachers, schools and regions is to be established – a feature which Pennycuick (1991) sees as important for developing countries. Indeed if this latter requirement does not obtain then an external examination might be fairer to students than poorly moderated continuous teacher assessments (Brooke and Oxenham, 1984).

A variant of this can be seen in Germany which, since 1954, has required teachers to grade their students formally twice a year using a national six-point scale (*Notenskala* – DES, 1986): 1 = very good; 2 = good; 3 = satisfactory; 4 = adequate; 5 = poor; 6 = very poor. Here teachers' gradings are a legal administrative act from the second year of primary education (Phillips, 1991).

A similar system can be observed in Saudi Arabian schools where a five-point scale is used – poor, acceptable, good, very good, excellent and in Italy where a ten-point scale is used for national examinations (Ferraris and Persico, 1990). Clearly a moderation exercise is required here if parity of standards and the reliability of results are to be ensured.

A balance between a uniform, objective national system or framework and a local assessment is an attempt to embrace the notion of parity of standards on the one hand and a person-centred approach to assessment which recognizes teachers' professionalism and the rights and individuality of students on the other.

It is possible to site the control of education not only at national and teacher levels but at the level of the students themselves, for example in the Records of Achievement (ROA) movement and its development into action planning and unit accreditation in the UK. In action planning students themselves set their own learning targets and review their achievements of these to complete a self-referenced report (an ipsative process); this process can be managed by introducing flexible learning arrangements (contingent upon resources and technology). In unit accreditation students and schools can have self-generated modules accredited towards an award given by a nationally approved accreditation or examination agency. The motivational potential for students is high here as this process involves them directly as decision-makers rather than as decision-receivers (cf. Kowalski's, 1990, evaluation of students' self-assessments in National Vocational Qualifications in the UK). Indeed Weston (1988) sees in ROAs a new dawn of motivation at an international level, though Hargreaves (1989) is less sanguine, arguing that ROAs are a sop to the disaffected in a time of an international crisis of motivation.

The implications of this analysis are to suggest that a balance can be struck between national and institutional control of assessment provided that the frameworks for this are clarified, and provided that adequate communication channels between all parties both exist and are used as part of an open, democratic process. The purposes of assessment need to be clarified and consensus reached on them; of particular import here is the debate about the legitimacy of using assessment for specified purposes, that is, addressing questions of validity and reliability and rationalizing the uses of assessment, developing new forms of assessment for emerging situations and keeping the uses of assessment close to the sources of assessment data.

THE STYLE OF ASSESSMENT

An international perspective on assessment reveals that the higher the significance which is accorded to assessment, the greater is the use of machine-scorable, closed-format styles of nationally prescribed examinations. The uniform rise in interest in assessment internationally has been met with limited diversity of response. At one extreme is the burgeoning rise of the closed multiple-choice, cloze procedure style and 'tick-box' forms of assessment which focus on low-level recall of factual knowledge, where content is elevated over skills and where assessment is largely undertaken by written examination. In Bulgaria this is taken a stage further (Sendov and Eskenasi, 1990: 61) where students work on multiple-choice tests which are displayed on a micro-computer rather than on a hard copy.

At the other extreme is the open-ended profile of achievements which teachers and students keep and which draws on a variety of assessment evidence – written or otherwise – and which is used to record the whole gamut of achievements of a student (for example, academic, social, extra-curricular).

One can detect an international trend in using a uniform type of assessment which has its roots in the behavioural objectives movement in the US. This style of assessment is evidenced in the concept of 'mastery learning', the use of checklists of 'competencies' and a 'blank-filling' style of examination, bringing with it the spectre of the commodification of curricula and a return to Taylorism (Smith, 1990). This objective style of assessment can be used to assess and compare vast numbers of students quickly, that is, to 'process' students.

The purchase of optical mark readers in the UK (Singer, 1990a) which are capable of scanning and processing up to 10,000 forms per hour, and the development of machine-scorable examinations in China (Singer, 1990b) and the US (Harnisch and Mabry, 1993) which are cheap to administer are indices of the increasing reliance on this style of assessment. Marks are aggregated to give an overall score, grade or level in a subject (for example in the assessment of a child's achievement of the National Curriculum in the UK or of examinations taken at the point of transition in Italy), a process which degrades data and thereby reduces validity.

The negative aspects of this style of assessment are legion: the diminishing of education to training students to perform certain prescribed behaviours, the emphasis on outcomes rather than processes (e.g. Nixon, 1990: 90), the passive nature of learning, the elevation of trivial, observable, measurable, short-term behaviours over serious, high-order, unmeasurable, creative, person-oriented, open-ended, lifelong aspects of education. One is reminded of Wittgenstein's words: 'when all *possible* scientific questions have been answered, the problems of life remain completely untouched' (Wittgenstein, 1961: 73). The move towards criterion-referenced assessments, whilst it addresses validity in requiring 'evidence' to inform teachers' assessments, does not herald a move away from behaviourism, rather it provides teachers with more to measure, more to assess.

At the opposite pole of behaviourism is the open-ended profile of students' achievements which is evidenced in ROAs in the UK. Here assessments include the 'non-cognitive' qualities of students, grades awarded in formal examination, and a whole profile of a student's achievements and awards – curricular and extra-curricular, personal, social, community-based and academic. Whilst these have the attraction of being a personalized portfolio which motivates their owners, they carry the risk of building in the prejudices and biases of teachers, of including illegitimate, value-laden and generalized statements (Law, 1984) and of being insufficiently discriminating in their coverage of the significant and the trivial. Furthermore, completing this open-ended record is time-consuming.

The rise of information technology threatens the open-ended profile or ROA as schools can draw upon word and phrase banks to comment on all aspects of a student – cognitive, affective, social, emotional etc. The use of technology risks the furtherance of a technicist mentality, where the desire to control – teachers, curricula, assessment – (Olson, 1989) is reproduced in the increased 'surveillance' of students (Hargreaves, 1989) afforded by profiling systems and the use of information technology in their development.

Where education has a high political profile the first casualties in assessment are validity and reliability. For example, the UK has witnessed criterion-referenced assessment data being used not as they were intended – for diagnostic and formative purposes – but being used normatively to compare school with school in a published 'league table' of results, a practice which is replicated in the US (Harnisch and Mabry, 1993). That this is a working out of a political ideology is evidenced in the expressed intention of the UK government to operate a market system in education and simply to ignore advice from those 'professionals' in education who express severe doubts about the validity and reliability of such assessments (Simon, 1988; James and Conner, 1992). Operating a market model of education with assessment at its core can be politically astute, as focusing attention on assessment can be used as a diversionary tactic to avoid attention being placed on resourcing schools. The full working out of a market model of education – an input/output model – will have to accept that attention to assessable output alone is insufficient; the input of resources is equally important.

Striking a balance between uniformity and diversity of styles of assessment requires the recognition of built-in limitations of specific assessment instruments. Furthermore the style of assessment has to take account of issues of equal opportunities. For example, in the UK the Department of Education and Science (DES, 1988) indicated that boys performed better in multiple-choice examinations than girls, and that girls performed better in written work than boys. Goulding (1992) indicated that continuous assessment of course work enabled a truer picture of girls' achievements in mathematics to be presented than that yielded by results on a written examination.

The issue to be addressed in selecting the style of assessment is 'fitness for purpose' – which types of assessment are most suitable for particular purposes of assessment. This is fundamental as it requires assessments to address construct, content and predictive validity and reliability. On an international plane one can see these principles being violated systematically – structurally – where inappropriate assessment evidence is used within and beyond education (Oxenham, 1984a), that is, where construct, content and predictive validity are violated. Validity is further threatened when a spurious score or measurement is accorded to a non-measurable quality, a very clear problem in attempting to assess non-cognitive characteristics in social and emotional development or qualities of personality (for example, leadership, cooperation, perseverance).

THE IMPORTANCE OF ASSESSMENT

According too little importance to assessment might result in its being seen as purposeless, providing little incentive for students to work hard (Rosenbaum and Kariya, 1991). According too much importance to assessment is also problematical. For example in Bhutan (Bailey, 1990), Italy (Ferraris and Persico, 1990) and Israel (Meir and Adler, 1990), progress to the next stage of schooling or to higher education hinges on the results of assessments. Successful achievement in the German system can provide automatic access to the next year of schooling, acceleration through the school, transfer to the next school and entrance to higher education (DES, 1986; OFSTED, 1993), a feature which is found in educational systems from Bahrain (Shirawi, 1989) to Denmark (Hansen, 1990). In Poland school leavers can apply for higher education upon successful completion of final examinations to obtain a Certificate of maturity (Siemak-Tylikowska, 1993). Unsuccessful achievement in the German system can result in students repeating a year or removing to another type of school. Unsatisfactory achievement in Niger can result in students leaving education altogether at the end of the period of elementary education (Goumandakoye, 1992: 54–5). Kellaghan (1988), reporting on Ethiopia, Lesotho, Malawi, Swaziland and Zambia, suggests that selection for higher education is seen by these countries as a legitimate purpose of the examination system in order to allocate scarce resources meritocratically. Assessments, then, have a very clear selective function regardless of whether the countries form part of the developing or developed world. Given this degree of importance, attention must be given to validity and reliability if fairness is to be addressed.

The use of assessments for selection does not remain simply in the field of education, that is, to enable students to have more education; assessments have a very powerful selective function in the jobs market. Rosenbaum and Kariya (1991) show that Japanese employers make much use of grades and complement these with their own aptitude tests, general knowledge tests and interviews (Okano, 1993). Rosenbaum and Kariya comment on the incentive that the extended use of grades provides for Japanese students, a feature which is not apparent amongst American youth, where employment is less reliant on grades.

In several countries the relationship between education and the employment market is paradoxical. Oxenham (1984) cites evidence from Sri Lanka, Tanzania, Ghana and China which suggests that, though one legitimate task of schools is to sort and select students for future employment and, thereby, for life chances, the nature of the assessments actually suppresses those qualities most needed for future employment. These include initiative, flexibility, adaptability, enterprise, creativity, problem-solving ability and autonomous working. In these countries, students at the point of examination are required to demonstrate the low-level recall of factual knowledge in multiple-choice questions as outlined earlier in this chapter. Predictive validity is reinterpreted here to mean using inappropriate data predictively. In these circumstances the validity of test items has to be developed.

Singh *et al.* (1988), in their study of Malaysian education, indicate that, whilst credentials still provide important criteria for job selection, employers – particularly those in the private sector – look for personal qualities and skill performance which are not tapped by qualifications. The ROA movement in the UK is an example of an assessment system which documents a wide range of achievements and experiences and which can be made available to potential employers upon request, thereby attempting to avoid the building-in of bias of undeclared criteria for job selection by employers.

This latter example goes to the very heart of assessment – the questions of validity and ethics of assessment – as information acquired for one set of purposes, for example motivation, diagnosis and action planning, in fact might be used for another set of purposes, for example selection, competition, employment and unemployment. The provision of an extended profile of achievements and personal qualities might simply provide employers and higher education with more evidence to use against a student rather than for the student as was intended.

Credentials and the results of assessments, then, can serve disparate purposes. The implications of this discussion are clear: it is necessary to ensure that the purposes of credentials are made very clear, that the significance accorded to them is fair, that they are used as they were intended to be used (and that this is made public to all participants and users), and that they are valid indicators of the qualities and abilities required by those using them – employers, teachers, Head Teachers, interviewers for higher education. There is a moral argument about civil liberties to be addressed in the use of assessment results which says that those whose results they are should have control over these data and the ways in which they may be used.

In striving to achieve a balance of importance afforded to assessments the criterion of fitness for purpose must be applied in order to avoid overburdening the results of assessments with implications that they are not able to sustain. In particular the roles, contents and range of educational qualifications and assessments in the jobs market is an agenda for research, clarification, debate and problematization.

The preceding argument has suggested that a uniformity of purposes of assessments has to be balanced by a diversity of ways of achieving these purposes, that infrastructures of support are in place, and that the machinery to manage such diversity is morally defensible. If assessments are to be used for prediction and selection then the contents of those assessments should fairly embody and address the elements of the post-selection activities for which they are being used, be this in relation to further and higher education, employment and adult life.

The continuity between purposes, contents and styles of assessment recognizes that manifold opportunities exist for the development of extensive, subtle, focused, differentiated, relevant, specific forms and contents of assessment and that these should derive from a careful and specific evaluation of the purpose of education and of the roles of assessment within it, for only crude use can be made of crude assessments. Opportunities are immense to extend the vision and development of assessment so that not only is fitness for purpose addressed but these purposes themselves are subject to scrutiny.

In this latter respect there are very serious questions to be put against the value of those international studies of educational achievement which strive to compare one nation's educational achievements with another's. These studies frequently rely on crude aggregations (Watson, 1992: 127) and generalizations which, though they might be politically useful, are educationally suspect, being simplistic, lacking in explanatory potential or diagnosis, ignoring context-specificity – human and cultural – of education, and furthering a competitive mentality and a market view of education. McLean's (1988) analysis of IEA studies of achievement in 17 countries exposes these problematical elements, echoed by Broadfoot and Osborn (1992) in their identification of problems of context, conceptual equivalence, equivalence of measurement and sampling in cross-cultural studies.

THE AMOUNT OF ASSESSMENT

The amount of assessment is clearly a function of the importance attached to it. Where there are vast quantities of assessment with a vast amount hinging on the results this can lead beyond the flourishing of private home tuition reported in Austria (Gruber, 1992) to the nightmare of the 'cram' schools (Goodman, 1992), 'examination hell' (Beauchamp, 1991), the 'grey youth' syndrome and the over-burdening of learning which is evidenced in Japan and which starves many young children of their childhood (Dore and Sako, 1989). Calvani (1990), commenting on the Italian system, sees the obsession with scoring everything as running a significant risk of fragmenting learning; one could add to this the fear that in such a situation people simply become a sum of their measurable parts.

One can see that the current increase in assessment inflates the credentialist spiral, operates from a zero-sum model of success and is a reaffirmation of human capital theory (cf. Oxenham, 1984) the value of which was questioned over a decade ago for its inability to address structural inequalities and privileges in society (cf. Hughes and Lauder, 1990). Here the work of Bourdieu on the 'cultural capital thesis' (Bourdieu, 1976), which charts very clearly how credentialism is socially reproductive rather than transformative, is brought up to date by Halsey (1992) who demonstrates that because of rising credentialism access to higher education becomes an arena for status struggles between social groups, the effects of which are to perpetuate economic inequality within and between nations.

On the other hand very little assessment can lead to poor diagnosis, poorly matched work and, as a result, an inappropriate, irrelevant curriculum and the lowering of standards of achievement. In the UK the growing attention which is being given to matching is accompanied by increased attention to assessment and diagnostic teaching (Bennett *et al.*, 1984; Schools Examination and Assessment Council, 1990).

Where assessment (continuous or staged) carries great significance it can exert permanent pressure on students and teachers. Further, it causes them to accord little significance to tasks which are not assessed. In Germany the uniformity of a system of assessment which is well understood by teachers, students and parents and which builds on the professionalism of teachers can cause problems of stress in students and fears of the negative aspects of accountability amongst teachers (Phillips, 1991). The undue weight given to assessment in systems like these exerts a conservative backwash effect on curricula, bringing lack of risk-taking by teachers and students and a de-personalization of curricula (cf. Dwyer's, 1988, and Harnisch and Mabry's, 1993, accounts of this in the US and McNaughton's (1988) account of this in New Zealand). Moreover, it is unclear whether the negative effects of undue assessment will undermine the expressed intention behind many of these types of assessment to drive up 'standards'.

Essentially what is being striven for is a balance between using insufficient and thereby invalid evidence formatively and so much assessment that it becomes 'interrogation without end' (Hargreaves, 1989) and a means of providing material to hold teachers accountable for aspects of students' development over which they exercise little or no control.

CONCLUSIONS – AN AGENDA FOR DEBATE

This paper has argued that the diverse issues in assessment are best served not by uniformity but diversity of response. Questions about assessment are contested and contestable yet the international analysis provided here indicates a marked uniformity of response. Opening the assessment issue to debate will address a range of issues:

- the balance of personal, institutional and national control of assessment, which makes full use of teacher professionalism and which builds on staff development;
- the examination of internal, external, construct, content and predictive validity of assessments;
- the clarification of the scope and purposes of assessment instruments;
- the balance of styles of assessment, in particular the reduction of testing and the increase of diagnostic forms of assessment;

- the balance of objective and subjective forms of assessment;
- the promotion of equal opportunities in and through assessment;
- the balance of motivational and demotivational aspects of assessment;
- the balance between over-assessment and under-assessment;
- the provision of infrastructures of support for a democratic approach to planning assessment;
- the identification and interrogation of political uses of assessment;
- the identification and interrogation of the appropriacy of different styles of assessment for selection within and beyond school;
- the examination of reliability of assessments;
- the dangers of credentialism.

What is being sought is an evaluation of assessment – its worth and its uses. Striking the balance between too little and too much assessment requires an identification of areas where assessments are and are not needed, the purposes of the assessment, the types of assessment required, and a move away from over-assessment. The touchstone here should be the clarification of (a) what is a necessary minimum of assessment rather than a possible maximum amount of assessment and (b) how assessment can promote the education of the whole person. Too little assessment is dangerous, too much assessment becomes a bureaucratic nightmare in which the thirst to measure erodes the creative spark in teaching and learning.

REFERENCES

Bailey, J. (1990) 'Educational developments in the mountain kingdom of Bhutan', in C. Bell and D. Harris (eds) (1990).

Beauchamp, E. R. (ed.) (1991) *Windows on Japanese Education*, Westport, CT: Greenwood Press.

Bennett, S. N., Desforges, C., Wilkinson, E. and Cockburn, A. (1984) *The Quality of Pupil Learning Experiences*, London: Lawrence Erlbaum.

Bourdieu, P. (1976) 'The school as a conservative force,' in R. Dale *et al.* (eds), *Schooling and Capitalism*, London: Routledge & Kegan Paul.

Broadfoot, P. and Osborn, M. (1992) 'French lessons: comparative perspectives on what it means to be a teacher', in D. Phillips (ed.) (1992).

Brooke, N. and Oxenham, J. (1984) 'The influence of certification and selection on teaching and learning', in J. Oxenham (ed.) (1984a).

Calvani, A. (1990) 'The area of social history: what to assess and how to assess it', in C. Bell and D. Harris (eds) (1990).

DES (Department of Education and Science) (1986) *Education in the Federal Republic of Germany*, London: HMSO.

—— (1988) *National Curriculum Task Group on Assessment and Testing: a Report*, London: HMSO.

Dore, R. P. (1976) *The Diploma Disease*, London: Unwin Education.

—— and Sako, M. (1989) *How the Japanese Learn to Work*, London: Routledge.

Dwyer, C. A. (1988) 'Trends in the assessment of teaching and learning: educational and methodological perspectives', in P. Broadfoot *et al.* (eds) (1990).

Ferraris, M. and Persico, D. (1990) 'The Italian school system', in C. Bell & D. Harris (eds) (1990).

Gipps, C. (1988) 'National assessment: a comparison of English and American trends', in: P. Broadfoot *et al.* (eds) (1990).

Goodman, R. (1992) 'Japan – pupil turned teacher?' in D. Phillips (ed.) (1992).

Goulding, M. (1992) 'Let's hear it for the girls', *Times Educational Supplement*, 21 February, p. 38.

Goumandakoye, A. Z. (1992) 'An evaluation of secondary education in Niger with particular reference to English language teaching', unpublished PhD thesis, School of Education, University of Durham.

Gruber, K. H. (1992) 'Unlearnt European lessons: why Austria abandoned the comprehensive school experiments and restored the *Gymnasium*', in D. Phillips (ed.) (1992).

Halsey, A. (1992) 'An international comparison of access to higher education', in D. Phillips (ed.) (1992).

Hargreaves, A. (1989) *Curriculum and Assessment Reform*, London: Basil Blackwell/ Open University Press.

Harnisch, D. L. and Mabry, L. (1993) 'Issues in the development and evaluation of alternative assessment', *Journal of Curriculum Studies*, 25: 179–87.

Hughes, D. and Lauder, H. (1990) 'Public examinations and the structuring of inequality', in H. Lauder and C. Wylie (eds), *Towards Successful Schooling*, Basingstoke: Falmer Press.

James, M. and Conner, C. (1993) 'Are reliability and validity achievable in National Curriculum assessment? Some observations on moderation at Key Stage 1 in 1992', *The Curriculum Journal*, 4: 50–20.

Kellaghan, T. (1988) 'Examination systems in Africa', in: P. Broadfoot *et al.* (eds) (1990).

Kowalski, R. (1990) 'Some implications of student choice of course content for the processes of learning, assessment and qualification', in C. Bell and D. Harris (eds) (1990).

Law, B. (1984) *Uses and Abuses of Profiling*, London: Harper & Row.

McLean, L. (1988) 'Possibilities and limitations in cross-national comparisons of educational achievement', in P. Broadfoot *et al.* (eds) (1990).

McNaughton, T. (1988) 'Exam questions: a consideration of consequences of reforms to examining and assessment in Great Britain and New Zealand', in: P. Broadfoot *et al.* (eds) (1990).

Meir, E. I. and Adler. N. (1990) 'Aptitude tests as predictor of success in the Israeli matriculation', in C. Bell and D. Harris (eds) (1990).

Nixon, N. J. (1990) 'Assessment issues in relation to experience-based learning on placements within courses', in C. Bell and D. Harris (eds) (1990).

Noah, H. J. and Eckstein, M. A. (1988) 'Trade-offs in examination policies: an international comparative perspective', in P. Broadfoot *et al.* (eds) (1990).

OFSTED (Office for Standards in Education) (1993) *The Initial Training of Teachers in Two German Länder: Hessen and Rheinland-Pfalz*, London: HMSO.

Okano, K. (1993) *School to Work Transition in Japan*, Clevedon: Multilingual Matters.

Olson, J. (1989) 'The persistence of technical rationality', in G. Milburn, I. Goodson and R. Clark (eds), *Re-interpreting Curriculum Research: Images and Argument*, Lewes: Falmer Press.

Oxenham, J. (ed.) (1984a) *Education Versus Qualification*, London: Unicorn Education.

—— (1984b) 'Employers, jobs and qualifications', in J. Oxenham (ed.) (1984a).

Parkes, D. (1990) 'Strategic planning in educational systems: a comparative perspective', *The Curriculum Journal*, 1: 333–42.

Pennycuick, D. (1991) 'Moderation of continuous assessment systems in developing countries', *Compare*, 21: 145–52.

Phillips, D. (1991) 'Assessment in German schools', *Journal of Curriculum Studies*, 23: 544–8.

—— (ed.) (1992) *Lessons of Cross-national Comparison in Education*, Wallingford: Triangle Books.

Rosenbaum, J. E. and Kariya, T. (1991) 'Do school achievements affect the early jobs of high school graduates in the United States and Japan?' *Sociology of Education*, 64: 78–95.

Schools Examination and Assessment Council (1990) *A Source Book of Teacher Assessment*, London: Heinemann Educational.

Sendov, B. and Eskenasi, A. (1990) 'Educational change and assessment in the age of information technology', in C. Bell and D. Harris (eds) (1990).

Shirawi, M. A. (1989) *Education in Bahrain*, Oxford: Ithaca Press.

Siemak-Tylikowska, A. (1993) 'Curriculum development in secondary education in Poland', *Journal of Curriculum Studies*, 25: 89–93.

Simon, B. (1988) *Bending the Rules: The Baker Reforms of Education*, London: Lawrence & Wishart.

Singer, R. (1990a) 'Profiling: the role of technology', in C. Bell and D. Harris (eds) (1990).

Singh, J. S., Marimuthu, T. and Mukherjee, H. (1988) 'Learning motivation and work: a Malaysian perspective', in P. Broadfoot *et al.* (eds) (1990).

Smith, D. (1990) 'Assessment, technology and the quality revolution', in C. Bell and D. Harris (eds) (1990).

Watson, K. (1992) 'Alternative funding of educational systems: some lessons from third world experiments', in D. Phillips (ed.) (1992).

Weston, P. (1988) 'Assessment, certification and the needs of young people: from badges of failure towards signs of success', in: P. Broadfoot *et al.* (eds) (1990).

Wittgenstein, L. (1961) *Tractatus Logico-Philosophicus*, London: Routledge & Kegan Paul.

Chapter 15

Authentic testing in mathematics

Barry Cooper

*In this chapter, Cooper describes and analyses the 1993 pilots of the SATs in mathematics for 11-year-olds, looking at the presentation of the material to children, and the boundary between common-sense, or everyday, knowledge, and mathematical discourse.**

INTRODUCTION

Mathematics is a key part of the curriculum in all developed educational systems. As such, alongside studies in the dominant language of a society, success and failure in it play an important role in the distribution of educational and more general opportunities to children and young people. Until fairly recently, in England and elsewhere, success in elementary school mathematics was achieved by demonstrating a capacity to memorize, reproduce and use relatively simple algorithms (e.g. for carrying out long division) (Griffiths and Howson, 1974). However, in recent years, there has been considerable change in school mathematics. A number of writers have begun to apply a variety of broadly sociological insights in analysing these changes. They have discussed both the origins of the changes and their consequences, and, more generally, the nature of school mathematics (e.g. Cooper, 1985a; Noss *et al.*, 1990; Abraham and Bibby, 1992). A particular concern has been the relationship between school mathematics and the social origins of pupils studying its various differentiated versions (e.g. Spradberry, 1976; Cooper, 1985b; Ruthven, 1986; Dowling, 1991). It is clear from these studies, as well as from more general considerations, that it is unhelpful to regard either mathematics education or mathematics *per se* as somehow above and beyond the social sphere (Mackenzie, 1981; Bloor, 1991; Restivo, 1991).

Previous studies of change in mathematics education have tended to concentrate on curriculum content and pedagogy, giving less attention to modes

* Originally published as 'Authentic testing in mathematics? The boundary between everyday and mathematical knowledge in National Curriculum testing in English schools', in *Assessment in Education*, vol. 1, no. 2 (1994), Oxford: Carfax Publishing Ltd.

of assessment (though see Griffiths and Howson, 1974; Pennycuick and Murphy, 1988). Now that, in England, we have national testing in mathematics and other subjects, to make possible the government's goal of being able to rank schools as more or less successful, it is of importance that we turn our attention to the nature of the tests and, also, to the likely responses to them of children from different social origins.

TESTING AND THE NATIONAL CURRICULUM IN ENGLAND

In an earlier paper, I discussed National Curriculum testing in mathematics at Key Stage 3 (for 14-year-olds) in relation to the social class of students (Cooper, 1992). In this paper, I want to discuss, against the background of the previous paper and some relevant sociological literature, some aspects of the 1993 mathematics Pilot Tests for Key Stage 2 (for 11-year-olds in the last year of their primary schooling). I will concentrate in particular on questions concerning their boundary between common-sense, everyday knowledge and mathematical discourse. However, before presenting the discussion of these mathematics tests, a brief account of the recent history of the testing component of the English National Curriculum (NC) is offered in order that the reader will be able to understand how the problems to be discussed have arisen.

The government made it clear in 1987 that there was to be a national programme of testing associated with the National Curriculum, to be introduced in the 1988 Education Act. A Task Group on Assessment and Testing (TGAT) was set up to advise on its nature (Gipps, 1992: 1). As Ball (1990: 189) has shown, the nature of the membership of TGAT enabled an 'educationalist' voice to be 're-admitted . . . into the formal corridors of policy making'. The TGAT proposals (DES/WO, 1988) are perhaps best seen as an attempt to argue for 'authentic assessment'[1] (Torrance, 1993) in a context where key political forces — especially those of the New Right advising the Conservative Government — were arguing for relatively simple paper and pencil tests of limited educational objectives as their preferred model of National Curriculum assessment (Ball, 1990). The proposed TGAT model emphasized continuous assessment by teachers which would be moderated by externally set Standard Assessment Tasks (SATs) at the end of four Key Stages (i.e. at ages 7, 11, 14, and 16). The subjects of the curriculum were to be set out via Attainment Targets (ATs) and associated Statements of Attainment (SoAs), with 10 levels of attainment, but it is important to stress, given later developments, that TGAT did not intend that all the ATs would be tested via the SATs but rather that a limited number of 'profile components' (within which various ATs would be grouped) would be the focus of testing.

The immediate debate over the proposals — in which the then Prime Minister Margaret Thatcher played a key role — led to a shift towards the privileging of external assessment over continuous assessment by teachers. Notwithstanding this, the SATs were still, at this stage, intended to be much more than paper and pencil tests. It was expected that they would involve a variety of practical and investigative activities. The TGAT proposals did not only, however, come under attack from Mrs Thatcher and the New Right. TGAT had originally intended that the SATs would sample a range of ATs but not that there would be comprehensive coverage of all of them. The intended purpose of the SATs was to moderate, at the level of the class, a teacher's own continuous assessment of pupils. However, government policy shifted this position to one where, by 1990/91, there was to be some written testing in controlled conditions of all pupils in each AT except where the nature of the AT made this obviously inappropriate[2] (Brown, 1992: 13–14). As a result of this political demand for more comprehensive testing, and given the relatively complex test items which TGAT's preference for 'authentic assessment' led to, the initial trials of the NC tests led to considerable teacher disquiet over 'excessive' workloads (Torrance, 1993). Eventually, as the trials spread from primary into secondary schools, this was to lead to a teacher boycott of testing in 1993 (with the result that, typically, although the tests to be discussed in this paper were often used by teachers with their pupils, their results were not reported to government). The results of these shifts, coupled with the pressure on test developers to respond to such changes within very tight deadlines (Brown, 1992), were that, by 1992, paper and pencil tests were being produced that involved contrived tasks which tended to compromise 'good practice' as set out, in the case of mathematics, in the influential Cockcroft Report[3] of 1982 (Cooper, 1992).

BERNSTEIN ON CLASSIFICATION AND FRAMING

Since Bernstein's theoretical work on educational knowledge codes has probably been the most significant single influence on recent work concerning the boundary between common-sense knowledge and school knowledge, I shall begin by briefly describing his analytic framework as it was originally set out in 1971, in order to be able to return to it after the discussion of particular mathematics test items in the middle section of the paper.

In his seminal paper, 'On the classification and framing of educational knowledge', Bernstein (1971) distinguished three component 'message systems' of formal educational knowledge: curriculum, pedagogy and evaluation. The first defined what counted as valid knowledge, the second what counted as a valid transmission of this knowledge and the third what 'counted as a valid realisation of this knowledge on the part of the taught'. It is with the last that this paper will be particularly concerned. He went on to introduce the term 'educational knowledge code' to refer to the 'underlying principles' shaping any particular configuration of curriculum, pedagogy and evaluation. The terms *classification* (referring to the degree of boundary maintenance between curriculum contents) and *framing* (referring to the degree of control teacher and pupil possess over the selection, organization and pacing of the knowledge transmitted and received in the pedagogical relationship) were then introduced to provide a way of conceptualizing the various codes. Two broad types of curriculum were described. One, the *collection type*, was characterized by having curriculum contents 'clearly bounded and insulated from each other', while in the case of the *integrated type* the strength of these boundary relations was less, with contents standing in a more open relationship with one another.[4]

A particular focus of his subsequent discussion was the relationship between the 'uncommonsense knowledge of the school and the common-sense knowledge, everyday community knowledge, of the pupil, his family and his peer group' (ibid.: 58). He wrote:

> I suggest that the frames of the collection code, very early in the child's life, socialise him into knowledge frames which discourage connections with everyday realities, or that there is a highly selective screening of the connection. Through such socialisation, the pupil soon learns what of the outside may be brought into the pedagogical frame. Such framing also makes of educational knowledge something not ordinary or mundane, but something esoteric which gives a special significance to those who possess it.

He went on to suggest that any weakening of this frame within school classrooms usually occurred with 'less able' children and for purposes of social control.

It seems that, although this relationship is discussed as an aspect of framing rather than classification, the point at stake concerns the strength and the policing of a particular boundary. Subsequently, drawing on Bernstein's insights, Dowling (1991), in a detailed examination of the much-used English secondary mathematics text SMP 11–16, has drawn our attention to the ways in which this boundary between everyday and mathematical discourse is treated differently in the SMP Y and G series, respectively aimed at different 'ability' groups (and therefore, implicitly at least, at pupils from different social origins).

CHANGES IN ENGLISH MATHEMATICS EDUCATION

It was during the period that Bernstein was developing these concepts that English mathematics education was undergoing a period of reform (Cooper, 1985a; Watson, 1976). Some of the individuals and groups involved in the movement to reform school mathematics, especially those involved with the Association of Teachers of Mathematics – partly under the influence of Piagetian psychological perspectives – were concerned to introduce more 'practical' work into school mathematics. When compared to the changes that occurred in curriculum content, their initial success was limited – especially within the secondary sector, probably because of the widespread assumption within English mathematics education that 'practical' work was only necessary for the 'less able' pupil (HMI, 1979, 1980; Cooper, 1985b). More recently however, as a result of the legitimation of 'practical', 'problem-solving' and 'investigational' approaches by the Cockcroft Report (1982) and their subsequent (perhaps temporary) institutionalization in the General Certificate of Secondary Education (GCSE) examination, those favouring such approaches in school mathematics have made considerable progress towards seeing their goals achieved (Cooper, 1994). As a result, although investigational work in particular was often situated entirely within 'esoteric' mathematical discourse[5], it had become more likely that children, in their 'mathematical' work, would have opportunities to import aspects of everyday 'non-mathematical' discourse into their classrooms. This shift, at least at the rhetorical level of official discourse about mathematics education, can be illustrated by a quotation from the follow-up by Her Majesty's Inspectorate (HMI, 1985) to the Cockcroft Report. Under the subheading of 'problem-solving', they wrote:

> The process of starting with a real problem, abstracting and solving a corresponding mathematical problem and then checking its solutions in the practical situation is often called mathematical modelling. It is worth stressing to pupils that, in real life, mathematical solutions to problems have often to be judged by criteria of a non-mathematical nature, some of which may be political, moral or social. For example, the most direct route for a proposed new stretch of motorway might be unacceptable as it would cut across a heavily built-up area.
>
> (1985: 41)

Associated with this shift there was also a move, again at least at the rhetorical level, away from the certainty of 'right answers' previously associated with school mathematics. Preceding the above quotation we find:

> Problems should be chosen with a range of possible outcomes: some problems have a unique solution; some have no solution; others would have a solution if more information were available; many will have several solutions and the merit of each may need to be assessed.
>
> (ibid.)

Teachers following HMI's guidance were clearly expected to encourage children to raise a range of questions and consider a wide range of possibilities when approaching 'problem-solving'. Notwithstanding the downgrading of Profile Component Three, which had been concerned with mathematical processes and personal qualities (Ball, 1990; Ernest, 1992: 47), in the early revisions of the draft mathematics National Curriculum, some of this concern remains under *Attainment Target 1: using and applying mathematics* and in particular in the original Non-Statutory Guidance issued to schools (NCC, 1989).

It is therefore possible, notwithstanding Bernstein's suggestion that, within collection codes, it is only very late in the learner's career that s/he is introduced to the provisionality of knowledge claims, that there was some shift in the 1980s towards a limited undermining of the authority of purely mathematical solutions to problems posed in mathematics classrooms. In those cases where such developments occurred, they will sometimes have existed as an 'add on' process, with the 'political, moral or social concerns' being addressed after mathematics proper had done its work. In other cases, a more integrated process may have occurred (see Frankenstein, 1989, for North American examples of such an approach).

Such developments in mathematics teaching are now threatened by those developments in testing associated with the introduction of the National Curriculum which I described earlier (Dowling and Noss, 1990). In the earlier paper, I attempted to show that the tests for 14-year-old pupils, piloted nationally in 1992, contained items that ran counter to much of the rhetoric concerning 'good practice' of the 1980s (Cooper, 1992). Here, after briefly illustrating the nature of the criticisms raised in that paper, I want to consider the pilot tests for 11-year-old pupils which were intended to be trialled in the summer of 1993. I want to consider the ways in which the boundary between the 'real' common-sense, everyday world and the world of purely mathematical discourse presents itself in these tests. I shall also consider, in an illustrative way, how the strength of this boundary varies with the particular National Curriculum level of achievement targeted by each test item. This will enable some light to be thrown on Bernstein's claims about the way in which the boundary between common-sense and school knowledge is drawn under the regime of a collection code – which the National Curriculum in England certainly is.

THE KEY STAGE 2 MATHEMATICS TESTS: AN INTRODUCTORY OUTLINE

It is important to note, straightaway, that the tests are not intended to test children's attainment in *Attainment Target 1: using and applying mathematics* (SEAC, 1993a). They are designed to test Mathematics Targets *2: number, 3: algebra, 4: shape and space,* and *5: handling data.* This characteristic is shared with the previous year's Key Stage 3 Pilot Tests. It is intended that AT1 will be assessed by different means.

More generally, the test items seem to have been designed on the assumption that children's skills in mathematics can be tested in a relatively compartmentalized way. Apart from the 'Quick response' section in which children are tested on number bonds via a flashcard approach, the items are

Table 15.1

	Book A (Ma2/Ma3)	Book B (Ma4/Ma5)
Target levels	1–2 (+ extension 3)	1–2 (+ extension 3)
Target levels	3,4,5	3,4,5

Book C This is an extension test which covers Ma2, 3, 4 and 5 at Level 6

Source: SEAC, 1993a

organized into five booklets, covering different Attainment Targets and different levels of attainment (see Table 15.1).

It is interesting to note that Book C, for level 6, represents a minor move towards less compartmentalization of skills in that the four Attainment Targets are located in one book as opposed to being split between two. However, this is more apparent than real since each item within Book C, as in the case of those in Books A and B, is associated in the marking scheme with a single Statement of Attainment (SoA).

The designers of the tests have positioned the items (in both versions of Books A and B but not, significantly, in Book C) in two 'real life' contexts – 'The School Trip' and 'Westwood School'. Partly as a result of this, and notwithstanding the explicit non-testing of AT1, many of the test items seem, to the 'common-sense' eye, concerned with the use and application of mathematics. Nevertheless, from an examination of the marking scheme, it would seem that children are implicitly expected, with very few exceptions, to bracket out any of their AT1-relevant 'skills' during these pencil and paper tests. Some examples of this will be discussed later. This decision thus to contextualize the items, presumably taken as a gesture in the direction of 'good practice' in the primary school, will be seen to raise similar potential difficulties to those characteristic of several KS3 items in 1992 (Cooper, 1992).

Alongside any difficulties caused by the compartmentalization of skills into five Attainment Targets (ATs), we also have to consider the problems raised by the attempt to characterize each AT by Statements of Attainment at different levels of difficulty. There has been a range of critical discussion of the way in which the National Curriculum is differentiated by 'attainment' via 10 levels of attainment, both generally (Davis, 1990) and in the case of mathematics in particular (Howson, 1989; Dowling and Noss, 1990). One of the difficulties – a lack of any clear and unambiguous progression between levels – can be illustrated by looking at an example which will receive more detailed discussion when particular test items are considered below. Under 'Probability', which is Strand (iii) of AT5, 'Handling Data', we have for levels 2, 3, 4, 5 and 6 respectively, the following statements of attainment:

- level 2: recognize that there is a degree of uncertainty about the outcome of some events but that others are certain or impossible;
- level 3: use appropriate language to justify decisions when placing events in order of 'likelihood';
- level 4: estimate and justify the probability of an event;
- level 5: use an appropriate method for estimating probabilities;
- level 6: identify all the outcomes of combining two independent events *and* know that the total probability of all the mutually exclusive outcomes of an event is 1.

Is there a clear progression as we move from levels 2 to 6? Consider levels 3, 4 and 5. While levels 4 and 5 seem to ask for more exactness than level 3, in that they refer to 'probability' – implying a number is required – rather than merely an ordering of 'likelihood', it is not so clear what the difference is between level 4 and level 5. Both require the estimation of 'probabilities'. Level 4 asks for a 'justifying' of this, while level 5 requests an 'appropriate' method. It seems at least arguable that justifying is a higher-order activity than merely choosing an appropriate method, that is that level 4 demands a higher-level skill here than 5. We shall see later in this paper how this problem is actually addressed in the design of the relevant test items. For now, it is enough to note that, because of the ambiguity inherent in these SoAs, there is considerable scope for the designers of test items and associated marking schemes to import their beliefs about mathematical 'ability' into their work.

THE 'REALITY' PROBLEM IN THE 1992 KS3 TESTS: AN ILLUSTRATION

Before moving on to discuss some aspects of the KS2 items, I want to consider one example from the 1992 KS3 tests (SEAC, 1992) in order to illustrate the kind of difficulties which arise from the current lack of clarity concerning the treatment of the boundary relationship between mathematical and everyday discourse by National Curriculum test designers. I have chosen an apparently simple item concerning a lift as illustration (see Fig. 15.1). I shall quote first from the previous paper (Cooper, 1992) but then add a diagrammatic representation of the problems such an item might cause a thoughtful student.

I wrote of this:

> This problem is to test the Statement of Attainment: 'Solve number problems with the aid of a calculator, interpreting the display' (2/4d).[6] The Marking Scheme (Band 1–4, Paper 1) gives as 'appropriate evidence' of achievement: 'Gives the answer to the division of 269 by 14 as 20, indicating that they have interpreted the calculator display to select the most appropriate whole number in this context. Do not accept 19 or 19.2.' This is basically a division exercise embedded in the context of a

15

This is the sign in a lift at an office block:

In the morning rush, 269 people want to go up in this lift.

How many times must it go up?

Figure 15.1
Source: SEAC, 1992

supposedly 'real life' problem. (But, note the 'catch'.) Now, does this reduce to 269 ÷ 14 rounded to the next largest whole number, as the Marking Scheme supplied with the tests implies? Well, possibly, if the child realises that it should not be treated as a *real* 'real life' problem. For example, the child has to assume, at least implicitly, in order to find the 'right' answer:

- That the lift is always full, except for the last trip. This is equivalent to there never being, except for the last trip, fewer than 14 people wishing to enter the lift. (The reference to the 'morning rush' is presumably meant to cover this, but it hardly guarantees it.)
- That nobody, in this 'morning rush' for the lift, gets fed up, and decides to use the stairs.
- That everyone involved uses the normal space associated with a person in a lift. Nobody here, amongst the 269, is, for example, in a wheelchair.

In other words, the child has to ignore the reference to the 'real world' in order to succeed at the piece of arithmetic, except for avoiding the 'catch' of merely dividing 269 by 14 and giving the 'unreal' answer of 19 or 19.2. Twenty, on the other hand, is the 'correct' answer! Some reference to the 'real' must be made, but not too much. A child who takes the setting of the problem (a lift in the morning rush) as signifying a piece of 'practical' mathematics, where s/he should begin by 'generating variables or features', 'selecting variables or pruning features', 'formulating questions', 'generating relations between variables', 'selecting relations' (the modelling skills listed in Burkhardt, 1981, quoted in Mason, 1988) is not likely to deal efficiently with this question. Rather, the child needs to see that the fact that this problem is set within the confines of this paper and pencil test signifies that the problem should not be treated in this way, but rather in a manner that ignores the implications of the 'real' setting.

(Cooper, 1992: 234–5)

It is possible to see the child, in such cases, as having to make a series of decisions about the questioner's intentions. In this particular case, to begin with, the child must decide whether the problem is to be seen as in any way located in a 'real' or 'everyday' setting. In fact, the marking scheme makes it clear that some use of 'common-sense' knowledge is required, in order to avoid the trap of merely dividing 269 by 14 and having the lift go up 19.21428571 times. However, the reference made to 'common-sense' must be no more than this, and this is where the child who recognizes this as a piece of a non-everyday discourse seems to be at an advantage. One possible set of choices about what the elements of the item signify can be represented in a diagram (Fig. 15.2).

In the earlier paper, after discussing several similar test items, I considered the possibility, drawing on Holland's (1981) Bernsteinian empirical work on children's classifying strategies as well as Keddie's (1971) more speculative comments on children's responses to school knowledge, that working-class children may experience particular difficulty in negotiating in acceptable ways

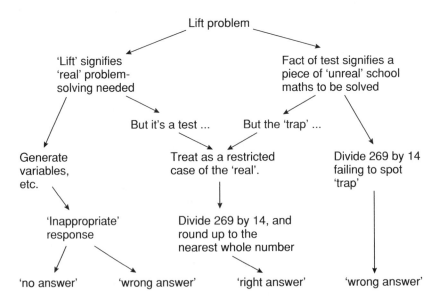

Figure 15.2

the types of decision mapped out in Fig. 15.2. The core of the argument, which I shall not reproduce here, concerned the possibility of there being a greater likelihood of their failing to disengage from an everyday common-sense perspective on these problems. Middle-class children, on the other hand, might be more prepared to read the test item as is intended by the test designers (for the argument, see Cooper, 1992: 239–42).

A more general form of the argument could be presented in terms of Bernstein's (1990) concepts of 'recognition and realisation rules', that is, 'the rules used by ... children to read the context, select their interactional practice, and create their texts' (104). A recent example of the use of this approach to explore social class differences in Portuguese children's responses to test items in science can be found in the work of Morais *et al.* (1992). In that case, the key difference explored was children's 'ability' to distinguish between items testing 'cognitive low-level competencies', that is, the acquisition of knowledge, and those testing 'cognitive high-level competencies', that is, those requiring the use of knowledge in new situations, typically *to explain.* Morais and her collaborators, on the basis of their empirical work, concluded:

> The results ... lead us to think that lower social groups have special difficulty in distinguishing the context of problem-solving from other contexts, that is they do not seem to have the recognition rules at this level.
>
> (Morais *et al.*, 1992: 267)

In her work, one element of this involved children's recourse to common-sense knowledge. There is considerable evidence in her paper that many children had great difficulty in moving outside of common-sense frames of reference when confronted with science test items requiring, for example, an explanation of why perspiration leads to skin feeling cooler (see also Driver, 1983). It is obviously dangerous to generalize from Portuguese work, especially given the relatively small samples involved, to the case of English children. Nevertheless, her work does seem to provide some support for the arguments developed in the discussion of KS3 items (Cooper, 1992), and certainly makes the task of analysing mathematics test items in terms of the boundary relationship between everyday and mathematical discourse seem worthwhile. I shall turn now to the KS2 test items themselves.

KEY STAGE 2 TESTS: DRAWING BOUNDARIES

There are many problematic aspects of the KS2 tests that I will not be able to discuss here. Some of the SoAs seem to be poorly operationalized in the test items. In some cases a child could clearly fail because of the need for some prior skill to be shown. There seems to be no clear pattern to the decision whether to award a mark for the 'right answer' and/or 'working out'.

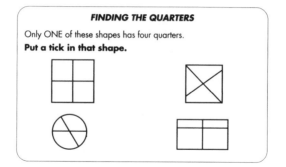

Figure 15.3
Source: SEAC, 1993a

There is some lack of clarity in wording. Lastly, there are cases where the 'right answer' provided could clearly be argued with. I shall mention one particularly noteworthy example because it seems to relate to my concerns here (see Fig. 15.3).

This follows an analogous item on 'halves'. The marking scheme, without any discussion, states 'only the one correct shape should be indicated in each case', and 'any unambiguous marking of the correct choice is acceptable'. The relevant SoA (2/2c) is to 'identify halves and quarters'. Now, since, from one perspective, all the shapes can be viewed as having four equal but undrawn quarters, one assumes that Level 2 children are not expected to worry themselves on this level of abstraction but rather to focus on the more concrete, visually available interpretation. Apparently here they are expected to remain on what might be seen as a relatively common-sense level, rather than move into a more esoteric discourse where all shapes might be seen as satisfying the condition whatever lines happen to have been drawn within their perimeters. Ironically, given the geometrical nature of the test item, the SoA lives under the strand 'knowledge and use of numbers' of *AT2: number* rather than under *AT4: shape and space*.

From the perspective of test designers, such problems – assuming they are not dismissed out of hand – might be seen as characteristic of *pilot* tests and susceptible to remedial treatment later. However, my concern here is with the underlying assumptions rather than the details. How is the boundary between everyday and mathematical discourse understood generally in these booklets and their marking scheme?

First of all, it is important to consider the possible consequences of the items in the mainstream booklets A and B being presented in a narrative framework perhaps signifying 'real life' events to children.

As the first example of how the narrative context might confuse children we can consider part of the School Trip Booklet (Book A, levels 3–5, p. 4:4).

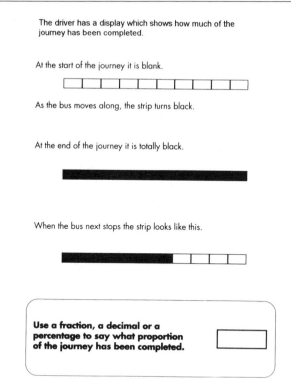

The driver has a display which shows how much of the journey has been completed.

At the start of the journey it is blank.

As the bus moves along, the strip turns black.

At the end of the journey it is totally black.

When the bus next stops the strip looks like this.

Use a fraction, a decimal or a percentage to say what proportion of the journey has been completed.

Figure 15.4

Source: SEAC, 1993a

Before this item is reached the child has been introduced to the idea of the trip, and has carried out calculations in order to determine the number of buses needed. S/he is then presented with the level 4 item shown in Fig. 15.4.

What is of interest here is the manner in which the flow of time is narratively presented. Following the text from top to bottom, the strip is blank when the bus starts its journey, then totally black when it finishes its journey, and then, *when it next stops*, the strip is partially black. In other words, one reading of the item – based on the convention that text is read left to right, top to bottom – might be expected to be very confusing for a child who has taken the narrative device of the trip seriously. To be successful here, the child has to recognize a different textual device – one quite common in mathematics texts – but one which inverts the apparent flow of time as represented in the narrative about the trip. If the child tries to interpret the item on the assumption that time flows monotonically with the text, s/he might well imagine that the strip starts to turn blank again from the right as the bus moves off (to the bus station?). Why not, given the imaginary nature of the distance recording device? On this reading, the 'correct' answer might be 40 per cent rather than the 60 per cent given by the Marking Scheme.

The SoA here (2/4c), 'use fractions, decimals or percentages as appropriate to describe situations', is presumably intended as a higher-level relative of the 'identify halves and quarters' SoA discussed earlier. In that case, at level 2, the child was apparently expected (and was required) to remain at a concrete, common-sense level. Here, at Level 4, we can see that a move out of the common-sense assumption about how time is conventionally represented in a narrative context seems to be required of the child. In other words, to succeed at the higher level, in the case of knowledge of fractions, does not require only a wider repertoire of fractions or their equivalents (6/10 as well as the more everyday 1/4 and 1/2) but also, possibly, a greater capacity to avoid the traps of common-sense interpretations. On the other hand, to move into esoteric mathematical discourse at level 2 might result in failure at that level.

The argument here is of course speculative and heavily dependent on children taking seriously the narrative devices of the 'School Trip' and 'Westwood School'. It must, therefore, be noted that there are aspects of the items that might lead them away from this reading. For example, in Book B (levels 1–2, p. 2:3), the children, in the 'first week of their project', are reported to have collected the objects shown in Table 15.2 from 'around their playground'.

Is this likely in their own school? On the previous page Gita and Katy are said to have made a written list of all the items they brought to school for recycling, before they went on to produce a tally chart (the test item for the children doing the test). This involved them writing 'can' five times, 'plastic bottle' four times, and so on – exactly the sort of task a tally chart is there to avoid. In Book A (levels 3–5, p. 5:5), Rashid and Gita manage to produce a result, during the activities involved in measuring the height of a tree, of 21,500 millimetres. The item continues, 'What is a more appropriate metric unit for measuring the height of the tree? Convert 21,500 mm into your metric unit'. It is assumed in this item (i) that millimetres are not appropriate units for measuring trees, and (ii) that Rashid and Gita have nevertheless used them. How they achieved this is a mystery to this reader and might be to the thoughtful child. Such contrived and artificial tasks are

Table 15.2

Item	Number
Plastic bottles	27
Cans	46
Glass jars	18
Newspapers	97
Magazines	33

SEAC, 1993a

common amongst the test items, and many other examples could be given. It is possible that some children will read these features as signifying that these items should not be approached in a common-sense manner and, furthermore, that this may be related to the children's social origins. Ultimately, this requires an empirical examination.

THE CASE OF ESTIMATING PROBABILITY

I want to spend much of the remainder of the chapter looking in more detail at the treatment of several related SoAs, at levels 4, 5 and 6. The first is 5/4d, 'estimate and justify the probability of an event'. The second, 5/5d, is 'use an appropriate method for estimating probabilities'. The third, at level 6, is 'identify all the outcomes of combining two independent events' (5/6c). In particular I want to consider how these items, and the associated marking scheme, present the boundary between everyday discourse and mathematical discourse as we rise through the levels.

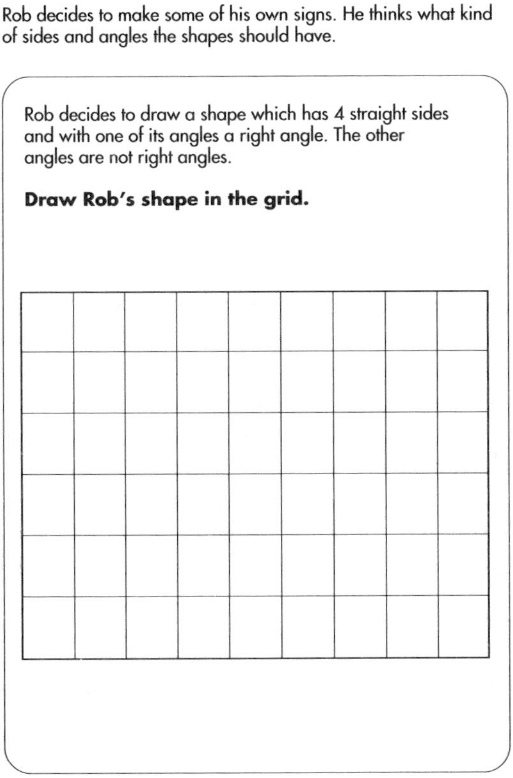

Rob decides to make some of his own signs. He thinks what kind of sides and angles the shapes should have.

Rob decides to draw a shape which has 4 straight sides and with one of its angles a right angle. The other angles are not right angles.

Draw Rob's shape in the grid.

Figure 15.5

Source: SEAC, 1993a

Rob's group cut out the shapes they are using to make signs.
They are:

6 traingles

1 square

2 rectangles

1 circle

They put their shapes into a bag.

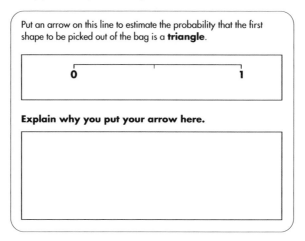

Put an arrow on this line to estimate the probability that the first shape to be picked out of the bag is a **triangle**.

> 0   1

Explain why you put your arrow here.

Figure 15.6
Source: SEAC, 1993a

The level 4 item was preceded by the item shown in Fig. 15.5 (Book B, levels 3–5, p. 4:5), allowing the shapes to be referred to in the probability item to appear 'naturally' within the narrative context. It was followed by the item shown in Fig. 15.6 (Book B, levels 3–5, p. 4:6).

It is not clear why the children would want to put their shapes into a bag (an act which might, after all, damage them). Perhaps they were to have a 'lucky dip' to help choose a winning sign? As in other parts of the book, the narrative context of 'Westwood School' is arguably little more than a gesture. What the marking scheme states for this item can be seen in Fig. 15.7.

What is of interest is that the child is not to be penalized for stepping outside of the esoteric discourse of mathematics. S/he is allowed – at level 4 – to make reference legitimately to more everyday concerns such as the suitability of shapes for signs[7]. It is also of interest to note that the child is apparently expected to accept the move into a 'lucky dip' situation but not to raise certain questions this might suggest. For example, would it not be 'fairer' to put the names of the shapes on the same-shaped cards and then choose them? They are, it seems, positioned here by the marking scheme as

Book B   Level 4 (Cont)

Page+	SoA	Answers	Notes
p4:6	5/4d		The SoA - 'Estimate and justify the probability of an event' is met by explanation and estimation corresponding with one another.
			In this question, information is given about the numbers of shapes, but the child may introduce additional factors which could prevent the outcomes being equally likely.
			Therefore, there are a range of acceptable estimations and explanations. e.g.
			'There are more triangles than anything'
			'Triangles are difficult to pick up'
			'They would feel for a circle because circles are better shapes for signs'.

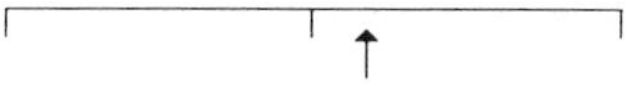

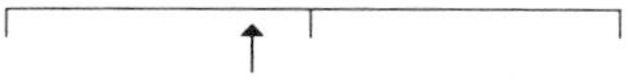

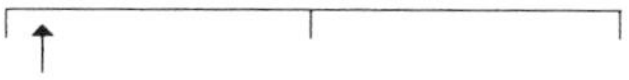

Figure 15.7
Source: SEAC, 1993a

liable to operate in a common-sense manner[8] and the possibility of their raising more abstract issues is not addressed.

The level 5 item is preceded by the item shown in Fig. 15.8 (Book B, levels 3–5, p. 5:4). The item itself is shown in Fig. 15.9 (Book B, levels 3–5, p. 5:5). The marking scheme gives 'David' as the correct answer,[9] adding 'the explanation should make reference to the fact that only David uses the information previously collected', and 'the arrow does not have to be exactly at the half-way mark'.

Comparing this to the marking scheme's comments on the level 4 shapes item we can detect a shift in the legitimacy of the move outside of the boundary of esoteric mathematical discourse as a means of solving the problem. Whereas the marking scheme for 5/4d gave three acceptable answers as illustration, here we have only one (though the arrow need not be exactly positioned!). It is not obvious that the child could not make moves outside

The children did a survey of the make of the cars in the car park at school.

They drew a graph of their results.

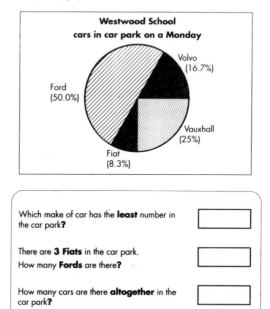

Westwood School
cars in car park on a Monday

Volvo (16.7%)

Ford (50.0%)

Vauxhall (25%)

Fiat (8.3%)

Which make of car has the **least** number in the car park?

There are **3 Fiats** in the car park. How many **Fords** are there?

How many cars are there **altogether** in the car park?

Figure 15.8
Source: SEAC, 1993a

of mathematical discourse as easily in this question as in the other. For example, perhaps Mr Jones always arrives early to do playground duty on a Monday, or maybe the Head Teacher arrives first and is more likely to own a Volvo. The fact that a possible move outside of mathematical discourse is not addressed in the marking scheme for a level 5 question when it previously has been at level 4, raises the interesting possibility that the child is being implicitly expected, as a condition of moving from level 4 to level 5, to better resist any temptation to move outside purely mathematical discourse when addressing 'apparently real' problems.

A look at the comparable items in Book C, that is, at level 6, suggests this progression is indeed accepted by the test designers, if only implicitly. In Book C, we have the item shown in Fig. 15.10 (Book C, p. 6:11). The marking scheme states that 'there should be exactly nine pairings, all different'.

This item seems to be based on the assumption that the children will not be misled by acting in a common-sense way – by imagining, for example,

Rashid's group try to predict which make of car will be the first to enter the school gates on the following Monday.

Ann says   **"I think it will be any of the makes because they will all have an equal chance."**

Gita says   **"I think it will be a Vauxhall because our teacher, Mr Jones, drives a Vauxhall."**

David says   **"I think it will be a Ford because there were more Fords in the car park last Monday than any other make."**

Who do you think is using the most appropriate method for predicting the first car through the school gates?

Explain why.

Use David's method to estimate the probability that the first car will be a Ford.

Put an **arrow** on the line to show your estimate.

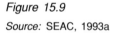

0   1

Figure 15.9
Source: SEAC, 1993a

that they might be acting physically on the 'names' on the cards in the context of an imagined 'realistic' competition. On the contrary, in order to be successful, they are expected, having abstracted the mathematical problem from its pictorial setting, to approach this in a Piagetian 'formal operational' mode. The problem is that, even where children are capable of undertaking the abstracted combinatorial act, they might not demonstrate it in this case. After all, objects put in such bags are normally there to be taken out (as, for example, in televised draws for the FA Cup).[10] If children were to operate on this assumption they would have, in their imagination, to put the 'names' back in order to generate all the possibilities. (In an empirical case, it could, in principle, given a run of bad luck, take a very long time to generate the nine possible pairs by this means.) It seems clear, therefore, that to achieve level 6, the child must treat this as a mental exercise in combining names and must be able to avoid being side-tracked by any element of the device used to test the SoA. The bags must not be taken to signify the request for the 'empirical' three pairs that might seem implicit in the physical act of removing names *without replacement* (as in the case of real draws for knock-out competitions), when a step into mathematical discourse *with replacement* can allow the production of nine.

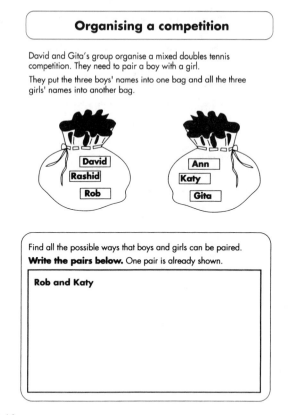

Organising a competition

David and Gita's group organise a mixed doubles tennis competition. They need to pair a boy with a girl.

They put the three boys' names into one bag and all the three girls' names into another bag.

David
Rashid
Rob

Ann
Katy
Gita

Find all the possible ways that boys and girls can be paired.
Write the pairs below. One pair is already shown.

Rob and Katy

Figure 15.10
Source: SEAC, 1993a

I hope I have done enough to illustrate the ways in which the levels of attainment for KS2 mathematics may be based on a set of assumptions about the proper relationship between everyday and mathematical discourse that is appropriate for different 'attainment' levels. In the case of probability, to achieve at higher levels, it seems, requires a progressive capacity to avoid a move into common-sense everyday frames of reference. It seems to be expected that children operating at level 4 will make this move, and the marking scheme allows them to succeed in spite of this. But, as we move into the level 5 and 6 items, it seems that success will be jeopardized by such a move. The nature of the comments in the marking scheme for the probability items discussed here certainly suggests that the boundary between level 4 and higher levels is related to children's ability to negotiate the boundary between the mundane and the esoteric in a particular way.

A NOTE ON THE ABSENT AT1: USING AND APPLYING MATHEMATICS

Given the above discussion of probability items spanning levels 4–6, it might be worth briefly mentioning what AT1 skills a child operating around these levels might be expected to display in their mathematical work, according to the National Curriculum map, and discussing the possible implications of this.[11] Taking level 4 as a guide, we have under the three strands of AT1 the following:

- level 4(a): identify and obtain information necessary to solve problems;
- level 4(b): interpret situations mathematically, using appropriate symbols or diagrams;
- level 4(c): give some justification for their solutions to problems;
- level 4(d): make generalizations.

It is noteworthy that 'justification' appears here at level 4. In the case of the probability items we saw that justification was asked for by the SoA at level 4 while, at level 5, an 'appropriate' method was required but without explicit reference to justification. However, what is of most relevance to my concern with the boundary between the everyday and the mathematical is 4(a). A child at level 4 and, presumably, at higher levels, is expected, in his or her general mathematical work, to 'identify and obtain information necessary to solve problems'.[12] This might often involve stepping outside of the given information and, in particular, in the case of 'real' problems, would often involve drawing on 'non-mathematical' knowledge in order to ensure that mathematics is used in fruitful ways.[13] In so far as there exist differences between schools in the stress laid on AT1 (and there are, see HMI, 1991, 1992), we can expect children, independently of their class-related socialization experiences, to handle the boundary negotiating procedures demanded by test items, like the probability ones discussed here, with different degrees of success as a consequence of the pedagogic preferences of their teachers.

CONCLUSION

I noted, in my brief description of Bernstein's (1971) concepts for analysing the curriculum, his argument that, under a collection code, 'very early in the child's life', the student would be discouraged from relating school knowledge to his or her everyday, common-sense knowledge.[14] He argued that the child would soon learn what could be brought from outside into the classroom context. Before the post-Cockcroft changes in school mathematics, this statement may well have described very well the situation in the classrooms of most 11-year-old English children, especially in those primary schools where mathematics was treated as a separate content, most typically by being taught by means of a 'scheme' such as 'Scottish Mathematics' (i.e. the texts of the Scottish Primary Mathematics Group) or 'Nuffield Mathematics'. Subsequently, however, there may have been moves away from rigid boundary maintenance between the 'everyday' and the 'mathematical' in those schools taking Cockcroft's and HMI's recommendations seriously. Some children, even where a collection code exists, may have received encouragement to cross the boundary, that is, to import more from outside esoteric mathematical discourse when working in 'mathematics'. Other children, working in schools where a more integrated curriculum approach has been used, will have probably experienced a weaker boundary between everyday and mathematical discourse as a result of 'mathematics' being embedded in topic work.[15]

What an exploratory analysis of KS2 test items allows is some insight into how the strength of boundary maintenance procedures between common-sense and mathematical discourse might now begin to vary with National Curriculum attainment level in the third of Bernstein's message systems of formal educational knowledge, that is, evaluation. We have seen that there is a tendency for the boundary to be seen, if only implicitly, as increasingly impermeable as the levels rise. Children are apparently expected, as they rise through the levels or, perhaps, *as a condition of being able to rise through the levels*, to be increasingly able to avoid 'irrelevant' steps into common-sense reasoning when faced with a 'mathematical' problem.

The analysis of KS2 items therefore suggests that what Bernstein pointed to in 1971 remains a key feature of the organization of educational knowledge in England. It appears to be the case that success in school, as measured by national testing in mathematics, will depend on the child's capacity or willingness to approach tasks with a particular orientation to meaning, one which brackets out everyday, common-sense knowledge as a resource. Holland's (1981) work on 8–10-year-olds suggests that working-class children will find this more problematic than middle-class children (Cooper, 1992). It may be that the embedding of test items in narrative contexts, while simultaneously requiring the child to avoid any move into common-sense reasoning as levels 5 and 6 are approached, might have the effect of preventing children from certain social origins from reaching these levels.

We can also note a problem for teachers. The use of mathematics to solve real problems has always involved difficult decisions about how much simplification of any real situation is appropriate in order to facilitate the resulting mathematical tasks. Teachers should have been discussing this problem with their students in respect of *AT1: using and applying mathematics*. They now have the additional problem of helping children decide when it is or is not appropriate to make reference outside of purely mathematical discourse when approaching an NC test item which only *appears* to address the 'real'. Given the ways in which this 'appropriateness' seems to vary with NC level of attainment in these pilot tests, and assuming teachers want the 'best' outcome for their school, this might prove a difficult pedagogic problem to solve.

Lastly, I want to consider the general lessons that we might learn from this critical discussion of the Key Stage 2 mathematics tests and my previous discussion of the earlier Key Stage 3 items (Cooper, 1992). The question of whether programmes of national testing can or will improve pupil learning has received considerable attention both in Britain and elsewhere (Broadfoot *et al.*, 1990; Gifford and O'Connor, 1992; Gipps, 1992; Torrance, 1993). In England, once a decision had been made to test all pupils across a wide range of objectives – rather than to sample both pupils and objectives – considerations of cost and teacher time soon led to attempts to simplify test items and their administration. This had occurred by 1992/93, facilitated by the strong preference of the influential New Right for simple paper and pencil tests of 'basic skills' which would allow the competitive ranking of schools, and by New Right's distrust of teachers as 'professionals' (Ball, 1990; Brown, 1993). Test developers have, nevertheless, attempted to produce items reflecting the 'good practice' of the 1980s by, for example, situating mathematics in apparently realistic contexts. This was always likely to lead to problems (Brown, 1992) and the results, if my critical discussion has any validity, suggest that this particular circle will not be squared at all easily. A number of writers have noted the unparalleled nature of the English experiment in national testing and suggested that the achievement of successful authentic assessment on such a scale was never likely to be easy (Murphy, 1990; Gipps, 1992). The English experience so far suggests that both much longer times scales to allow the lessons of research and experience to play a greater role, and less political interference in the development of tests, will be needed to enable the delivery of accountability without simultaneously causing damage to the development of school mathematics as a discipline.

NOTES

I would like to thank Stephanie Cant, Pat Drake, Colin Lacey, David Longman, Martyn Hammersley and Harry Torrance for their critical comments on a previous draft of this paper.

1 Torrance (1993: 81) writes of this, 'it has also been increasingly argued on both sides of the Atlantic that assessment must take account of higher order skills and competencies such as problem-solving, investigation, and analysis and thus must involve far more 'authentic' or realistic tasks than have traditionally been employed in the field'.
2 As in the case of *AT1: using and applying mathematics* (SEAC, 1993a).
3 Paragraph 243 of this Government Report became a new orthodoxy within English mathematics education during the 1980s. It read: Mathematics teaching at all levels should include opportunities for:

- exposition by the teacher;
- discussion between teacher and pupils and between pupils themselves;
- appropriate practical work;
- consolidation and practice of fundamental skills and routines;

- problem-solving, including the application of mathematics to everyday situations;
- investigational work.

4 For a critical discussion of Bernstein's 1971 paper, see Gibson (1977).

5 Examples would be the various investigations drawn from the field of number theory. Furthermore, even where a problem seems to have a 'real' setting this is often merely a device to get a piece of pure mathematics going, as is the case in the commonly set problem of how many ways a certain number of milk bottles can be arranged in a partially full milk crate.

6 The 2/4d refers to the SoAs in the NCC (1991) document, *Mathematics in the National Curriculum*, and subsequent documents.

7 We might note that the example given – that circles make good signs – doesn't lend any support to Rob's decision, after thinking about 'what kind of sides and angles the shapes should have', to use a rather unusual shape for a sign. Neither do any of the shape names describe the one Rob drew.

8 In the sense of being likely to move outside of the esoteric 'mathematical' domain.

9 As, implicitly, does the preference for David's method shown in the item itself.

10 This points to possible gender issues which could be explored in these test items.

11 Especially, as elsewhere, SEAC does not seem to compartmentalize mathematics quite as it does in these tests. For example, 'Ma1 is about using and applying the knowledge, understanding and skills contained in Ma2–5. Work related to Ma1 cannot be tackled in isolation from the rest of the programmes of study. Opportunities to assess Ma1 should, therefore, be present in all work in mathematics. All activities which allow pupils to show their achievements in Ma1 should relate to one or more of the other attainment targets. Most of these will naturally also allow pupils to show attainment in aspects of Ma2–5' (SEAC, 1993b: 3).

12 The equivalent level 3 SoA (3a) is 'find ways of overcoming difficulties when solving problems'.

13 In so far as the arguments of this paper are correct, therefore, there might be some tension between 4a and 4b, that is, in so far as 4b might require an avoidance of the step into common-sense discourse.

14 Since his 1971 paper, Bernstein has done considerable work on his general codes thesis (Bernstein, 1990), reworking the ideas in terms of the general ideas of the recognition and realization rules which regulate the production of texts, in a general sense, in contexts. Elaborated codes, originally defined in broadly sociolinguistic terms, are now described as the media which allow the thinking of the 'unthinkable', 'because the meanings they give rise to go beyond local time, space, context and embed and relate the latter to transcendental space, time, context' (p. 182). This form of description is much easier to bring into line with his analysis of curriculum than the very early version of the codes (see, for example, Cooper, 1976; Edwards, 1981). He has also extended his discussion of the ways in which the school distributes 'forms of consciousness' differentially through the population (Bernstein, 1990: ch. 5).

15 Clearly, this will only be the case where the integration has, in some sense, been 'genuine' rather than rhetorical.

REFERENCES

Abraham, J. and Bibby, N. (1992) 'Mathematics and society: ethnomathematics and the public educator curriculum', in M. Nickson and S. Lerman (eds), *The Social Context of Mathematics Education: Theory and Practice*, London: South Bank University Press.

Ball, S. J. (1990) *Politics and Policy Making in Education*, London: Routledge.

Bernstein, B. (1971) 'On the classification and framing of educational knowledge', in M. F. D. Young (ed.), *Knowledge and Control*, London: Collier-Macmillan.

—— (1990) *The Structuring of Pedagogic Discourse*, London: Routledge.

Bloor, D. (1991) *Knowledge and Social Imagery*, 2nd edn, Chicago: Chicago University Press.

Broadfoot, P., Murphy, R. and Torrance, H. (eds) (1990) *Changing Educational Assessment: International Perspectives and Trends*, London: Routledge.

Brown, M. (1992) 'Elaborate nonsense? The muddled tale of Standard Assessment Tasks at Key Stage 3', in C. Gipps (ed.), *Developing Assessment for the National Curriculum*, London: Kogan Page/London University Institute of Education.

—— (1993) 'Clashing epistemologies: the battle for control of the National Curriculum and its assessment', professional inaugural lecture, King's College, London.

Cockcroft, W. H. (1982) *Mathematics Counts*, London: HMSO.

Cooper, B. (1976) 'Bernstein's codes: a classroom study', University of Sussex Education Area, Occasional Paper No. 6.

—— (1985a) *Renegotiating Secondary School Mathematics*, Basingstoke: Falmer Press.

—— (1985b) 'Secondary school mathematics since 1950: reconstructing differentiation', in I. F. GOODSON (ed.), *Social Histories of the Secondary Curriculum*, Barcombe: Falmer Press).

—— (1992)'Testing National Curriculum mathematics: some critical comments on the treatment of "real" contexts for mathematics', *The Curriculum Journal*, 3: 231–43.

—— (1994) 'Secondary mathematics education in England: recent changes and their historical context', in M. Selinger (ed.), *Teaching Mathematics*, London: Routledge.

Davis, A. (1990) 'Logical defects of the TGAT report', *British Journal of Educational Studies*, XXXVIII: 237–50.

DES/WO (1988) *National Curriculum: Task Group on Assessment and Testing: A Report*, London: HMSO).

Dowling, P. (1991) 'A touch of class: ability, social class and intertext in SMP 11-16', in D. Pimm and E. Love (eds), *Teaching and Learning School Mathematics*, London: Hodder & Stoughton.

—— and Noss, R. (eds) (1990) *Mathematics Versus the National Curriculum*, Basingstoke: Falmer Press.

Driver, R. (1983) *The Pupil as Scientist*, Milton Keynes: Open University Press.

Ernest, P. (1992) 'The National Curriculum in mathematics: its aims and philosophy', in M. Nickson and S. Lerman (eds), *The Social Context of Mathematics Education*, London: South Bank University Press.

Frankenstein, M. (1989) *Relearning Mathematics: A Different Third R-radical Maths*, London: Free Association Books.

Gifford, B. and O'Connor, M. (eds) (1992) *Changing Assessments: Alternative Views of Aptitude, Achievement and Instruction*, Boston: Kluwer.

Gipps, C. (ed.) (1992) *Developing Assessment for the National Curriculum*, London: Kogan Page/London University Institute of Education.

Griffiths, H. B. and Howson, A. G. (1974) *Mathematics: Society and Curricula* (Cambridge: Cambridge University Press.

HMI (1979) *Aspects of Secondary Education in England*, London: HMSO.

—— (1980) *Aspects of Secondary Education in England: Supplementary Information on Mathematics*, London: HMSO.

—— (1991) *Mathematics: Key Stages 1 and 3: A Report by HM Inspectorate on the First Year, 1989-90*, London: HMSO.

—— (1992) *Mathematics: Key Stages 1, 2 and 3: A Report by HM Inspectorate on the Second Year*, 1990–91, London: HMSO.

Holland, J. (1981) 'Social class and changes in orientation to meaning', *Sociology*, 15: 1–18.

Howson, A. G. (1989) *Maths Problem: Can More Pupils Reach Higher Standards?* London: Centre for Policy Studies.

Keddie, N. (1971) 'Classroom knowledge', in M. F. D. Young (ed.), *Knowledge and Control*, London: Collier-Macmillan.

Mackenzie, D. (1981) *Statistics in Britain: 1865–1930*, Edinburgh: Edinburgh University Press.

Morais, A., Fontinhas, F. and Neves, I. (1992) 'Recognition and realisation rules in acquiring school science: the contribution of pedagogy and social background of students', *British Journal of Sociology of Education*, 13: 247–70.

Murphy, R. (1990) 'National assessment proposals: analysing the debate', in M. Flude and M. Hammer (eds), *The Education Reform Act 1988: Its Origins and Implications*, London: Falmer Press.

NCC (National Curriculum Council) (1989) *Mathematics: Non-statutory Guidance*, York: NCC.

—— (1991) *NCC Consultation Report: Mathematics*, York: NCC.

Noss, R. *et al.* (1990) (eds) *Political Dimensions of Mathematics Education: Action and Critique*, London: University of London Institute of Education.

Pennycuick, D. and Murphy, R. (1988) *The Impact of Graded Tests*, London: Falmer Press.

Restivo, S. (1991) *The Sociological Worldview*, Oxford: Blackwell.

Ruthven, K. (1986) 'Differentiation in mathematics: a critique of *Mathematics Counts* and *Better Schools*', *Cambridge Journal of Education*, 16: 41–5.

SEAC (1992) *Mathematics Tests, 1992, Key Stage 3*, London: SEAC/University of London.

—— (1993a) *Pilot Standard Tests: Key Stage 2: Mathematics*, London: SEAC/University of Leeds.

Spradberry, J. (1976) 'Conservative pupils? Pupil resistance to a curriculum innovation in mathematics', in: M. F. D. Young and G. Whitty (eds), *Explorations in the Politics of School Knowledge*, Driffield: Nafferton.

Torrance, H. (1993) 'Combining measurement-driven instruction with authentic assessment: some initial observations of national assessment in England and Wales', *Educational Evaluation and Policy Analysis*, 15: 81–90.

Watson, F.R. (1976) *Developments in Mathematics Teaching*, London: Open Books.

Chapter 16

The challenge of the 1990s

Andrew Pollard

In this chapter, originally published in 1990,* Andrew Pollard attempts to foretell the challenges of the 1990s. He foresees, among other things, potential difficulties as well as power in putting formative, teacher assessment at the heart of the planning and teaching process. He also predicts the need for primary teachers to become more familiar and confident in the subjects of the school curriculum.

Education is currently facing its biggest challenge this century. The National Curriculum and the new ways of managing schools and teachers are explicitly intended to increase educational 'standards' and the quality of children's education. However, it is by no means certain that they will succeed – indeed, the search for improved standards of education is comparable to that for the Holy Grail. In ten years' time we may still be looking for it! In the case of education, the reason for the constant search is usually that we change our minds about what, precisely, we are looking for.

In any event, the 1990s will be a decade in which we will all have the opportunity to test the propositions and goals that are now enshrined in legislation. The new curricular structures and assessment procedures will become part of our children's lives and the test of them will thus be directly empirical. They will be visible to every family with young children and to every adult who takes the time to become involved in the life of a school. For our children's sake, we must all sincerely hope that the new structures will be a success and, in general terms, the challenge of the 1990s is to ensure that this is the case.

However, it would be naive and irresponsible to leave the discussion there, because there are a number of potential difficulties that must be addressed if we are to make progress. In this chapter, I therefore want to raise a few of the most important challenges that we face – challenges that we *must* overcome if we are to make progress, and challenges that we can *only* overcome if parents, governors and teachers collaborate together. As a vehicle for this,

* Originally published in A. Pollard, *Learning in Primary Schools*, London: Cassell.

and to reassert the point that children themselves ultimately control their own learning, we can turn to the case of Naomi and her new shoes.

NAOMI'S NOTE

She wrote:

> I'm happy, I'm happy.
> I know I am. I'm sure I am.
> I'm happy because I got new shoes.

Thinking of Naomi here is important because her simple message conveys some of the realities of children's learning – the qualities of openness and immediacy, the links between children's development, experience and growing competence, the importance of trusting relationships between adults and children. If we are really concerned about learning, these are things that matter enormously. Curriculum attainment targets, assessment procedures, local management of schools, performance indicators, and all the rest, may be important but they are simply adjuncts of the learning process. They should be in its service – supporting, facilitating, enabling – as each child gradually constructs his or her understanding of the world. The danger is that they may become an encumbrance, a set of diversions and a framework of constraints that have little resonance with children's immediate needs. Indeed, the 1988 Education Reform Act could produce a bureaucratic 'clutter' for the 1990s, which would be really very damaging. I will consider some of the challenges that are now posed.

PROGRAMMES OF STUDY AND CHILDREN'S LEARNING

Taken as a whole, the specification of programmes of study in the National Curriculum must be a positive advance. It will ensure breadth of experience and should also provide progression. However, there is a danger that programmes of study could become a straitjacket, for there is now a lot of evidence that much of children's learning does not proceed in a generalizable, linear way. Ultimately, all children are unique and will learn in their own ways, through their own routes to understanding. True, it is responsible and necessary for adults to provide a supportive structure, but we have to be *very* careful that this does not become a conveyor belt that processes children and from which no one can escape. If the potential richness, variety and excitement of the curriculum become reduced to a trek from attainment target to attainment target then we will have failed our children. In this context, we should very much fear the results of the massive plans by some publishers to produce 'work schemes' for the subjects specified by the National Curriculum.

ASSESSMENT AND CHILDREN'S LEARNING

Assessment can be seen as being at the centre of the learning process. When it is devoted to that end, with an emphasis on ongoing, formative, teacher assessment, it is likely to be a considerable help in developing the quality of understanding of children and of what is provided for them. However, assessment could also become a diversionary pressure, an intrusion and a threat.

It could be a diversionary pressure if it comes to take up such a large proportion of teacher time that teachers have little scope for other important aspects of their role. We know that this has happened in parts of the United States so it is a real concern. Should Naomi's teacher have recorded the detail of her emerging competence at writing or should she have talked to her or written back?

Assessment could become an intrusion if it begins to sour relationships between children and teachers. Children, being clever and canny, will know what is going on and will be aware when teachers are forming judgements about them. Given that the basis of close relationships must be trust and a mutual exchange of dignity, the assessment process could easily change the whole quality of classroom experience for both children and teachers. Since this quality has been one of the great strengths of primary education over many years, it must not be allowed to alter – Naomi wrote because she wanted to share her excitement with her teacher.

Assessment could become a threat because of the possible use and consequences of reported results. It is naive to pretend that children will not soon know of the 'levels of attainment' that have been attributed to them – ask any infant school child to compare how he or she is getting on at reading with the progress of one of his or her friends. The result, for some children, must inevitably be a sense of relative failure and a loss of self-esteem. There is also a very real danger of social stigma. How would public reporting of results have affected Naomi and her classmates? Public reporting is a possibility even for infant schools and is a legal requirement at the end of other key stages.

The new assessment procedures are thus very powerful. They could do a lot of good, but they could be very damaging too. Given the delicacy and inter-personal subtlety of many learning processes in classrooms, assessment will have to be handled with extreme care.

TEACHER PROFESSIONALISM

How the legislation is interpreted and enacted will depend on professional judgement, skill, knowledge and commitment. The profession shows many strengths and some weaknesses. For instance, there is a considerable body of research evidence that demonstrates the sophistication of teachers' thinking, the ways in which judgement is exercised and the skills that are developed.

Yet many of these judgements and skills seem to be primarily focused on managing classrooms from the control point of view rather than on children's learning *per se*. Similarly, the actual subject knowledge of many primary teachers is a little shaky in some areas, such as science, and this inevitably causes some difficulties in interpreting the challenge of learning tasks and in diagnosing each child's needs. It is clear that support and help for teachers as they develop their professional expertise must be provided.

This will not be easy because we have a shortage of teachers, and morale at the start of the decade is low. However, teachers derive great personal satisfaction from their work with children and are likely to respond positively if their work is respected and valued appropriately. Naomi trusted and valued her teacher – it is not a great deal to ask that other people should do so too.

LOCAL MANAGEMENT OF SCHOOLS

Control of the greater part of a school's budget will bring considerable autonomy to governors and Head Teachers. It is to be hoped that, after inevitable initial teething problems, this greater budgetary control will enable schools to match their specific needs against expenditure with more precision than in the past.

Local management of schools could become a major administrative pressure, however, and we do not yet know the extent to which it will divert Head Teachers from their primary responsibility for the children's learning. To lead their staff teams effectively, Head Teachers need to stay in touch, to teach some of the time, to have opportunities to talk to people. 'Management by wandering about' is not sufficient for a Head Teacher in the 1990s, but it does remain necessary for the person-centred environments that schools are. Like Naomi, her teacher also has need of praise, encouragement and guidance, and this could not be given if her Head Teacher was buried under computer print-outs in her office. It thus remains to be seen if some administrative services would be more effectively coordinated centrally.

RESOURCES FOR LEARNING

The devolution of budgetary control to schools says nothing about the absolute level of the funding that is provided and one of the biggest challenges for the 1990s is undoubtedly that of increasing resources for primary education. The present imbalance between primary, secondary and tertiary education reflects historical precedent rather than any real appreciation of what it would really cost to meet the needs of young children. With the introduction of the National Curriculum, teachers in primary schools are going to be under enormous pressure and the resources available to them are, in my view, totally unrealistic. In particular, in addition to the actual process of teaching, they need more time to liaise, plan, prepare, monitor, record, report and discuss the children's learning. If the present levels of contact-time with children continue, the work that teachers are now being asked to do will simply not be possible.

The most positive way forward is to move to a system of 'activity-led' staffing, in which the time needed to do the job is calculated and then provided. This would cost significant sums of money and it will need a sustained campaign over the next decade to provide it. If it is not forthcoming, the Naomis of the future may discover that their teachers hardly have time to read their notes, let alone reply.

EQUAL OPPORTUNITIES

For many years, people in the education service have consciously worked to provide equality of educational opportunity for all children. However, given the seeming intractability of the conditions and social relationships that give rise to social differences, most people would recognize that enormous scope for improvement with regard to gender, race, social class and disability remains. The recent 'recommendation' from the Council of Europe on *Teaching and Learning about Human Rights in Primary Schools* reinforces this point and draws on the European Convention of Human Rights. Equal opportunities thus remains a very important concern for the 1990s.

Unfortunately, some provisions of the 1988 Education Reform Act seem likely to increase inequalities, particularly in provision between schools. This essentially arises because of the choice of the market mechanism as a means of improving educational standards. To make a market operate, there needs to be both information and choice. With regard to schools, information is to be provided by the publication of assessment results and school brochures, and through annual meetings for parents. To achieve choice, a new policy of 'open enrolment' is being introduced. This requires schools to admit pupils on demand up to their planned admission levels. The resourcing of schools is then to be largely based on the numbers of pupils attending. Popular schools should thus flourish and less popular schools will, so the theory goes, have to consider the reasons for their difficulties and improve.

Perhaps this might work if all the 'reasons' for differences in levels of performance were under the control of schools, if the practicalities of family life made it possible for all parents to send their children anywhere and if no parent ever made judgements about the work of schools for educationally unsound reasons. However, none of these conditions can realistically be satisfied. The result is that the consequences of the use of market mechanism could be very damaging. Children's entitlement – their right to a high level of provision whichever school they attend – is, in my view, at risk. In the long term it may well be that social divisions of race, as well as class, will be reinforced by this reliance on market forces.

I would suggest that Naomi and her generation will not be best served for their future, or for their contribution to our development in the next century, by the reinforcement of the unjustifiable indignities of the British social class system that seems to be in store for us. However, balancing the individual rights and responsibilities of parents regarding their children with wider social, economic and ethical imperatives remains the prime duty of government. It is thus to future governments that we must look if the fears I have expressed above do materialize – and, of course, it is for us to elect and influence governments.

CONCLUSION

Despite concerns such as those outlined above, and perhaps because of them, we owe it to our children to think, co-operate and act constructively. I believe that we must face the legislation squarely, must monitor and address any weaknesses as they emerge, and must support teachers in developing their professionalism. We must secure appropriate funding for primary education. We can only realistically succeed in these challenges by taking the new opportunities that are open to us and by sharing and drawing together in a collaborative spirit.

Above all, we need the resolution and determination to work positively to develop the learning and learning experiences of all young children. Through this collective endeavour parents, governors and teachers can play major parts in constructing our future.

REFERENCES

Bennett, N. and Kell, J. (1989) *A Good Start? Four-year-olds in Infant Schools*, Oxford: Blackwell.

Blyth, A. (1984) *Development, Experience and Curriculum in Primary Education*, London: Croom Helm.

Caldwell, B. J. and Spinks, J. M. (1988) *The Self-Managing School*, Lewes: Falmer.

Council of Europe (1985) *Teaching and Learning about Human Rights in Schools*, Recommendation no. R(85)7 of the Committee of Ministers, Strasbourg: Council of Europe.

HMI (1987) *Primary Schools: Some Aspects of Good Practice*, London: HMSO.

Pollard, A. and Tann, S. (1987) *Reflective Teaching in the Primary School*, London: Cassell.

Rowland, S. (1987) 'Child in control: towards an interpretive model of teaching and learning', in A. Pollard (ed.), *Children and Their Primary Schools*, London: Falmer Press.

Tizard, B. and Hughes, M. (1984) *Young Children Learning*, London: Fontana.

Part IV

Into the twenty-first century

Chapter 17

The third revolution?

Robin Alexander

Drawing on a range of empirical research, including the findings of the Leeds survey published in 1991 and which played a key role in the revisions to the National Curriculum in primary schools, Robin Alexander puts forward in this piece a wide-ranging agenda for changing primary practice in the twenty-first century. *

Set against a historical analysis of the roots of primary philosophy in England, he calls for a redefinition of a rationale for primary education, and for the divisions between the sectors of education, a reconception of the funding arrangements for primary and secondary schools based on task rather than age, the redefinition of teacher roles in primary schools, the need to underpin primary practice with intellectual reflection on theoretical frameworks, rather than attachment to dogma, the continued development of pedagogy based on classroom research findings, continued redefinition of the scope of the primary curriculum, and emphasises the need to reconsider which are really going to be the basic skills for the twenty-first century.

THE THIRD REVOLUTION?

We can think of primary education as having undergone at least three revolutions in the last three generations. With 1839 as a starting point we capture both the free-for-all of pre-universal elementary education and the roots of subsequent reform. The 1870 and 1902 Education Acts signalled the achievement of universal elementary education. Hadow in 1931 and Plowden in 1967 expressed the growing unease at the limited educational vision which was the price paid for this achievement and offered a richer alternative; they also legitimated 'primary' as a distinctive part of a longer endeavour to replace 'elementary' as the sum total of that endeavour. Finally we saw, and are still experiencing, the rejection of progressive ideals and their replacement, riding

---

* From R. Alexander (1995) *Versions of Primary Education*, London: Routledge (edited slightly for this volume).

triumphantly on the tide of Thatcherism from 1988 or so, by an updated version of the earlier instrumentality, consolidated in 1995 for the remainder of the century, or so at least Dearing hoped (the third revolution).

Elsewhere (Alexander, 1995), I have tried to identify some of the ideas and events which have proved particularly influential in shaping our current system of primary education, ideas and events which have their resonances in all four of the empirical studies in that volume. In doing so I have confronted a choice about how these matters might be portrayed and explained. To some – notably, the dominant political group of the 1980s – educational history is a tale of constant transformation and progress, not to say revolution, as the elementary archetype is ousted by progressivism which in turn gives way to economic pragmatism and enlightened common sense. This view tends to generate an inflated faith in current achievements and future intentions, a dismissive attitude towards the recent past and an unquestioning presumption of consensus: means may be debated, but not ends. To others, the history of this phase of education is more properly seen as a pendulum which swings back and forth between the poles of 'traditional' and 'progressive', leaving in its wake the polarization and adversarialism that these two terms connote. In contrast to both, the hybrid model espoused here highlights continuity rather than transformation; conflict, paradox and dilemma rather than consensus; and invites a more cautious evaluation of what has been and what might be achieved because of the inertia thus generated.

The weakness of the hybrid model is that in looking forward it becomes weighed down by its sense of the problematic, seeing no answers, only questions (while in the other models there tend to be no questions, only answers). Nevertheless, albeit unfortunately, the current case of primary education seems indeed sufficiently problematic to justify this stance.

Thus, we have the persistence of the elementary legacies of grossly discrepant funding, adverse pupil–teacher ratios, an inflexible and possibly outmoded model of staffing, a narrow view of what is 'basic' to education at this stage, and an over-sharp gulf between these 'basics' and the rest of the curriculum, all embedded within an educational culture in which paternalism/maternalism, deference, dependence and a fair measure of anti-intellectualism continue to exert what some may regard as a surprisingly strong influence over the lives and outlooks of many primary teachers. Neither of the two recent revolutions (or quasi-revolutions) in primary education, progressivism and Thatcherism, has done much more than chip at the surface of legacies such as these – and indeed each has to some extent reinforced them – and the tensions and dilemmas for those teachers who seek to pursue an agenda more comprehensive than simply doing what others require remain as sharp as ever.

Thus, therefore, the considerable achievements of progressivism – transformed physical and interpersonal contexts for learning, heuristic approaches to teaching, reduced curriculum boundaries, a focus on the affective and the creative – have by and large left intact, or have been diluted by, the more fundamental institutional and curricular structures inherited from the nine-teenth century. If we turn now to the Thatcherite revolution, if that is what it will turn out to be, or the period since the 1988 Act, we see a similar tendency. Questions have been raised about the structure, content and manageability of the curriculum, but not about its longer-term rationale. The curriculum thus restructured combines the partial modernization of science, technology and information technology with the reaffirmation not just of the elementary curriculum but also of its grammar-school counterpart, as the various subject lobbies extend their hegemony from secondary to primary education. Assessment is defined in the traditional form of the test, and – significantly – the test points (7, 11, 14 and 16) are exactly those proposed in the anti-progressive Black Papers of the 1960s and 1970s (specifically, Cox and Boyson, 1975). Indeed, the extent to which the 1980s policy agenda was in part a final and comprehensive assault on progressivism is manifested almost daily in the political rhetoric of the time, from Prime Minister Major's gauntlet-throwing 'The progressives have had their say, and they've had their day' to his triumphalist Eastbourne litany of 'Knowledge. Discipline. Tables. Sums. Dates. Shakespeare. British history. Standard English. Grammar. Spelling. Marks. Tests. Good manners' (Major, 1992) – all of them, according to the right-wing demonology, despised and rejected by the progressives. At the same time, Dearing uses the device of the Key Stage to confirm the rigidity of the traditional infant/junior/primary/ secondary structure, and the government underscores this by refusing to intervene in the matter of secondary/primary funding discrepancies, thus making it difficult to explore more than marginal staffing alternatives to the class-teacher model, and by continuing to stonewall on the matter of primary pupil–teacher ratios and class sizes.

I have used the word 'revolution' to describe what has happened since 1988, though cautiously. Clearly, the Conservative governments of the 1980s and 1990s would have their policies and legislation rated as nothing less. In reality is far too early to form a judgement about this, especially as the price politi-cians have to accept for politicizing education to this extent and imposing reform with such cavalier ruthlessness is that their policies can be overturned, equally ruthlessly and equally quickly.

Moreover, there is no simple measure for assessing the impact of a major educational initiative or movement. In the 1970s and 1980s there was pretty widespread espousal, within the primary professional community at least, of progressive *ideas*; yet at the levels of school and classroom *practice* and in the curriculum as experienced by primary children, the picture was far less convincing. Similarly, though by the mid-1990s a National Curriculum of nine subjects was in place in every primary school, together with attendant procedures for assessment, budgetary delegation and school governance, such empirical research as by that time was beginning to examine the working-out of the National Curriculum in the classroom suggested an emerging picture of complexity and unevenness which could eventually match that of the 1970s and 1980s, notwithstanding the surface uniformity which the imposition of the National Curriculum Orders produced.

This is probably just as well. Though neither group would wish to acknowledge the similarity, the government which introduced the 1988 reforms and many of the key figures in the post-war progressive movement had one characteristic in common: the unshakeable belief that they, and they alone, were right, and that being so they could legitimately expect teachers in primary schools to conform to their views. Such hubris should never go unchallenged and in any case usually carries the seeds of its own downfall.

The challenge to the 1988 reforms has come on a number of fronts. The manner of their introduction provoked widespread opposition at its apparent disregard for democratic principles and the extent to which it shifted the balance of power towards central government and eliminated the system's checks and balances (for example, Simon and Chitty, 1993). The National Curriculum was challenged on empirical grounds in respect of the viability and manageability of its content (for instance, Campbell and Neill, 1994) and the validity of its contingent assessment programme (for example Gipps, 1993). It was criticized on fundamental ethical and conceptual grounds (for instance Kelly, 1990; O'Hear and White, 1993). At the same time, both commentators and practitioners have demonstrated a fair measure of ambivalence towards the changes. Thus, to some, the prescriptions of national government were a much-needed corrective to the local culture of patronage and political correctness; in place of confusion about exactly what the primary curriculum should constitute, there was relative clarity; instead of the hand-to-mouth improvisation which often characterized curriculum planning in other than historically codified areas like mathematics there was a welcome degree of structure and guidance at the levels of both overall framework and operational detail; and even the least popular provisions, those concerning assessment, had their supporters.

The main source of the pressure to conform to particular values and practices, to which primary teachers, one way or another, have long been subject, has shifted in certain important areas from inside the profession to outside it. This could make the handling of such dilemmas more rather than less straightforward in as far as they might generate collective solidarity rather than individual *Angst*. By the same token, though in matters like curriculum content teachers obviously have less autonomy than in the days when decisions about curriculum and assessment were left to LEAs and schools, in less obvious repects they may actually have greater autonomy than hitherto. For within the new framework of legal requirements there may be a greater-than-anticipated room for manoeuvre at the level of the curriculum as transacted in classrooms now that the locus of power and influence has shifted from the LEA to the school, and from the Head as keeper of ethos, curriculum and pedagogy to the staff as collective decision-makers and problem-solvers.

TOWARDS THE MILLENNIUM

Not only is a perspective on the past a prerequisite for understanding the present – in primary education no less than in other aspects of this country's culture – but it also conditions one's view of the future. If a study of the emergence of our present system of primary education teaches us to be cautious in our claims about what has been achieved so far, then we need to be equally careful in how we approach the period to come.

Means or ends?

Despite this slightly pessimistic sentiment, nothing in education should be taken as given or predetermined, and I want to continue by tentatively identifying those aspects of primary education where choices are both necessary and possible. These fall into two contingent groups, a set of questions about *means*, and a set of questions about purposes or *ends*. The latter are in a fundamental sense of far greater importance, and indeed should properly speaking be resolved before one considers the manner in which primary education should be presented. Nevertheless, it is with the means that I wish to start, because it can fairly be argued that the structural, organizational and pedagogical context of schooling does not merely reflect educational values, but also shapes them, and in this sense educational means and ends are inseparable. If, therefore, so much about the future is unknowable we need above all to define structures for primary education which will *enable* rather than constrain, and it is to this principle that I now turn in identifying what seem to be some of the dilemmas to be confronted and resolved as we seek to construct a version of primary education which will meet the demands of the twenty-first century.

Schooling continuous or divided?

How far are the established divisions between infant, junior and secondary still valid? The divisions are rooted in the pre-war rationalization of the muddled administrative legacy of the nineteenth century; but they were reinforced by the 1988 Education Reform Act's delineation of Key Stages and sharpened up in the interim and final Dearing Reports. The tension here, it seems, is between preserving what is seen as the distinctive but vulnerable ethos and agenda of pre-adolescent education, especially early years education, and addressing notions of educational continuity, progression and coherence (these latter being, perhaps, among the more important contributions of HMI before it was subsumed within OFSTED). The tension is acute because of the historical tendency for primary schools to be subservient – in terms of status, finance and power – to secondary, and for secondary imperatives to shape primary decisions on curriculum, assessment and organization, most notably during the period of 11-plus selection, but also, in the view of some, after the arrival of the National Curriculum. Such subservience was paralleled among teachers themselves, until the demise of the training colleges (where until the 1970s nearly all primary teachers were trained), and the shift in the balance of undergraduate and graduate training began to erode the double divide of culture and professional qualification. Awareness of these legacies, and the ever-present threat of secondary hegemony in respect of values, curriculum, assessment and pedagogy, prompt many in primary education to opt for separatism – and indeed for the erection of defensive barriers to resist any dilution of what is thought to be most distinctively and vulnerably 'primary'. However, separatism, whatever its benefits, also produces isolation and parochialism. Separatism, moreover, legitimates discrepancies in funding.

The same dilemma is becoming increasingly prominent within the primary phase itself. Elsewhere (Alexander, 1995) I have argued that the first stage of primary education has always been a distinctive and even a semi-detached one, and how the 1988 Act's Key Stages legitimated and consolidated the division between 'infants' and 'juniors'. The Act has had another consequence, that of marshalling early years commentators against the established holistic notion of primary education. This has happened because the idea of a subject-based curriculum, let alone a curriculum of nine such subjects, was much more alien to early years thinking and practice than to that of later years, being seen as diametrically opposed to prevailing developmental models of learning. Moreover, some of the more prominent classroom research in which recent critiques of primary pedagogy have been grounded (for example, the influential ORACLE and ILEA studies of Galton *et al.*, 1980, Galton and Simon, 1980 and Mortimore *et al.*, 1988) have focused on the 7–11 age range. Some in the early years movement have felt their values threatened further by the apparent acquiescence shown by their later years colleagues, and this has since been heightened by gender-consciousness as a mostly female early years community sees in later years education, and more generally in the professional hierarchy of primary education and indeed the academic study of primary education, the dominance of male agendas, values, language, realities and of course power.[1] In the face of such a double betrayal – by government and by others in primary education – the establishment of early years education as an institutionally as well as philosophically separate stage of education becomes increasingly attractive to some of its proponents, especially when the growth of pre-school and nursery provision and its increasing political prominence provide those working in the Key Stage 1 area (5–7) with both an alternative and perhaps more appropriate reference group to Key Stage 2 (7–11) and a more promising power-base.[2]

The choices to be confronted, therefore, are several. Is unity of purpose throughout compulsory education appropriate? If so, should it be reflected in unity of structure (bearing in mind, for example, that the separation of primary schooling from secondary is by no means a universal practice outside

Britain)? If structural separation is appropriate, where should it come – at age 11 as argued by Hadow, at age 13 as postulated by Plowden; and within the phases so organized, is further division appropriate, and if so at what points: age 5, age 7 or age 9? What should be the relationship between what are currently defined as statutory and non-statutory early years provision – that is to say, Key Stage 1 on the one hand and pre-school and nursery provision on the other? How far should such subdivisions be taken: to the extent of an appropriate level of age-range differentiation within a common structure and a common framework of purposes and values, producing a unitary phase of pre-adolescent education; or to the extent of a sharper differentiation between, say, autonomous and distinct early years schools or centres catering for children aged 2 or 3 to 7 and truncated 7–11 schools sandwiched between the contrasting structures and philosophies of early years and secondary education?

Personally, I believe that fragmentation of the primary phase would be disastrous, for it would not only militate against coherence and progression in the young child's education and consolidate the current debilitating funding discrepancies, but it would also greatly weaken the impact of the primary community as an effective lobby just at the point when its influence is beginning to be felt in National Curriculum deliberations, in teacher education, in the Commons Education Committee, and even, up to a point, in government. I understand the growing sense of frustration among early years experts at the continuing failure of policy-makers, and indeed others in primary education, to acknowledge – let alone to speak to – their condition. The charge of secondary hegemony in respect of the National Curriculum in primary schools is well merited, especially as it bears on children in Key Stage 1 and those 4- and 5-year-olds not yet subject to the National Curriculum but already inevitably affected by its provisions. However, the solution to these problems is not secession from the primary 'union' but a much more strenuous effort by both early and later years practitioners and researchers to understand and accommodate to each other's perspectives and reach a shared and coherent definition of the purposes and character of pre-secondary education.

Funding: historical precedent or future need?

At the time of writing it is generally accepted – except by central government – that primary schools are seriously underfunded in respect of the tasks they are required to undertake, and this is true whether their tasks are defined narrowly, as in the Dearing Report, or more generously, as is actually implied in the first chapter of the 1988 Education Reform Act from which the National Curriculum, and hence Dearing's revisions, stem. The range and complexity of the learning agenda for primary schools as currently conceived cannot adequately be delivered by the combination of large classes and the singularly inflexible class-teacher system which primary schools have inherited from their elementary forebears. The evidence presented to the 1994 enquiry of the Commons Select Committee on Education strongly supports this proposition. At the same time we know that any significant easing of the current financial climate is unlikely, and that the economic and political risks of a policy commitment to activity-led funding for primary as well as for secondary schools are considerable. There are, after all, some 20,000 primary schools in England, compared with 4,000 secondary; some 4.5 million primary pupils compared with under 3 million secondary. But this does not weaken the argument as such. Even on a forward projection of the current National Curriculum, the notion that schools delivering the first two Key Stages of a nine- or ten-subject compulsory curriculum need up to half the resources given to schools delivering the second two Key Stages of the same curriculum is difficult, if not impossible to defend. The question to be confronted here, therefore, is whether primary education should continue to be funded on the basis of historical precedent allied to suspect claims about the relative 'needs' of younger and older pupils, or on the basis of a proper reassessment of the tasks which primary and secondary schools have to undertake and the kinds and quantities of expertise and other resources which these require. Since many of the needs-based claims are essentially circular – that is, to say that a 16-year-old needs specialist teaching in small classes while a 9-year-old does not is simply to say that because history has thrown up such discrepancies then they have *ipso facto* educational validity, and since it is manifestly the case that the tasks of primary schools are now considerably more complex and diverse than they were when the current funding discrepancies first emerged, then the argument for a total reassessment of the relationship between tasks and resources in the two phases of compulsory education is essential. At the time of writing, the government has just announced that it is not prepared to undertake such a reassessment (House of Commons, 1994b).

Teaching roles: the whole or the parts?

The origins of the prevailing teaching role in primary schools – the class teacher who teaches the whole curriculum to all children in his or her class for a year or more – are economic rather than educational. However, generations of primary teachers have not only come to terms with the challenges and constraints of the class-teacher system, but have also identified in the system considerable advantages both for them and their pupils, most of which can be encapsulated in the notion of holism.

I do not wish to rehearse here my earlier and fairly substantial critique of the class-teacher system (Alexander, 1984; chs 2 and 3); nor, however, do I wish to imply that the holistic concern with the child's development, learning and curriculum is misplaced. Rather, I wish to argue that here, too, there are dilemmas.

Thus, for example, we must confront the question of how far the scope and complexity of the modern primary curriculum exceeds what it is reasonable to expect the professional knowledge of the one-class teacher to encompass. The 1992 DES primary discussion paper (Alexander, Rose and Woodhead, 1992; paras 146–9), drawing on the Leeds research (Alexander, 1992: 204) identified a continuum of four teaching roles (as opposed to the existing two of class teacher and subject coordinator) which between them could accommodate the requirements of a modern primary curriculum, in both its early and later years manifestations: *generalist, consultant, semi-specialist* and *specialist*. It did not argue – as some claimed – for the abandoning of the class-teacher system any more than it argued that this system should at all costs be preserved. Nor did it say – as, again was claimed – that children in years five and six should be taught by specialists. Instead it proposed an approach to primary staffing which takes no primary teaching role – generalist, specialist or other – as given and starts instead with each school analysing its range of educational tasks, identifying the kinds of expertise these require, and constructing a profile of professional roles which match them as closely as possible.

What is now clear is that the primary discussion paper's continuum, novel though it was at the time, conceals an even greater range of variants on the themes of both full and partial responsibility (Richards, 1994), and that the notions of generalist/specialist can apply to aspects of the work of primary schools other than the curriculum. Some of these variants, though subject to the severe constraints of historical funding formulas, have been explored by primary schools in the period since the 1992 primary discussion paper. The debate on this matter remains open, though for as long as funding is tied, as it currently is, to an assumption that the class-teacher role is the sole or dominant one in primary schools, there will be limited room for manoeuvre.

Pedagogy: fitness for what purpose?

From being 'historically neglected' in Britain (Simon, 1983), pedagogy has assumed much greater prominence in recent years as a field for research, study and debate. Enquiry into primary teaching has grown extensively in the years since Bennett's lone and controversial foray of 1976. By 1992 it was possible for the DES primary discussion paper to bring together a set of propositions about the likely prerequisites for improved classroom practice (Alexander, Rose and Woodhead, 1992: 37–41) based on a synthesis of what by the winter of 1991 was a considerable body of empirical material. The specific propositions related to the following themes:

- teacher professional knowledge: of children, individually and collectively, of subject matter, of pedagogical practices and of the social, institutional and cultural contexts of teaching and learning;

- curriculum planning: at the levels of the whole school and the individual class; for pedagogy broadly defined rather than content alone; and for the long, medium and short term;
- curriculum balance as a multifaceted concept, encompassing curriculum areas and subjects; parity in quality among these; the way content is conceived and encountered (subjects, themes and topics); and the cross-curricular generic activities of which learning tasks are constituted;
- the context of classroom values, norms and relationships;
- expectations of individual children and assumptions about particular groups of children;
- the deployment of teacher time in the classroom, particularly relating to pupil diagnosis and assessment;
- the construction of learning tasks which promote different kinds and levels of learning: revision, practice, new skills and understanding; creative and imaginative activity;
- assessing children's learning, both formative and summative, and focusing on learning processes as well as their outcomes;
- providing pupils with constructive and informative feedback;
- the nature and application of a pedagogical repertoire for primary education, and the judgement to deploy this appropriately, on the basis of 'fitness for purpose';
- the specific strategies of whole-class teaching, groupwork, including collaborative groupwork, and teaching one to one;
- the generic teaching techniques, underpinning all broad teaching strategies, of observation and listening; asking different kinds of questions; explaining; instructing; providing oral and written feedback; managing space, time and behaviour.

The propositions in this section of the primary discussion paper were grounded in an extensive trawl of the classroom research undertaken in the previous decade or so, mainly in the United Kingdom, and with reference to both published and unpublished material from HMI. Lest that imply that the list offered was simply an atheoretical 'best buy' based on a random and not necessarily compatible collection of research studies, let it be stressed that the propositions also had a consistent theoretical perspective grounded, in part, in a reassessment of the dominant pedagogical ideas of the 1960s and 1970s, particularly the influence on these of Jean Piaget, the Swiss zoologist-turned-psychologist whose massive output provided much of the theoretical core of the training received by that generation of primary teachers for whom, in turn, the Plowden Report of 1967 provided both inspiration and legitimation.

Because the Piagetian model isolated in considerable detail the stages, characteristics and approximate ages of cognitive *development*, together with attendant stage-independent processes like assimilation and accommodation, the theory of *teaching* derived from this was essentially applied child development rather than pedagogy in its broader sense; and since Piaget's studies had been of individual children interacting with materials and/or with adults on a one-to-one basis, the derived theory of teaching sought to replicate this individualization in settings – large classes – where clearly this was difficult if not impossible, and had little guidance to offer on the practice of teaching other than that it should provide an environment and stimulus for such individualized and essentially self-directed learning. In contrast, where this theory focused on the interaction of learners and their environment, its revaluation highlighted the interaction of learners with one another and with the teacher, stressing the social nature of learning and the critical role of talk. Where the earlier model implied that the learning task should be matched to the child's existing stage of development and legitimated the notion of 'readiness', the alternative argued that the function of teaching was to accelerate development rather than merely keep pace with it (and indeed this counter to the 1960s/1970s view, a paraphrase of Vygotsky, was offered as the final proposition in the 1992 primary discussion paper's list referred to above). Where earlier models of teaching had tended to encourage a 'hands-off' role of teacher-as-facilitator, the alternative presented the teacher as intervener, fulfilling a critical role in mediating between pupil and task. Where the earlier model saw developed knowledge structures as incompatible with the developing child's ways of making sense of the world, its successor viewed these as a continuum, able to be bridged, and needing to be bridged, by 'scaffolded' learning tasks provided by the teacher which carry the child's understanding forward across the 'zone of proximal development'.

Such ideas were not new: Vygotsky, the key figure in what Bruner and Haste (1987) called the 'quiet revolution' in developmental psychology which generated these ideas, died as long ago as 1934, and though his work was for many years banned by the Soviet authorities it has been available in the west since the 1960s (Vygotsky, 1962, 1978), the era during which the very different perspectives of Piaget were beginning to exert their maximum influence on primary education in the United Kingdom, especially through teacher-training courses and published schemes in mathematics. Bruner himself had presaged the 'revolution' in his seminal texts, arguing the essentially social nature of learning and the accessibility of knowledge structures 'to any child at any stage of development' subject to the teacher's ability to provide a 'courteous translation' of the knowledge to be encountered (Bruner, 1963, 1966), ideas which were influential in several of the Schools Council curriculum projects in the 1970s. This raises the interesting question, which I have explored in detail elsewhere (Alexander, 1984: chs 2 and 4) of why Piaget's work was adopted with such uncritical enthusiasm (while Vygotsky's and Bruner's was relegated to textbook footnotes) during an era when, generally, theory and research bearing on education were viewed by many teachers as largely irrelevant to their task.

Be that as it may, by the late 1980s an alternative, 'constructivist' learning paradigm was emerging and, equally important, the now substantial body of observational data on primary teachers and children at work in classrooms – ethnographic, qualititative and quantitative – provided evidence from several different starting points to support the new paradigm's emphasis on the context of social interaction. It therefore seemed to offer the prospect of squaring the circle of pedagogical theory, for the time being at least. The 1992 primary discussion paper's synthesis of pedagogical propositions referred to above reflected these developments as they were documented by late 1991.

In looking ahead, we have now to ask where the pedagogy of primary education should be heading. For some, the key questions about learning and effective teaching are largely settled and the most important – and difficult – task now is to translate these into strategies for helping teachers currently in post to develop their pedagogic skill and understanding, and for training the next generation of teachers more effectively than the last (which of course is a comment on teacher training, not on teachers). Thus, Bennett, Wragg and their colleagues at Exeter have produced a succession of texts and training manuals on some of the generic teaching skills such as questioning, explaining and organizing collaborative groupwork (Dunne and Bennett, 1990; Bennett and Carré, 1993; Wragg, 1993a, 1993b; Wragg and Brown, 1993; Wragg and Dunne, 1994).

Work such as this not only focuses on the core interactions of which teaching is constituted, but is also premised on the importance of knowledge of curriculum subject matter (Shulman, 1986, 1987), in turn grounded in a comprehensive 'map' of the subject as a whole, thus underscoring the constructivist view that the gap between the child's developing understandings and developed subject structures can and should be bridged. Behind such a view is a concept of education as being concerned with cultural engagement and cultural transmission, so that learning in schools requires the interaction of the learner and the world of ideas, not merely the learner and the physical environment.

Others are less sanguine. Galton (1989, 1994), another leading figure in the primary classroom research movement of the 1980s, sees primary teaching as in a continuing state of crisis and is strongly critical of the models of pedagogy which he believed underpinned the Leeds research and the 1992 primary discussion paper, though rather ignoring the fact that his own ORACLE project (Galton et al., 1980, Galton and Simon, 1980) itself exemplified some of the conceptual and empirical weaknesses of which he was so critical in the work of others. For Kelly (1990) a model of teacher education which makes subject-matter pre-eminent – as had government requirements since 1984 (DES, 1984, 1989; DFE, 1992, 1993) – was simply taking as given the subject-led version of the primary curriculum espoused for party-political reasons by central government, and distorting or denying the developmental imperatives which should be at the heart of the early years teacher's task. For

Drummond (1993), the burgeoning teacher-effectiveness industry carried dangers of presenting pedagogy as mere technique, disembedded from questions of educational value and purpose.

The debate, therefore, is far from over, and in any event, even if one distances oneself a little from the quest for unitary pedagogical paradigms there remains a formidable list of problems in primary classrooms which need to be addressed, by both researchers and practitioners. Thus, on the basis of the Leeds research and other studies (see Alexander, 1975), we identified the following agenda (Alexander, 1992: 195):

Improving our understanding of the children we teach

- Raising teacher expectations of all children.
- Eliminating stereotyping.
- Focusing on the full range of pupil needs.
- Looking at children's potential as well as their problems.
- Sharpening the skills of diagnosis and assessment.
- Adopting classroom strategies which maximize teachers' time to exercise these skills.

Promoting children's learning

- Shifting the thrust of debate about classroom practice from teacher style and physical context to interaction, learning processes and outcomes.
- Rethinking groupwork.
- Rethinking multiple curriculum focus teaching.
- Maximizing opportunities for productive teacher–pupil and pupil–pupil interaction.
- Making teacher–pupil talk task-focused and cognitively challenging.
- Balancing encouragement with informative, and formative, feedback.
- Managing time in the classroom as economically as possible.
- Matching learning task and child.
- Matching learning task and classroom context.

Defining and organizing the curriculum

- Addressing curriculum balance as a system-wide issue.
- Ensuring that all subjects, regardless of their time allocation or perceived importance, receive the attention and resources they need in order to secure quality in their teaching.
- Examining curriculum balance in the classroom in terms of the mix and balance of cross-curricular generic activities as well as subjects and the hours and minutes these are allocated.

The wider school context

- Exploiting and developing each teacher's specialist skills.
- Extending the cross-school roles of teaching staff, especially in relation to curriculum support, review and development.
- Delegating responsibilities and securing participative decision-making.
- Addressing management as a whole-school rather than a merely hierarchical issue – all teachers are, or can be, managers.
- Making questions of management strategy contingent on prior questions of educational purpose.
- Giving professional development high priority and securing a mixed INSET economy.

Schools and parents

- Developing parent–teacher relationships which reconcile the rhetoric of partnership with the distinct responsibilities of each.

Of course, much of the latter part of this list is not about pedagogy as usually defined, but I have left it intact to remind us that however coherent and convincing a theory of teaching, its successful application in classrooms cannot ignore the wider school context within which the teacher works, and the power of this context to influence and/or constrain what the teacher does within what some perhaps erroneously call the 'privacy' of their classrooms. In this respect, it is perhaps offering the note of caution that a model of teaching defined too exclusively in terms of classroom interaction may be as likely to founder in its application as one which focuses too exclusively on processes of child development.

However, though the Leeds research portrayed and sought to explain classroom action not just in its own terms but also as a response to the culture of the school and LEA, it – like all pedagogic research – was constrained by the limitations of the methods it employed, and, even more fundamental, by the model of teaching which informed these methods and the particular aspects of teaching it selected for study. Thus, for example, systematic observation tends to atomize classroom action and divest it of the meanings it has for the actors; qualitative research may be both in obvious senses highly subjective (though of course subjective judgement plays a part in every single research paradigm yet identified or likely to be identified) and over-restricted by the small number of cases used; much research on pedagogy focuses far more – and perhaps to excess – on the teacher rather than the learner, thereby neglecting, for example, the extent to which pedagogy is a function of the child's strategies as well as the teacher's, the considerable diversity of understandings which members of a class or group of children bring to, and take from, a given teaching encounter, and the element of negotiation which characterizes the whole enterprise. Nor is the broader debate about whether teaching is an art, a craft or a science as pointless as some suggest, since the dominant research paradigms tend, often tacitly, to opt for the latter and therefore to impose adult scientific rationality on activities which may be shaped – and therefore best explained – by entirely other means, and indeed may be more subtle than any such paradigm is able to encompass.

All this any researcher knows well enough, and it is standard fare in critiques of classroom research. Unfortunately, what some such critiques offer, however, is not so much a constructive nudge towards a better balance in the studies they criticize, born of a shared recognition that none of us in this business can do more than provide an incomplete picture of that which we seek to portray, as an insistence that their own bias, their own methodology, and their own definitions of what teaching is about are somehow more comprehensive, more neutral, and more correct than anybody else's. In fact, the best they can offer is a different picture, a different shot at the truth, a different selection of pieces from the vast and complex jigsaw that is teaching: it may be better, it may be worse, or it may just be different. Galton's surprisingly virulent and misinformed attack on the Leeds research and the 1992 primary discussion paper (Galton 1994) seems to display just this lapse in consciousness.

The task ahead for those involved in the study of pedagogy is essentially one of continuing the journey in the hope that each attempt will add to the sum of our collective insights and contribute to the task of improving the quality of teaching and learning. In particular, I would like to see the common ground between radically different approaches to classroom study – for example Bennett (1984), Pollard (1985) and Armstrong (1980), to cite three which are very different yet in their different ways equally illuminating – more carefully, and less aggressively, explored than hitherto. Especially, though the 1970s and 1980s saw a movement away from child study towards a focus on the teacher and the strategies the teacher deployed (a necessary corrective, as argued above, to the 'applied child development' model of pedagogy), the balance needs now to be tilted back, especially now that study of the learner can apply a wider range of perspectives than was on offer during the developmentalist 1960s. Moreover, the legal reality of the National Curriculum makes it essential that we build up our understanding of how the young learner engages with versions of curriculum which were peripheral to the concerns of the earlier studies.

Perhaps even more important, though we can and must isolate the processes and skills which a teacher needs in order successfully to promote learning, pedagogy is not simply a technical matter, reducible to some ostensibly value-free science. Pedagogy is perhaps the most powerful and pervasive way in which a school expresses and helps the child engage with the values and purposes which drive and shape both the curriculum in the classroom and the wider community of the school. The 1992 primary discussion paper's use of the craft principle of 'fitness for purpose' was taken by some (such as

Drummond, 1993; Carr, 1994) to invite an unprincipled and narrowly prag-matic approach to teaching. This was certainly not its intention (though the political climate of the time may have encouraged such an interpretation). On the contrary, it sought to make precisely the opposite point, that the most basic test of the rightness of one's teaching is the degree to which it is true to the educational values which the teaching claims to manifest. It is to these matters, therefore, that we should now turn.

Curriculum: what basics, whose balance?

In December 1993, the final Dearing Report (1993b) argued that after the trauma of implementing a new and in some respects unmanageable National Curriculum, teachers and children were entitled to a period of stability, and that, once implemented, the 1995 statutory orders should remain unchanged for five years. While for battle-scarred primary teachers such a ceasefire was undoubtedly welcome, Dearing – in this recommendation and throughout his two reports – presumed, in my view both wrongly and dangerously, that the more fundamental questions about the character of the primary curriculum should now be regarded as settled. If there *is* to be a period of relative stability, therefore, I would wish to see it used, in part, to look to the next century and address the kinds of questions which government educa-tional policy from 1987 so effectively pre-empted.

Thus, if we take the principles of 'breadth' and 'balance' which emerged first in HMI documents during the 1980s and were subsequently offered as guiding principles for the National Curriculum, we should note immediately that the ineffable blandness of what Kelly and Blenkin (1993) have called 'breadthandbalance' (like 'aimsandobjectives' in the sixties, one portmanteau term to elide and make meaningless two concepts which are related yet also quite distinct), conceals value questions of profound importance. Since 1987, the *breadth* or scope of the primary curriculum has been defined in terms of a canon of nine subjects, and its *balance* has been conceived quantitatively in terms of time notionally allocated to each of these. The result is a curious definition of 'balance': three subjects get the lion's share of the time avail-able, the nine are arranged in a temporal pecking order (as they always have been, of course), and the vital questions about the educational values which inform these arrangements are avoided. The rationale goes, tautologically, as follows: every child is entitled to a broad and balanced curriculum; the National Curriculum is every child's statutory entitlement; therefore the National Curriculum is a broad and balanced curriculum. From 1988, then, curriculum breadth and balance became non-negotiable concepts: they meant what government and its agencies said they meant. For schools, there-fore, breadth and balance became *logistical* rather than *philosophical* imperatives – the challenge of fitting all that was required by law into the time available.

The Dearing moratorium – if it is observed (and five years is an exceptionally long time in educational politics) – allows us to consider alternative notions of breadth and balance. Elsewhere (Alexander, 1994) I suggested three of the several possible starting points for this alternative analysis. The first was to develop and apply the notion of generic curriculum activities which emerged from the Leeds research. For example, we noted there that the large amounts of time devoted to mathematics and language seemed to be the least efficiently used and that those curriculum activities which most successfully maintained children's attention were those which involved interaction with other people. This prompted us to question not just the assumption that by allocating large amounts of time to these subjects one ensures their quality, but also the more fundamental supposition that apportioning time is all that curriculum balance is about. Beyond this, the notion of generic activities allows us to ask another question: which 'reality' of curriculum – as conceived by government and teachers or as experienced by children – matters most when we are debating questions of curricular breadth and balance? It also prompts us to examine the extent to which the questions concern pedagogy more broadly defined rather than content alone. For the importance we attach to the generic activities of, say, structured talk and collaboration, must in part be conditioned first by our knowledge that they both happen to be essential tools of learning – any learning, in any subject – and in part by the practical realization that well-organized collaborative work can help the teacher manage time more effectively. Thus, regardless of broader assumptions about the place in the National Curriculum of speaking and listening (English Attainment Target 1) there could be an overriding *pedagogical* imperative to ensure that it features more prominently and pervasively than its presentation as a component of one subject allows.

The second starting point for reassessing breadth and balance which I proposed was also grounded in the Leeds research. In the final report on the Leeds project we noted

> At each level of the system we found claims to breadth and balance liable to be undermined by countervailing policies and practices: by LEA special projects favouring some curriculum areas at the expense of others; in INSET provision; in funding allocations; in the distribution of posts of responsibility in schools; in the status of postholders and the time they had to undertake their curriculum leadership responsibilities; in the areas of the curriculum subjected to curriculum review and development; in teacher expertise; and above all in the quality of children's classroom experiences. In the end, curriculum breadth and balance are less about time allocation than the diversity and challenge of what the child encounters; and *if the goals of breadth and balance are to be achieved in the classroom they must be pursued at every other level of the system as well.*
>
> (Alexander, 1992: 141, my italics)

Curriculum balance, then, is a product of decisions taken across the system as a whole, not merely within the school and classroom. It is a matter for policy-makers as well as teachers.

Third, I proposed that we should cease to treat the important and universal notion of a core curriculum as synonymous with English, mathematics and science, and instead conceive of the core in more comprehensive and less bounded terms. In few other countries is the core curriculum defined so narrowly, and the commoner approach is to have a more generous notion of core which at the same time is specified in rather less detail. The problem with defining the core of the curriculum as core subjects is the 'winner takes all' effect on the curriculum as a whole: every aspect of mathematics, for example, however peripheral in relation even to political objectives like the country's economic vitality it actually is, becomes by this inclusive formula more important than aspects of other subjects which by any reasonable definition are of much greater significance.

We have this country's historical 3Rs fixation to thank for this somewhat restricted concept of a core curriculum, and perceptions will be slow to change. On this Dearing appeared at first to provide a window of opportunity. In recommending (Dearing, 1993a) that each of the original subject orders be revised to divide its existing content into a statutory core and optional studies, he appeared to allow for the possibility of moving to a notion of a core curriculum which includes a far wider array of critically important knowledge, understanding and skill, drawn from the curriculum as a whole, than the idea of core subjects allows. This interpretation was soon scotched as it became clear that the core/options idea was simply a device for consolidating and securing the more effective delivery of the National Curriculum as first conceived, and that this was to be achieved by strengthening the three-subject core at the expense of the other six subjects. However, treating core curriculum and core subjects as synonymous is so palpably suspect, on conceptual as well as educational grounds, that it requires reappraisal. In practice, too, it might be argued that the core/non-core distinction has proved as damaging to curriculum coherence and consistency (two more 1980s HMI watchwords neutralized by adopting them as policy) as the old but perennially powerful basics/non-basics distinction.

Nor can the long-standing notion of 'the basics' continue to escape scrutiny. We have to ask how far a nineteenth-century preoccupation with a narrow spectrum of literacy and numeracy provides all that should be implied by a notion of 'basic skills' for the twenty-first century.[3] What, beyond this, is implied if we accept that tomorrow's adults will have needs, every bit as pressing, for the broader skills which will enable them to cope with the complexities and tensions of life in a pluralist and divided society, with the challenges of living in a fragile democracy set within an overcrowded world, with the need to relate to other people constructively and with empathy, with the need to engage with and benefit from imaginative and creative endeavour, with the need to find common cause with the rest of humanity, and with the need to invest life with meaning and purpose?

To argue for a reassessment of the basics is not to assert that the perennial commitment to the 3Rs is wrong. Oracy and literacy, in particular, seem to me to retain an unshakeable case for being accorded the highest priority, for they not only underpin the rest of the curriculum and therefore enable the child's learning across a wide spectrum of activities, but they are also vital ingredients in human discourse and the individual's meaningful participation in society. Rather, it seems reasonable to ask whether as a judgement of what is 'basic' to a modern education the 3Rs definition can be regarded, after over a century of continuous and unquestioned use, as adequate. In any event, it rests on unexamined but suspect assumptions about the separation of cognition from affectivity, and skills from their application. It is also worth reminding ourselves that the 3Rs view of the basics was directed not at the social and cultural plurality which is typical of today's primary schools, but at the working classes alone; and it was devised not to enable or liberate those working classes, but to contain and control them.

There are, therefore, two kinds of question to ask about the received definition of the basics in relation to future models of the primary curriculum and their relationship to life in the twenty-first century. First, even if this definition is seen to retain its validity, what can be said about the particular understandings and skills which it incorporates: for example, the heavy emphasis on computation, reading and writing, and the relatively lower value placed on other aspects of language, notably the spoken word, and other forms of literacy – for example, in respect of information technology, film, television and other audio-visual media?[4] Second, how far are its boundaries too sharply drawn when one looks to the claims of other skills and understandings necessary for learning and for life?

Primary education for what?

It will be understood that none of the questions I have posed so far can be adequately addressed without prior or simultaneous consideration of questions of value and purpose. It will also be recognized that the centralization of key educational decisions on curriculum and assessment from the late 1980s allowed such questions to be annexed and pre-empted as part and parcel of educational policy. On that basis the electoral system was deemed to have given government a monopoly over the enterprise of raising educational value-questions as such and a mandate for imposing on the schools the answers it alone gave to the questions it alone asked. The only question which was regarded as open to those in the education service was how, through the curriculum, these values should be transmitted.

Such a view is of course both presumptuous and dangerous, and it is to the credit of the independent National Commission, set up in 1991 with the blessing but not the tangible support of government, that it sought to define afresh a value-orientation for the British educational system, grounded not in political or technocratic determinism but a careful analysis of future trends and needs. On that basis (National Commission, 1993), the Commission identified the main global and national problems this country faces over the next few decades and urged a drive to use education and training to improve the country's economic performance. It argued that the tendency of our education system to educate a minority extremely well but fail the majority must be reversed and showed how this might be done, and that the debilitating divisions between education and training, and between the academic and vocational should be eliminated. The report deserves, and repays, careful study. Yet, apart from arguing for universal nursery education and the reduction of primary school class sizes, its recommendations for the primary stage were not particularly radical. Indeed, given the Commission's concern about the extent of under-achievement in English education, the modest attention they gave to the substance of primary education was somewhat surprising, for, of course, under-achievement does not start at age 11. The core curriculum at Key Stage 1 (age 5–7), argued the Commission, should consist of English, mathematics, science and technology together with 'other areas of study chosen at the discretion of the school' – in other words, a slightly modified version of the National Curriculum. At Key Stage 2 (age 7–11) the curriculum should include a widened core, taking about 70 per cent of the available time, which includes English, mathematics, science, technology, citizenship and a modern foreign language, together with a minimum of one subject from the arts and one from the humanities.

Apart from the upgrading of technology, the addition of a foreign language and the emphasis on citizenship – modifications which would bring our primary curriculum more into line with those of some other countries – the diet is a familiar one. It accepts without question the division of compulsory education into four Key Stages along the historically established lines which we questioned above. It accepts the concept of a curriculum divided into a high-status core and a lower-status residue. It accepts the notion that the curriculum, for primary as for secondary, for early years as for later, is best defined as a canon of subjects. Like the National Curriculum, it is at the same time modernizing and conservative. Like the National Curriculum, it implies that the challenges and tasks ahead are technical more than they are moral. Like the National Curriculum, it sees the humanities and arts as peripheral to the main thrust of education, especially in the early years. Like the National Curriculum, it does not really engage with the fundamental educational challenge of achieving a balance between meeting societal needs and fostering individual autonomy; though unlike the National Curriculum the National Commission does at least underpin its definition of 'citizenship' with principles like 'community' and 'democracy', even if they do look more comfortable in print than they are in practice. Perhaps, in the end, the

Commission's understandable desire to achieve a broad consensus frustrated the need to be genuinely radical, about primary education at any rate. Or perhaps the Commission's report simply demonstrates this chapter's thesis about the immense durability of the structures and values which underpinned elementary education.

Comprehensively redefining the purposes of primary education for the twenty-first century demands a range of understanding and skill beyond the scope of one person; indeed, in a pluralist society it can only be undertaken by many people, working both separately and together. That of course was the unachieved promise of the National Commission. All an individual like myself can do is to assert the urgency of the task and nominate some of the key questions to be addressed.

Primary education as preparation

Being the first stage of education, primary education constitutes, however it is defined and structured, a preparation. The question is, for what? For subsequent education, especially secondary? For the world of work? For the rounded life, of which work, paid work at least, is but a part? In considering these questions it is salutary to note current predictions that advances in medicine will ensure longer life expectancy for more and more people; that people can expect to change their jobs more frequently and radically than hitherto, and that the combination of these factors may therefore produce a situation in which for many people the longest phase of their lives is that spent in what, currently, we call 'retirement'. Should primary education attempt to provide a foundation for all this? Should it set itself more modest goals? Or should it eschew the social determinism that all notions of 'preparation' imply and reassert instead the progressives' belief in the value of education, for its own sake, here and now.

Primary education and culture

Education is one of the most important manifestations of, or mirrors to, a culture. But what version of culture should primary education reflect? One which is static, monolithic and consensual? One which is changing, pluralist and characterized by tension? One which is local? One which is national? One which is international or global? Having gained a purchase on the notion of culture, what particular aspects of culture should primary education engage with: for example, economic, political, intellectual, ethical, artistic, scientific, technical, spiritual, material? And what should be the character of that engagement: to depict; to transmit faithfully as heritage, generation to generation; to examine critically on the basis that culture must be actively shaped and reshaped?

Future and past

We have the lessons and the images of the past before us: universal, but uncompromisingly instrumental, elementary education; progressivism's attempt to provide an individually liberating alternative. How far do these provide pointers to the future? To what extent can the efforts to revisit and update the elementary model, which is arguably what government policy has invested some at least of its energies in since 1979, be regarded as appropriate for the twenty-first century? To what extent is a reassessment and reconstruction of the progressive model both useful as a counterbalance and viable as a version of primary education in its own right? Or can neither of these historical paradigms, however modified, provide a basis for the future and is it more appropriate to try to devise a version of primary education that – if possible, which I doubt – is totally new?

Coda

As I come to the end of this text I am in the middle of collecting material for a comparative study of primary education in five cultures which I hope will help me understand and more successfully address some of the problems of purpose and practice in British primary education, and especially the broader questions of value. So far this project has taken me to two countries very different from Britain, where I have talked with those who make and enact national educational policy in general, and primary education policy in particular, and those who implement it in schools. I have spent many hours observing, filming and making notes in primary classrooms in these countries and in talking with children, their teachers and their parents. I have also observed and spoken with the some of the next generation of primary teachers currently undergoing their training. The project has taken two years to plan and negotiate; it will be several months before the data-gathering stage is completed, and, I suspect, several years before I have made sense of all that I have seen and heard and have translated it into publishable form. But the longer I spend in these countries the more convinced I become of the truth of four deceptively simple propositions.

First, in international terms much of what we do in our primary schools is both educationally ambitious and operationally impressive – often exceptionally so. This is no mere paternalistic platitude of the kind politicians give us before delivering yet another blow to educators' self-esteem, but an observable and testable truth, and one worth putting on record. Second, though wholesale educational transplants are not to be recommended, we can learn a great deal from other countries in our quest for alternative versions of primary education, at every level from policy to practice, and from the identification of broad purposes and values to the fine detail of classroom transactions. Third, in Britain we are sometimes extraordinarily parochial and insular in our thinking about primary education, and far too ensnared by the powerful historical legacies which have featured in this chapter, and the values, ideas, habits and practices which they carry in their train: somehow we have to escape from them, or at least stand back somewhat and view them for what they are. Fourth, the historical tendency of British primary education to stand outside the mainstream of the nation's intellectual life has been, and remains, a serious handicap.

We know why this last is the case. Elementary education set out to provide basic skills but under no circumstances to offer intellectual or cultural enfranchisement. Progressivism was rooted in anti-enlightenment values, and though it had roots, too, in political dissent and religious nonconformity of an often invigorating kind, these were soon diluted by a more generalized and unfocused romanticism which turned its back on the social and ethical issues which fed early progressive thinking. Primary teacher training for long reflected both these strands: at first primary teachers were given no more than a low-level apprenticeship, later it became an induction into progressive ideas and practices; but in neither context were intellectual engagement or critical dialectic fostered or for that matter countenanced. Even when primary education, and primary teacher training, began to end their professional and intellectual isolation, there was the more general problem of the marginalization of educational study as a whole within the universities, to contend with. In the face of this, secondary teachers were at least part of the wider communities of subjects and subject study central to the university tradition which for many was the defining intellectual springboard for adult life. Finally, it is only relatively recently that primary education became part of the personal experience of those with power and influence, political, intellectual and cultural.

Those of us interested in reconstructing a system of primary education for the twenty-first century must, for better or worse, end our isolation, look outwards to cultures other than our own, and engage the shapers of ideas and opinions in this country on their own ground and in their own terms.

NOTES

1   Sometimes the charge that early years realities and needs are neglected is overstated and the early years and gender issues can be invoked needlessly and gratuitously. For example, when David, Curtis and Siraj-Blatchford (1992) wrote their riposte to the 1992 primary discussion paper of Alexander, Rose and Woodhead (1992), their fundamental criticism that it ignored early years rather missed the point that its remit was to concentrate on Key Stage 2. Their – valid – objection to the lack of a woman among the paper's authors and their exploitation of the 'three wise men' label ignored the fact that the discussion paper's authors were not self-selected, had themselves unsuccessfully questioned the wisdom of an all-male team, and had vainly tried to resist the epiphanic silliness of 'three wise men'.

2 It is the fate of nursery education to be more frequently advocated yet more frequently ignored than any other phase of education. At the time of writing, a new head of steam appears to be building up, following the Rumbold Report (DES 1990), the strong endorsement of the principle of universal nursery education provided by the 1993 National Commission Report, and the Labour Party's acceptance of this position. The government's initial reaction, voiced by Secretary of State Patten, was to reject the National Commission proposals as far too expensive. However, Prime Minister Major soon contradicted this with a strong expression of support for nursery education. However, as on previous occasions, no commitments were given as to timing or funding.

3 It is interesting to note an apparent shift from the hard-line 3Rs position taken by Dearing in his 1993 interim report to the more extended definition of 'basic skills' in his final report (Dearing 1993b): reading, writing, speaking, listening, number and information technology. In this respect the final Dearing position is close to that of the National Commission. The government view of the basics, however, remained unreconstructedly elementary, as Prime Minister Major repeatedly exhorted teachers to concentrate on getting children to 'read, write and do sums'. Dearing's revised definition was clearly a response to views expressed within the education profession, but the Prime Minister was targeting the more powerful constituencies of backbench and public opinion.

4 The question of the boundaries of English, as one of the traditional basics, was explored by participants in the 1993 Commission of Enquiry into English sponsored by the British Film Institute and *The Times Educational Supplement* (Bazalgette, 1994).

REFERENCES

Alexander, R. J. (1984) *Primary Teaching*, London: Cassell.

—— (1991) *Primary Education in Leeds: Twelfth and Final Report from the Primary Needs Independent Evaluation Project*, University of Leeds.

—— (1992) *Policy and Practice in Primary Education*, London: Routledge.

—— (1995) *Versions of Primary Education*, London: Routledge.

—— Rose, A. J. and Woodhead, C. (1992) *Curriculum Organization and Classroom Practice in Primary Schools: A Discussion Paper*, London: DES.

Bazalgette, C. (ed.) (1994) *Report of the Commission of Enquiry into English: Balancing Literature, Language and Media in the National Curriculum*, London: BFI Publishing.

Bennett, S. N. (1976) *Teaching Styles and Pupil Progress*, London: Open Books.

—— and Carré, C. (1993) *Learning to Teach*, London: Routledge.

Bruner, J. S. (1963) *The Process of Education*, New York: Random House.

—— (1966) *Toward a Theory of Instruction*, Cambridge, Mass.: Harvard University Press.

—— and Haste, H. (1987) *Making Sense: The Child's Construction of the World*, London: Methuen.

Campbell, R. J. and Neill, S. R. St J. (1994) *Curriculum Reform at Key Stage 1: Teacher Commitment and Policy Failure*, London: Longman.

Carr, D. (1994) 'Wise men and clever tricks', *Cambridge Journal of Education*, 24(1).

Cox, B. and Boyson, R. (1975) 'Letter to MPs and parents', in B. Cox and A. E. Dyson, *The Fight for Education: Black Paper 1975*, London: J. M. Dent.

Dearing, R. (1993a) *The National Curriculum and its Assessment: Interim Report*, York and London: NCC and SEAC.

—— (1993b) *The National Curriculum and its Assessment: Final Report*, London: School Curriculum and Assessment Authority.

DES (Department of Education and Science) (1984) *Initial Teacher Training: Approval of Courses* (Circular 3/84), London: DES.

—— (1989) *Initial Teacher Training: Approval of Courses* (Circular 24/89), London: DES.

—— (1990) *Starting with Quality: Report of the Committee of Enquiry into the Quality of Educational Experience Offered to 3- and 4-Year Olds* (Rumbold Report), London: HMSO.

DFE (Department for Education) (1992) *Initial Teacher Training (Secondary Phase)* (Circular 9/92), London: DFE.

—— (1993) *The Initial Training of Primary School Teachers: New Criteria for Courses*, London: DFE.

Drummond, M. J. (1993) *Assessing Children's Learning*, London: David Fulton.

Dunne E. and Bennett, S. N. (1990) *Talking and Learning in Groups*, London: Routledge.

Galton, M. (1989) *Teaching in the Primary School*, London: David Fulton.

—— (1994) *Crisis in the Primary Classroom*, London: David Fulton.

Galton, M. and Simon, B. (1980) *Progress and Performance in the Primary Classroom*, London: Routledge.

Galton, M., Simon, B. and Croll, P. (1980) *Inside the Primary Classroom*, London: Routledge.

Gipps, C. (1993) 'The structure for assessment and recording', in P. O'Hear and J. White (eds) *Assessing the National Curriculum*, London: Paul Chapman Publishing.

House of Commons (1994a) *The Disparity in Funding Between Primary and Secondary Schools: Education Committee Second Report*, London: HMSO.

—— (1994b) *Education Committee Third Special Report: Government Response to the Second Report from the Committee, Session 1993–4 (The Disparity in Funding Between Primary and Secondary Schools)*, London: HMSO.

Kelly, A. V. (1990) *The National Curriculum: A Critical Review*, London: Paul Chapman.

—— and Blenkin, G. V. (1993) 'Never mind the quality, feel the breadth and balance', in R. J. Campbell (ed.) *Breadth and Balance in the Primary Curriculum*, London: Falmer Press.

Major, J. (1992) Speech to the Conservative Women's Conference, Eastbourne.

Mortimore, P., Sammons, P., Stoll, L., Lewis, D. and Ecob, R. (1988) *School Matters: The Junior Years*, London: Open Books.

National Commission on Education (1993) *Learning to Succeed*, London: Heinemann.

O'Hear, P. and White, J. (eds) (1993) *Assessing the National Curriculum*, London: Paul Chapman Publishing.

Pollard, A. (1985) *The Social World of the Primary School*, London: Holt-Saunders.

Richards, C. M. (1994) 'Subject expertise and its deployment in primary schools: a discussion paper', *Education 3–13*, 22(1).

Shulman, L. S. (1986) 'Those who understand: knowledge growth in teaching', *Education Researcher*, 15(2).

—— (1987) 'Knowledge and teaching: foundations of the new reforms', *Harvard Educational Review*, 57.

Simon, B. (1983) 'The study of education as a university subject in Britain', *Studies in Higher Education*, 8(1).

—— and Chitty, C. (1993) *SOS: Save Our Schools*, London: Lawrence & Wishart.

Vygotsky, L. S. (1962) *Thought and Language*, Cambridge, Mass.: MIT Press.

—— (1978) *Mind in Society: The Development of the Higher Psychological Processes*, Cambridge, Mass.: Harvard University Press.
Wragg, E. C. (1993a) *Class Management*, London: Routledge.
—— (1993b) *An Introduction to Classroom Observation*, London: Routledge.
—— and Brown, G. (1993) *Explaining*, London: Routledge.
—— and Dunn, R. (1994) *Effective Teaching*, London: Routledge.

Chapter 18

Four-year-olds in school
Cause for concern

Jenefer Joseph

Jenefer Joseph charts and comments on the trend in England and Wales whereby by 1993, 78 per cent of the 3- and 4-year-olds who are having some kind of educational provision, are in infant classes. Her argument is that school is an inappropriate learning environment for under 5s.* All emphases in the chapter are the author's original ones.

Let's start with a few facts:

1   Over 347,000 children in England and Wales, aged 4 at 31 August 1991 were admitted to infant classes in maintained primary schools, in the autumn term of the 1991/92 school year. All of them were below compulsory school age and nearly half (170,000) were admitted more than a term before they reached compulsory school age.
2   In addition 119,000 children aged 4 at the end of December were admitted to infant classes in January 1992 – a term or more before they reached compulsory school age.
3   Between 1983 and 1992, the number of pupils below compulsory school age in infant classes rose consistently every year – a rise of 43 per cent since 1983.
4   Over 90 per cent of 4-year-olds in infant schools attend full time.
5   In addition in January 1992 there were 45,900 such pupils in independent schools in England – a rise of 56 per cent since 1983 (DFE, 1993).

Thus of all 3- and 4-year-olds in England having some educational provision, a **minimum of 78 per cent are in infant classes.**

Based on this, it is reasonable to say that 4 is now the unofficially acknowledged and accepted age at which children start formal schooling in England and Wales. This makes us unenviably unique in the world, 5, 6 and 7 being the norm in all other countries.

---

* Originally published in P. Gammage and J. Meighan (1993) *Early Childhood Education: Taking Stock: An Education Now Special Report*, Derbyshire: Education Now Publishing Co-operative (slightly edited for this volume).

How has this reprehensible situation come about? Historically, in spite of the pioneering work in nursery education started by the McMillan sisters at the turn of the century, there has never been a real commitment to the promotion of early years education by any government, whatever its colour. There have been many promises, normally trotted out in election run-ups, but time after time, opportunities have been missed (or rather avoided), and our meagre state nursery schooling has largely slipped in through the back door whilst nobody was quite watching.

The Government White Paper of 1972 aimed to provide nursery education for all 3- and 4-year-olds whose parents wanted it. This too became a promise unfulfilled and, soon after, nursery classes attached to primary schools began to proliferate, and to act as substitutes for traditional nursery schools. During the whole of the Thatcher years, monetary considerations plus falling rolls were used to encourage LEAs to admit children from 4 years plus into infant/reception classes.

As to current reasons – some, of course, arise from the historical developments themselves. For example, the continued lack of sufficient nursery provision has made it possible for authorities to claim that 4-year-olds are better off in infant classes than having no educational experience at all. The fact that, so often, reception class provision is inappropriate for 4-year-olds, is brushed aside in favour of inflating the statistics of under 5s provision.

Further grounds include the fact that:

- it clearly costs less to have 4-year-olds in a reception class, with a teacher/pupil ratio of, say, 1:30, than to run a nursery class with two staff, where the accepted ratio is closer to 1:15.
- if a school admits children early, it is less likely to lose them to other schools in the neighbourhood.
- there are now more working mothers who, finding no nursery places available, press for their children to be admitted early.

The effects of these various aspects are already considerable, and in order to judge whether they are likely to be beneficial or detrimental to the welfare and educational progress of the children, we start by considering their needs.

THE NEEDS OF 4-YEAR-OLDS

Whilst one should never generalize about human behaviour, it is fair to say that, especially in young children, there are aspects, such as specific needs, which can be demonstrated to be characteristic of certain stages of development, and which can guide us in providing educational settings which are appropriate for them.

1 **Four-year-olds need space.** They are active beings, and need space to move, run, jump, build, climb. They also need the kind of space which

allows for intimate, cosy areas, where they can enjoy being peaceful and undisturbed.

2   **Four-year-olds need plenty of opportunity for self-chosen social interactions** both with their peers and with adults. This socialization is of the kind which arises naturally during children's activities and which varies and flows from one-to-one encounters to small groups. Young children are trying to understand and cope with the differing social situations which they meet, testing out and clarifying the roles and demands of others, and their own relationship to them. This includes adults as well as children – they need to feel safe and secure in the support of understanding and caring adults and to have the enrichment of experiencing their diverse talents and abilities.

3   **Four-year-olds need time** – to do things in their own way, at their own pace, without being rushed or pressurized. This is an aspect of young children's lives which is often overlooked, especially during routine times, when children are hurriedly prepared for the next event. Children are in learning situations almost all the time at this age, and they need to be able to concentrate for as long as they like, and to remain involved in absorbing pursuits with as little interruption as possible, so that they can complete tasks to their own satisfaction. They also need time for reflection, to think about what they have done, or are going to do, and generally have the opportunities for contemplation which adults themselves seek.

4   **Four-year-olds need to be able to follow their own interests** – to be able to indulge in and concentrate on their own intentions, whether they be creative, social or whatever. They learn in diverse ways, are curious about a great number of things, and they need the freedom, within a secure framework, to explore, investigate and generally pursue what is of significance to them.

5   **Four-year-olds need endless opportunities to enhance their language development**, and their verbal facility in particular. We know that children acquire language largely within the context of the activities and the concerns which are engaging them at the time. We also know that children's language experiences before they go to school vary enormously, so the linguistic environment, which is provided for them at school, has to be rich, and allow for a great many conversational exchanges both in small groups and in relaxed one-to-one situations, where the adult is doing as much listening as talking.

6   **Above all, four-year-olds need the freedom and encouragement to play.** Central to children's all-round development is their need for spontaneous play activities. It is through their play that they make their social adjustments, and learn to cope with their emotions. Moreover, through play children juggle with ideas, 'develop what they know, . . . dare to take risks, negotiate, solve problems, initiate, anticipate, . . . reflect on and consolidate their knowledge and understanding' (EYCG, 1989: 2).

HOW, WITHIN THE EDUCATION SYSTEM, ARE WE TO BEST CATER FOR THESE NEEDS?

We will examine the three types of provision presently available to 4-year-olds.

Nursery schools are designed and geared to meet these needs and promote the all-round development of 4-year-olds.

- They have the *space*, both indoors and out, which gives the children the freedom to pursue their interests actively, and to experience a wide variety of equipment and materials especially appropriate to their needs and capabilities.
- They offer a *timetable* which is both loosely structured and flexible, which is geared for individuals rather than groups, and where the groups are predominantly self-selected, small and random. This encourages children to use their initiative, to achieve independence of thought and to take responsibility for their actions.
- They offer a *curriculum* which encourages children to explore any areas of knowledge which attract and influence them. This, together with the staff ensuring that language, mathematical and scientific development is fostered, gives these young children a broad and sound initiation into the world of knowledge from which they can begin to pursue their individual interests.
- They maintain an *adult–child ratio* of 1:10/12.
- *The staff are specially trained,* having the detailed knowledge of child development needed to understand young children's behaviour, together with the teaching skills and techniques appropriate for such young children.
- *The staff maintain close contact with parents,* welcome them as observers in the school, and encourage them to be actively involved with the children when and where appropriate.

All these factors make it possible for the children to learn through their play, the importance of which, in the all-round development of young children, has already been emphasized.

Nursery classes

Whilst some of these are able to offer much of what the nursery schools do, many have to contend with considerable restrictions on space; often have to modify their timetables to accommodate to the demands of the rest of the primary school; and are likely to have to share outdoor space with the rest of the school. This last means offering dauntingly bare areas of tarmac, bereft of the safety and security that a more intimate and appropriately furnished area gives.

Clearly then, nursery schools and (some) nursery classes provide the educational ambience to meet the needs of 4 year-olds.

Reception classes differ in various aspects.

Space

The class is usually in one room in part of the primary school. There may be a small anteroom, and the corridor may be used in spite of constantly passing traffic. Indoor space, being limited, cannot offer the sorts of facilities available in nursery schools. Outdoor play space is merely part of the whole playground, inhospitably tarmacked and with inappropriate equipment.

Timetabling and curriculum

Inevitably, timetabling has to be tighter and more structured. There is a clear division between 'work' and 'play', the latter usually being allowed when the 'serious' work of dealing with the exigencies of the 3Rs has been completed, and children are entitled to indulge themselves in somewhat 'non-serious' play activities, such as creative work, block building and imaginative games. In contrast to nursery provision, the daily programme is dominated by teacher rather than child-chosen activities, and there is more group work than individual one-to-one interchanges. Moreover, because of the above factors, much important equipment and material is omitted. For example, sand and water, two fundamentally important resources for children's sensory, mathematical, scientific and imaginative development, are seldom available.

Opportunities for play

Arising from all this, it is clear that a reception class can offer very limited opportunities for genuinely spontaneous play, and this is profoundly antipathetic to the needs of 4-year-olds. As Mari Guha says:

> to give time for play in school, is not to give a 'break' or rest from learning; it is not a concession to immature minds. Rather it is a way of making teaching and learning more productive. . . . We do not know what the knowledge is, and the skills are, that the children of today will most need in the future. Flexibility, confidence and the ability to think for oneself – these are the attributes one hopes will not let them down. If play is conducive to the development of these, we had better have it in the school.
>
> (1988: 78–9)

The skills of the teacher

We know that a qualified teacher is supposedly capable of teaching any child. We also know that specialist knowledge and understanding is crucial for teachers to really succeed with different age groups, and this applies equally to those teaching under-5s. Anyone who knows anything about the under-8 age group understands that there is a great deal of difference between the skills, knowledge and capabilities of children between 4 years 1 month and 5 years 11 months, the developmental range which can now be found in reception classes. The teacher of 4-year-olds, therefore, needs to understand fully how they learn, and be able to cater for it, at the same time as trying to satisfy the equally important needs and demands of the 5-year-olds. She has to allow for the children's need for exploratory play; to be able to diagnose and then discuss the children's intentions with them; provide inspired materials at critical moments; help children reflect on their experiences. All these are paramount in promoting and enhancing the children's cognitive progress, and ensuring the quality of their learning. Such highly professional skills emanate primarily from the teacher's sound knowledge and experience of child development at this particular age, and from her commitment to the notion that children's play is intrinsic to their all-round development.

So without underestimating the skills, knowledge and professionalism of reception teachers, by and large they are not as *au fait* with 4-year-olds as they could be. Moreover, because of the restrictions and pressures which the national system puts upon them, many find themselves unable to educate the children as they would, in fact, prefer. It must be said that many reception teachers do try to offer programmes which are genuinely more appropriate for very young children, but lack of support in the form of resources and staff hinders them. They recognize the stress and fears which 'big school' often brings, and are concerned and worried for the children. Moreover, 'Most reception class teachers accept that they have been asked to undertake an impossible task ... [and] feel pressured by colleagues and parents to "get the children on"' (NCNE, 1993: p. 3).

Clearly, then, it is not the fault of the teachers, but of the education system which has encouraged the admittance of 4-year-olds, at same time as making less authentic nursery provision available. It should be added that research evidence into different types of provision for the under-5s showed that:

1 Children in LEA nursery schools scored consistently higher in tests than children who had other types of pre-school experience.
2 Children with **no** pre-school experience scored lowest on tests.
3 Most worryingly, the 4-year-olds in reception classes performed at the same levels as with the children who had had *no* pre-school experience.

4   Children who have attended reception classes as young 4-year-olds have
    no evidence of educational or behavioural advantage over children who
    started school after their fifth birthday (Osborn and Millbank, 1987:
    p. 210).

Martin Woodhead (1989: 2) highlights the folly of the policy of admitting
very young 4-year-olds to school: 'the equivalent might be if some universities proposed to admit young people from the age of 14, rather than 18'.

THE EFFECTS ON PARENTS AND NURSERY SCHOOLS

The advent of both the National Curriculum and the early admission of
4-year-olds has made parents uneasy and anxious about their children's
schooling at this crucial first stage. Whilst many appear clearly satisfied with
what their children are gaining from the nursery school, they are also
concerned that their children's chances of success in the Attainment Tests at
7 might be jeopardized if they don't enter the reception class as young 4s.
They are also under pressure from primary schools who offer early places,
and worry that non-acceptance might hinder their child's future progress.
As a result, many parents succumb to these influences and remove their
children too soon for them to have gained the full educational benefits of
the nursery school. This, in turn, adversely affects the balance between
the 3- and 4-year-olds in the nursery schools. The 3-year-olds are denied the
role models of the 4s and: 'The four-year-olds lose the opportunity to be the
oldest most responsible members of the group. In the reception class they
become "babies" again, which is particularly undermining for summer born
children' (NCNE, 1993). Moreover, it is difficult for nursery school staff to
keep satisfactory records on children who are with them for much less than
three terms.

   Furthermore, the specialist training facilities, which nursery schools offer
to nursery nurse and teacher students-in-training, are diminished when there
are too few 4-year-olds in the school to demonstrate the true qualities of a
distinctive nursery school programme. Not least of all, 'The professional
reward for nursery staff has been seriously undermined by the removal of
four year olds. . . . Their skills are not used to the full [and they] feel that
they have been devalued' (ibid.).

WHAT IS TO BE DONE ABOUT THIS SORRY STATE OF AFFAIRS?

People working in Early Years Education have, in the past, been notoriously
reticent about actively opposing state edicts which they have considered to
be detrimental to the education and welfare of young children. This is partly
because the importance of early childhood has never really been acknowledged

and has been resolutely undervalued, and so working with young children has always had a somewhat low status. This in turn revolves around the fact that early education has been almost entirely undertaken by women. One can't explore the historical and sociological reasons for this here. But the two factors combined have helped to undermine any resolve to resist, with any degree of assertiveness, government policies which the profession believed was not in the best interests of the child.

It is this attitude which must be overcome. Until the government is made to understand that these policies are bad for children, and that teachers have strong arguments that justify such a claim, Ministers of State will continue to bring about situations which are politically expedient but educationally retrograde.

The recent clashes between teachers and the government over testing are an indication that the profession is sick and tired of the proliferation of rules and regulations with which they have had to contend since the Education Reform Act. These confrontations are already encouraging nursery and primary school teachers to make vociferous and country-wide objections to another new proposal to create 'A one year course for parents and other mature students ... who wish to train to teach nursery and infant pupils only' (DFE, 1993: 12) – a further indication of the lack of understanding of the considerable teaching skills required for early-years education.

One hopes that all those working in the early years will be further provoked to join together in force to persuade the powers that be:

- To reverse their ill-conceived decision to allow 4-year-olds into reception classes.
- To increase financial and other help to nursery schools and classes so that they can become even more viable alternatives to having 4-year-olds in reception classes.
- To ensure that reception classes which already have 4-year-olds in them are made to conform to DFE guidelines for *nursery* provision with regard to curriculum and specialist staff suited to nursery children.
- To ensure that parents are not subjected to pressures from any source to send their children to primary school before they feel it right for the children to go.

Persuading the authorities to take action means taking action ourselves. It means writing, organising meetings, rallying parents and the media, lobbying MPs and councillors – generally demonstrating strong and justifiable objections. There is clear evidence that the only occasions on which governmental or local schemes have been reversed have been those when a huge public outcry has forced the issue. Early childhood educators 'need to be articulate, organised and skilful in acting as a voice for young children. ... They need to become political advocates on behalf of young children' (Pascal, 1992).

Erich Fromm said 'People today are yearning for human beings who have wisdom and convictions and the courage to act according to their convictions' (1978).

Those human beings could be the educators of our vulnerable young children.

REFERENCES

DFE (1993) Statistical Bulletin, No. 11/93.

EYCG (Early Years Curriculum Group) (1989) *Early Childhood Education, The Early Years Curriculum and the National Curriculum*, Stoke-on-Trent: Trentham Books.

Fromm, Erich (1978) *To Have Or To Be*, London: Jonathan Cape.

Guha, M. in G. Blenkin and A. V. Kelly (1988) *Early Childhood Education*, London: Paul Chapman Publishing.

NCNE (National Campaign for Nursery Education) (1993) *Four Year Olds in Reception Classes*, London: NCNE.

Osborn, A. F. and Milbank, J. E. (1987) *The Effects of Early Education*, Oxford: Clarendon Press.

Pascal, C. (1992) 'Advocacy, Quality and the Education of the Young Child,' Inaugural Professorial Lecture, Worcester College of Higher Education.

Woodhead, M. (1989) 'School starts at five ... or four years old?', *Journal of Educational Policy*, 4 (1): 2.

Chapter 19

Managing access and entitlement in primary education

Barbara MacGilchrist

Access to the totality of learning in primary schools for all pupils, regardless of socio-economic, ethnic or age background, seems likely to continue to exercise teachers and schools into the twenty-first century. Barbara MacGilchrist emphasizes that awareness of disadvantage, and legislation for access and entitlement through the National Curriculum, are insufficient on their own to ensure equality of opportunity. Set against the background of change within primary education policy in England and Wales, she argues that Head Teachers need to create a strategic vision for enabling access to the whole curriculum for all pupils, in partnership with their staff and also parents.*

SUMMARY

Legislating for access and entitlement in primary education (DES, 1988) will not of itself ensure equality of educational opportunity for all children. Managing access and entitlement to the curriculum requires strategic management by all those concerned. This is a collective responsibility that should be perceived as a 'partnership for entitlement'. Improving the progress and attainment of all children as well as closing the achievement gap between the lowest and the highest achievers is a major challenge . . . Schools and those who teach in them hold the master key to access and entitlement. To enable the key to be used to unlock the door to raising achievement requires the different partners – those within the school and those beyond the school gate – to take action in respect of policy decisions over which they can exercise direct control . . .

* Originally published as a much longer paper: *ASPE Paper No. 3: Managing Access and Entitlement in Primary Education*, Stoke-on-Trent: ASPE/Trentham Books (edited for this volume).

PRACTICAL STRATEGIES FOR MANAGING ACCESS AND ENTITLEMENT

1   The process and content of learning are vital factors in ensuring equality of opportunity. It is the quality of these opportunities that determines levels of achievement. The role of the teacher is central as it is the teacher in the classroom who decides how best to match the curriculum to the learner. Parents themselves also have a role to play.

2   There is a link between disadvantage and underachievement which can affect children's life chances and influence teachers' expectations of children's capacity to learn.

3   Schools matter. They can improve progress and so raise the achievement levels of all the children in a school. They can further help to combat disadvantage by narrowing the difference between the highest and the lowest achieving groups. Good quality early years education has a vital role to play.

4   Improving achievement levels of children regardless of background factors is very complex. Assessing the effectiveness of a school on test results alone can mask the reality for individuals and groups. Complacency or unwarranted criticism could ensue.

5   Managing access and entitlement is essential, because it will not happen by chance.

. . . To achieve access and entitlement requires good management. Essentially it is the schools themselves that have it within their control to make a major impact on levels of achievement. Schools do not improve simply because of new legislation and because of LEA policy. They do not improve simply because an inspector or an advisory teacher comes to call. They can and do improve substantially as a result of the actions taken by those who work within them. It is the will to improve and the quality and expertise of the staff that are so important.

It is Heads and teachers who have shown what is possible and the findings of the Junior School Project illustrate this quite dramatically. The National Curriculum has made a significant contribution but it will be the schools themselves that will determine the success of its implementation. At the end of the day the evidence of research points to the fact that it is the quality of the leadership provided by the Head Teacher that can be, and so often is, the overriding factor in school effectiveness (Thomas, 1985; Nias and Southworth, 1992). Nevertheless schools cannot do it alone. The responsibility for raising levels of achievement by improving progress must be a collective one – a partnership for entitlement between those involved. A partnership between teacher and child; between class teacher and the Head and other colleagues on the staff; between the home and school; between the school and the LEA; between the LEA and central government. LMS has strengthened the role of the school in this partnership but to fulfil this increased responsibility schools need a good quality service from those with responsibility beyond the school gate. The teacher and child in the classroom must ultimately be the focus of the partnership. Each of the partners involved will have different roles to play but they share the same task – to ensure quality – to provide access and entitlement for all. To make the partnership work there needs to be openness and trust and a commitment to translating policy into practice in such a way that children really are 'at the heart of the educational process'.

MANAGING ACCESS AND ENTITLEMENT – PRACTICAL STRATEGIES FOR SCHOOLS

Managing access and entitlement requires Heads and teachers to have a clear idea about: what it is they want to achieve; how well they are doing at present; what needs to be done next. Any discussions about policy and practice in school need to be informed by general principles that are shared by all the staff. For example, it is important for a school to be explicit about how children best learn and to define achievement. The school's general view about the curriculum also needs to be made clear. No less important is the school's view about equal opportunities. The kinds of progress and perform-ance indicators to be used and the evidence of progress and performance the school intends to collect and share with children, parents, governors and others need to be decided. Both qualitative and quantitative data will be important.

Once general principles have been clarified the task of managing access and entitlement can be approached in three different ways although in prac-tice the three are interdependent.

Establishing general whole-school policies to support and extend achievement

At the level of the whole school it is possible to identify which factors in the school have an impact on achievement and require a policy that every-one agrees to put into practice. The Junior School Project is just one example of how a school can be helped to achieve this. The research identified twelve key factors that relate to effectiveness. By using these as an aide-memoire a school can soon assess how well it is doing and what needs to be improved. Record keeping, for example, was one of the factors. It may well be that a school decides to broaden the present system so that it becomes a record of achievement that is contributed to and shared by children and parents.

Identifying specific whole-school policies to combat underachievement

In recognition of the research evidence that whilst an effective school can raise achievement levels in general, groups and individuals may well be under-achieving, a school can identify very practical steps that can be taken to address this key issue. These might include:

- rigorous monitoring and review of the progress of specific individuals and groups who could be vulnerable, for example, bilingual learners, summer-born children, children with disabilities, children from certain social and ethnic backgrounds;
- early identification of underachievement and the establishment of a detailed action plan for improvement for each child concerned;
- close scrutiny of resources to ensure they are appropriate for all pupils and do not contain damaging stereotypes or materials that disadvantage some children;
- combating potential low expectations of teachers and other adults in the school through moderation activities, inservice education courses, visits to other schools;
- planned use of adults other than the class-teacher within the school, and good communication about children's progress.

Improving classroom practice

It should go without saying that the acid test of any policy is the extent to which it can be seen in action in the classroom and the impact it is making on the progress of individual learners. Policy established at the level of the whole school needs to be translated into practical, manageable steps that support and guide the work of teachers in the classroom.

It is not possible here to cite all the practical strategies a teacher can adopt to ensure access and entitlement for each child. Research evidence and HMI reports drawn from direct observation of teachers in classrooms have identified many of the essential elements of good practice (DES, 1987). Elements such as curriculum planning, assessment, record-keeping, classroom talk, management and organization, and expectations and relationships have been reported on in detail. When considering these and others, all important is the quality of the day-to-day decisions a teacher takes in relation to the next learning step for a child. The key role of the teacher in matching the process and the content of learning has already been examined. The National Curriculum and assessment requirements have raised the profile of teacher assessment. Much good can come of this providing improved planning and assessment go hand in hand. Improving a teacher's ability to identify what children can do and can go on to learn next is at the hub of teaching and learning. Practical steps such as helping children to set manageable targets, making explicit the achievements expected, and collecting evidence of that achievement can all contribute to improving progress and attainment.

Managing access and entitlement at these three levels will require a systematic approach to school improvement by the Head and staff. The processes of development planning outlined in the DES publications (DES, 1989b, 1991) provide a systematic approach to improvement and enable schools to set themselves realistic and achievable targets. The LEA has an important role in supporting the school in this process. It is essential that, just as teachers need to establish a range of strategies to ensure effective learning in the classroom, the LEA also should establish strategies for helping schools to make themselves more effective. Shared performance indicators, shared monitoring and assessment and quality inservice training can all make an important contribution.

FUTURE CONCERNS

In the context of access and entitlement it is worth raising four particular concerns for the future.

The need for more nursery places

The importance of the early years has been identified, yet a commitment to provide nursery places for all who need them is not forthcoming. The financial constraints facing LEAs at present place what nursery education there is at risk.

The need to break down phase barriers

Primary and secondary schools need to collaborate much more in the future. The National Curriculum makes this even more urgent. Primary education can no longer be perceived as simply a preparation for secondary school. It is of vital importance in its own right and if continuity and progression are to be assured then good communication between schools will be essential. It is also the case that primary teachers lack curriculum subject expertise in several areas (DES, 1992) which is understandable. Secondary schools have that expertise and ways need to be found to share it with primary colleagues. Primary teachers have a good knowledge of classroom practice and in turn can assist secondary teachers with mixed ability teaching.

The need to recruit and retain quality teachers

Initial training and inservice training are key factors in enhancing the professionalism of teachers. Access and entitlement require good teachers. Good teachers will not come into the profession or remain in it unless they are valued, supported and given positive encouragement to improve.

Levelling – down or up?

Not all children can achieve the same educational level. However, there is a potential danger in the national assessment arrangements that have been put in place. The requirement to allocate each child to a level and so label a child, for example, as level 1, level 2 or level 3 could result in teachers teaching to the level and grouping children accordingly. This in turn could lower teachers' expectations and in the longer term lead to levelling down as opposed to levelling up. The very principles of entitlement written into the National Curriculum could be defeated. A powerful statement by Entwistle (1978) acts as a sharp reminder of the need to avoid such a scenario at all costs.

> Though notions of educational ceilings (i.e. absolute limits on anyone's development) may be useful in certain contexts, the likelihood is that these are usually a good deal higher for most people than elitist educational theorists are apt to suppose. For their own good reasons (if only to survive in an unpromising social environment) individuals may build their own cognitive ceilings very low, opting for an anti-intellectual, cognitively impoverished stance on life. But no one has the right to be architect of anyone else's low-ceilinged educational hovel, and the existence of late developers who break through the educational roof is all the justification necessary for the view that for anyone, educationally, only the sky is the limit. For once the possibility of rationality and critical awareness is allowed in relation to any of life's enterprises, there can be no guarantee that the germ of rationality in any life can be sterilised once it has begun to fructify.

REFERENCES

DES (Department of Education and Science) (1987) *Primary Schools: Some Aspects of Good Practice*, London: HMSO.
—— (1988) *The Education Reform Act*, ch. 1, part 1, London: HMSO.
—— (1989) *Planning for School Development*, London: HMSO.
—— (1991) *Development Planning: A Practical Guide*, London: HMSO.
—— (1992) *Curriculum Organisation and Classroom Practice in Primary Schools*, London: HMSO.
Entwistle, H. (1978), *Class Culture and Education*, London: Methuen.
Nias, J. and Southworth, G. (1992) *Whole School Curriculum Development in the Primary School*, Lewes: Falmer Press.
Thomas, N. *et al.* (1985) *Improving Primary Schools*, London: ILEA.

Index